P9-EEB-294

GREEK TRAGEDY

GREEK TRAGEDY

882.009
L565

ALBIN LESKY

Translated by
H. A. FRANKFORT

With Foreword by
PROFESSOR E. G. TURNER

SECOND EDITION

LONDON · ERNEST BENN LIMITED

NEW YORK · BARNES & NOBLE · INC

LIBRARY ST. MARY'S COLLEGE

First published in Germany by
Alfred Kroener Verlag, Stuttgart
under the title Albin Lesky *Die Griechische Tragoedie*
Third revised edition © Alfred Kroener Verlag 1964
First English edition published 1965
Second (corrected) impression 1967
by Ernest Benn Limited
Bouverie House · Fleet Street · London · EC4
and Barnes & Noble Inc. 105 Fifth Avenue · New York 10003
Distributed in Canada by
The General Publishing Company Limited · Toronto
English translation © Ernest Benn Limited 1965, 1967
Printed in Great Britain

65-9616

To

Eva and Victor Ehrenberg

Foreword

THE FORTUNATE traveller seated in reverie on the hard stone benches of the theatre of Dionysus at Athens is conscious of the strangeness of the outer trappings of Greek tragedy. As he looks downhill at the wide circular orchestra and the foundations of stage-buildings the sun gets into his eyes. Greek drama was played out of doors, in a large open area without curtain or even raised stage, in full daylight, lacking the illusions created by artificial lighting. Its actors wore painted masks, concentrating attention on the formalised external appearance of the character, the *dramatis persona*. Yet even the stay-at-home who knows A. E. Housman's parody will be aware of oddities in its literary form. In dialogue exchanges, no matter how banal or momentous the question, a whole line and no more than a line must be spoken. The constant presence in the orchestra of a chorus impeded the development of secret intrigue and inhibited the presentation of violent action. But the traveller will have an advantage over the arm-chair critic. He will have noted the ceremonial chair of the priest of Dionysus and the god's altar and realised that drama was also ritual, and the columns that bear trophies of dramatic victories, the Acropolis towering above, the Areopagus and Pnyx hard by will have reminded him that these annual spring competitions were an integral part of Athenian life. In them an Athenian audience will have felt the solemn associations and overtones of religious ceremonial and rite, yet not have been overawed; as connoisseurs of the spoken word they will have welcomed rhetoric as natural in a play, shown quick-witted appreciation of a well-contrived action, and learned by heart from relatives in the chorus such lyrics as took their fancy.

Origin in ritual, development as an organic portion of a city's life, the conventions of stage-production: the strangeness of these factors, relatively easy to seize, should put us on our guard against assuming that in our approach to its less tangible characteristics our assumptions are the same as those of the Athenian dramatists themselves. The great figures of Greek tragedy seem to speak to us directly across the centuries. We should not want to learn more about them had we not somehow felt their continuing power to move and amaze:

> What's Hecuba to him or he to Hecuba
> That he should weep for her?

Yet just because we seem to be on familiar ground we are in danger of carrying our modern attitudes and preconceptions into our appreciation and judgment of this ancient art form. Our notions must be tested against the account of Athenian attitudes and habits which scholarship can supply; against the practice of the tragic poets and the views of the earliest dramatic critics.

This is where Professor Lesky's book comes to our aid. It would save us, for example, from foisting psychological motivation of character into a stage production of the Oresteia (as was recently done in a much-admired London production). The author makes it clear that for Aeschylus unseen forces, whether gods, former wrongs or the weight of a family curse, are at least as effective contributors to the dramatic tension as the actors who move before us. In Sophocles, no doubt, we begin to be more conscious of the actors as characters. Yet they are still far from constituting autonomous beings (see pp. 114–118), and the plays in which they figure cannot be treated without reserve (in William Empson's phrase about A. C. Bradley) as the historical evidence for their biographies. It is even doubtful whether we do right to import our psychologising into judgments about Euripides. Professor Lesky summarises the difficulty very briefly in his discussion of our modern revulsion at Admetus' complacent acceptance of Alcestis' self-sacrifice in his place (p. 140). Even here it is legitimate to hold that an ancient Athenian would not have felt our difficulty, that the behaviour of the character is part of the logic of the action, and the story being a familiar one, disbelief is readily suspended.

Professor Lesky does not claim anything more for his book than that it is an introductory essay. Yet it is amazing how much he has crammed into it. Origins, history, background of ideas, stage practice receive a proper and balanced treatment from one who knows scholarly polemic but does not practice it, and whose encyclopedic History of Greek Literature has become a familiar and trusted work of reference. He has a gift for clear exposition of the points at issue, and pays his reader the compliment of intelligent discussion.

Yet his principal interest is that of a lover of great literature, responding to emotions and ideas and their magnificent expression. Rightly so: he is analysing masterpieces and the seminal germ of other masterpieces. He interprets each of the surviving plays, asks what makes it a tragedy, and shows the inadequacy of any single formula of exegesis. In an introductory essay he discusses the substance of tragedy, and keeps his categories clearly before the reader throughout. He is well equipped for this task: a man of sensitive mind; of wide sympathies, and widely read; no stranger to English or American scholarship, and a welcome visitor to English-speaking countries. Yet the particular value of his essay and its particular appeal in translation may well be that it puts readers restricted to the English language in touch with a way of looking at Greek tragedy informed by familiarity with and reflection on Winckelmann, Lessing, Goethe, Grillparzer and Jaspers rather than Shakespeare, Johnson, Jebb and A. C. Bradley. It is good to be reminded that no one school of critics has a monopoly of the truth.

Professor Lesky's book was first published in 1938; it was radically overhauled in a second edition dated 1958 (the copy from which this translation has been made, though it bears the note '3rd edition 1964', differs from the second edition only in carrying an up-to-date bibliography, which has been specially adapted for English readers). But though brought up to date, this essay still retains its youthful freshness. Occasionally, it may be, a passage (such as that on page 53 where Gestalt psychology is invoked to justify analysis of a work of art) will show traces of the date of writing. But Professor Lesky has missed very little that is significant up to 1957, and his appendix alludes to work done since then. Of course no book of this kind can be completely up to the minute. One preoccupation of criticism at the moment this foreword was written is with the idea of the tragic hero, and a determined attempt is being made to oust the concept as a Romantic notion foisted on to Aristotle. Another school has joined battle against the notion that Aeschylus was a profound religious thinker. Professor Lesky does not share the view of the new iconoclasts. The excavations of the late Dr. John Papadimitriou at Brauron have thrown an interesting new light on the Attic cult of Iphigeneia, page 176.

E. G. TURNER

1965

Contents

Acknowledgements

MOST OF the extracts from the tragedies are quoted, by kind permission of the University of Chicago Press, from the translations in *The Complete Greek Tragedies*, edited by David Grene and Richmond Lattimore. Thanks are also due to the publishers of other translations to whom credit is given below the relevant extracts.

The publishers are particularly grateful to Professor David Grene for the specially commissioned translation from Aeschylus' *Diktyoulkoi* on page 91. They would like to thank Professor E. G. Turner, of University College, London, and Professor William M. Calder, of Columbia University, N.Y. (who was also responsible for the translation from Aeschylus' *Danaids* on page 70), for their advice and suggestions on the translation of the German text.

Acknowledgements to Second Edition

THE publishers wish to record their grateful thanks again to Professor E. G. Turner, to Professor Bernard Knox of the Center of Hellenic Studies, Washington, D.C., and to Mrs Valerie L. Chandler, who compiled the index, and to Mr C. S. Walker for most helpful and constructive suggestions towards improvements of the English text.

CHAPTER ONE

What is Tragedy?

IN A SHORT introductory chapter it is out of the question to survey the problem of tragedy in its full depth. Rather, we shall try to bring one question of central importance into focus, in such a way that the account which follows can be related to an already prepared theme, and unity maintained in our inquiry. Likewise, we shall not attempt to define the essence of tragedy in a slick formula, but merely to illustrate an important part of a problem which must in some aspects remain unsolved.

The complex nature of tragedy makes it inevitable that the closer we get to the actual phenomenon the more any hope of grasping it with the aid of definition fades. Only one example need be quoted from a wealth of literature on the subject: Benno von Wiese, in his study of German tragedy from Lessing to Hebbel, states emphatically, and quite rightly, that even for this comparatively restricted period he has refrained from giving a 'magic formula for interpretation.' We shall follow his example and ask first of all how our problem fits into the cultural history of the West.

All problems concerning the tragic, however wide their scope, begin and end with Attic tragedy. We shall discuss later how this perplexing form of art developed, out of various rather elusive and rudimentary stages, into the three different types of perfection which it reached in the fifth century B.C. We also hope to show that its formal elements give an important clue to its historical development.

Is the substance of tragedy, in the general sense of the word, so closely bound up with tragedy as a form of art that it first found expression in this framework? Or can we find in earlier Greek poetry elements which foreshadow that first and most perfect expression, embodied in fifth-century drama, of the tragic view of life? Since we can now view the *Iliad* and the *Odyssey* again for what they are, namely as works of art, moulded out of diverse traditional material into a superb design, this question has been raised with renewed urgency in relation to both these epics. Karl Jaspers, for instance, mentions as the earliest examples of tragic awareness which he has noted: Homer, the Edda, Icelandic sagas and the ubiquitous heroic legends which range from Western Europe to China. This undoubtedly implies that the type of heroic song, mostly transmitted by word of mouth, whose wide divulgation and strong similarities have been examined by Sir Maurice Bowra,[1] shows tragic elements also. The central figure of such songs is always the radiant hero and conqueror, the splendour of his weapons, of his acts; but he appears against the sombre background of inevitable death, a death which will tear him away from his joys and plunge him into nothingness; or, a fate no better, into a mouldering world of shadows. In this contrast, only indicated here, but deeply experienced throughout the heroic songs, we must indeed recognise a tragic motif, but one which was insufficient for Homer. The theme of heroic man, doomed to succumb to the futility of all things human, is rounded off and given an added intensity in Homeric poetry by the contrast between humanity and the gods. The blessed immortals may indeed, if they feel so inclined, graciously stoop towards a mortal and assist him when in need. But at any moment they may turn away and reveal the immeasurable gulf which separates their state of blessedness from the anguish of those doomed to die. Hephaestus, for instance, complains in the first book of the *Iliad* because a banquet of the immortals has been disturbed by a wrangle about mere miserable mortals, while Apollo, in the battle of the gods, refuses to fight with Poseidon for the sake of so decrepit a race. Moreover, this fighting of gods with gods is no more than a wanton brawl, a good joke, which the Father of the gods approves with a laugh. But men on the battlefield stake all they possess in combat, risking its loss for ever in bitter death.

We have, however, not yet mentioned the most significant of those adumbrations of authentic tragedy in Homer, which distinguish the *Iliad* from other typically heroic sagas. Bruno Snell[2] has shown that what characterises epic is the perception of life as

[1] *Heroic Poetry* (London, 1952).
[2] *The Discovery of the Mind* (Oxford, 1953).

a chain of events. This image of a chain with its smooth sequence of links, which recalls the well-known cliché of the epic stream, does indeed touch on something of essential importance for epic in general. Even in Homer we find sections which remind us of the successive links in a chain. But what raises the *Iliad* to a level of artistic achievement beyond the range of typical epic, what enables the poet to take the first steps in the direction of tragedy, is the forging not of a chain of events but of a deep connection between events and single passionate man.

The very concentration of events, in both Homeric epics, within the space of a few days, means a departure from simple concatenation. And how closely is individual action bound up with the destiny of others – friends, comrades in arms, whole nations – when the fate of the individual is seen as part of a dramatic sequence which leads inevitably to tragic events. It was a stroke of genius on Homer's part to make the motif of anger the crystallisation of the entire poem, since it lent to Achilles his tragic stature. The very excess of the hero's wrath, which turned to *hybris* when he rejected the envoys' petition, became the cause of his greatest suffering: the death of the person he loved above all, his friend Patroclus. Suffering quenches his anger and all that remains is a desire for revenge, but the revenge wreaked on Hector proves to be fatally connected with Achilles' own death. Even in the case of the two men who are so closely related to him in love and hate, tragic elements are accentuated. Patroclus goes into battle well warned, but at the crucial moment he ignores the restraint imposed on him and finds his death. For Hector it is the greatest day of his life when the Greeks, driven back to the camp near their ships, await their fate with fear. He wants to press the attack still further and in a delirium of victory rebuffs Polydamas, who, trying to warn him, bars his way three times. He reaches the climax of his triumph when he dons the arms of Achilles, which he has taken from his victim Patroclus. In an incomparable scene the poet has unfolded the fateful tragedy. Zeus looking down on Hector, a knowing god seeing man triumphant and deluded, feels compassion. He grants him one more hour in which to overreach himself. But when Achilles has swept the battlefield bare, when the gates of Troy are closed behind the fugitives and Hector at last in dreadful loneliness awaits his ruthless opponent outside the walls, then he must reckon with his fate, realising what sin he atones for with death.

When the ancient critics[1] called Homer the Father of Tragedy, or merely considered his poetry a type of tragedy, they chiefly had in mind the mimetic element in epic, especially the dialogues. But when, in the relief of Archelaus of Priene whose subject is the Apotheosis of Homer, we find Tragedy paying tribute to the poet, the connection is the deeper one we have already seen.

The Homeric epic is, however, merely a significant prelude to those works of art in which tragedy has found a fully articulate expression. We must start with drama in our quest for its essential features. Here these features take on their authentic form, as all who can respond to it will acknowledge, especially in the West. Its influence has been deep and lasting and Creizenach is fully justified when he calls the rebirth of tragedy in the West the greatest event in modern literary history. It is true that the word 'tragic' has become divorced from the art with which it was linked in classical Greece and has come to denote the fateful course of certain human lives which appear to have a special depth of meaning. This requires examination. The word is also used to qualify a particular world-view, for instance that of Sören Kierkegaard, for whom our world remains separated from God by an unbridgeable chasm. Fundamentally tragic concepts of the world occur long before our era, but it is not surprising that such ideas should be astir at the present time. Yet, in reply to the specific historical question when and in what context the idea of tragedy first gained its wider significance, we must plead ignorance. Careful historical investigation is still needed here.

One thing, however, may be confidently asserted. Though the Greeks created tragedy, a great form of art and one of mankind's most significant achievements, they never developed a theory of the tragic which, reaching beyond the phenomenon of drama, might touch on man's spiritual attitude towards the world as a whole. Further, the lofty conception of tragic events which manifests itself in Greek drama, variously refracted but with overwhelming grandeur, was largely lost to the Greeks of a later period. We shall presently see how this happened. The history of the word τραγικός, a term which needs closer examination, shows the change very

[1] Pl. *Rep.* 10. 595b–c, 598d; (Plu.) *de Hom.* II, 213.

clearly. When Aristotle used the word in the sense of 'solemn' or even 'exalted', he probably still conformed to the linguistic conventions of his day. Gradually, however, one notices a change of meaning, mainly in two directions. *τραγικός* may mean dreadful, horrifying; for instance when Dio Cassius calls the murder of Agrippina a tragedy. Here he is not thinking of man fatally caught in the snares of passion, or of a particular condition of the world which allows or even causes such things to happen. The word is simply intended to convey: terrible, cruel, blood-thirsty. And when in the Hellenistic period historians turn history into written tragedy this is not, as with Herodotus and Thucydides, a sign of a tragic interpretation of history; they merely aim at heightening the effect of their gaudily colourful stories. The other change that has been mentioned occurs when the word begins to mean turgid, bombastic, but always in the sense of exceeding the normal. In late antiquity the term never bears the important philosophical connotation which it has acquired in our time – even when casually used. This fate it shares with the word 'classic', which also refers to a definite historical phenomenon (the highest peak of Attic culture), but which may be used in a much wider sense and is then apt to become meaningless.

There is a work of Aristotle on the subject of poetry which deals mainly with tragedy, and which has exerted an astonishingly potent influence over the centuries. May we not expect to find in the *Poetics* the earliest signs of an insight into tragedy that reaches beyond a technical analysis of works of art; and does not Aristotle's statement about *κάθαρσις* ('purgation') as the purpose of tragic poetry give us the key to our problem: the essence of tragedy? The definition of tragedy in the *Poetics* is worth quoting in full: 'Tragedy, then, is an imitation of an action that is serious, complete and of a certain magnitude; in language embellished with each kind of artistic ornament, the several kinds being found in separate parts of the play; in the form of action, not of narrative; through pity and fear effecting the proper purgation of these emotions.'[1] The long story of the misinterpretation of the last phrase (*δι' ἐλέου καὶ φόβου περαίνουσα τὴν τῶν τοιούτων παθημάτων κάθαρσιν*) need not be repeated, although this would in fact throw a remarkable

[1] S. H. Butcher, *Aristotle's Theory of Poetry and Fine Art* (4e. New York, 1951), p.23.

sidelight on cultural history. The spectators are neither meant to be purged from those passions, which the tragic figures experience in excess and for which they atone with their ruin, nor to be made better by an increase in compassion or the discarding of exaggerated emotions. The origin of the controversial term *catharsis* has in fact been traced to the realm of medicine and it has been proved through a comparison with other passages that the actual meaning of the word is a pleasurable relief from the emotions in question. We also agree with modern scholars when they maintain that Aristotle did not expect any moral effect from this kind of *catharsis*. On the other hand he had no misgivings about it and this places him clearly – though unavowedly – in opposition to Plato, who views tragedy as a moral danger to the citizens of his ideal state, from which he rigorously bans it.

We have only discussed the problem of Aristotelian *catharsis* as far as was necessary to show that it has no connection with a conception of the tragic in the modern, more philosophical sense. The same holds good for a passage in the *Poetics* (1453 a 29) which at first sight appears promising. Here Euripides is called the 'most tragic' (*τραγικώτατος*) of the Attic dramatists. The phrase is quoted as often as it is variously interpreted. But when the passage is read in its context it is obvious that Aristotle only refers to the unhappy ending of Euripides' plays and that he therefore uses the word 'tragic' in a sense which anticipates its later application mentioned above.

Max Kommerell, in his book on Lessing and Aristotle, sums up his conclusions as follows: 'The entire method of enquiry (used in the *Poetics*) . . . is descriptive and summarising and stops short of the tragic as a phenomenon, which it explains but does not evaluate.' In general, our conclusions are similar, but Aristotle may in one instance have transcended these limitations, thereby anticipating modern views. The passage will prove important in another connection. When Aristotle develops, in the 13th chapter of the *Poetics*, his theory of the 'sudden change' (*μεταβολή*) of fate as the core of tragic myth and with it his idea that 'average' characters are the most suitable for tragedy, he says that if we are meant to experience such a ruinous downfall as tragic, it should not result from a moral defect but *δι' ἁμαρτίαν τινά*. In this particular context the phrase is undoubtedly borrowed from the realm of epic and signifies a failure – due to human frailty – to discern what is right and resolutely to guide oneself towards it. Thus man, if not wrecked by moral inadequacy, will yet be destroyed because within the limits of his human nature he is incapable of dealing with certain tasks and situations.

Here we may ask if Aristotle's phrase does not imply that the human situation is fundamentally tragic. But all we have to go by is this one remark, which is indeed thought-provoking. When in the same sentence Oedipus is quoted as a typical case, we understand the choice of such a striking example, but the mention of Thyestes as a parallel shows how the fragmentary preservation of classical tragedy has limited our understanding. The definition of tragedy as 'the catastrophe of heroic fate,' made by Theophrastus, the most gifted pupil of Aristotle, is purely descriptive, and largely rests on his master's concept of *metabole*. This brief phrase *ἡρωϊκῆς τύχης περίστασις* is astonishingly eloquent as regards the status of the persons concerned and the contrast between their high rank and the powers of destiny.

Antonio Sebastiano Minturno had his six books on poetics printed in Venice in 1559 and his *Arte Poetica* in 1563. Between these two dates J. C. Scaliger's *Poetics* appeared, published in 1561. In Scaliger, the emphasis lay on the rational evaluation of the emotions and on the conviction that when controlled they could be beneficial to man. Minturno, on the other hand, was aware of that dark background of life, of the constant threat to all who are in an eminent or favoured position, and of the possibility of errors which may plunge even the great into misery. Such ideas, in which man's vulnerability, the failure of his spiritual defences against overpowering hostile forces, is seen as the source of tragic events, also occur in studies on poetry of the Baroque period. Here the main concept is the *error ex alienatione*, man's delusions, arising from different sources, about himself and others, and the ever present danger that such delusions may cause disaster and suffering. Only in turning to God can man be secure, but, the world being what it is, his life on this earth is from the start exposed to deception, to appearances which hide reality from him, to illusions which beckon him to ruin. Thoughts of this kind, which take for granted the fact that human existence is treacherous and exposed to danger, could hardly find response in the Age of Enlightenment.

So we may forestall any future and more detailed history of the concept by stating that the revival of humanism in the early nineteenth century also meant a re-emergence, from past treatises long forgotten, of the question: what is the essence of tragedy? For it was at this time that a new and most fruitful relation with Greek tragedy developed.

Any attempt to define tragedy should begin with the words spoken by Goethe on the 6th of June 1824, to Chancellor Müller: 'All tragedy depends on an insoluble conflict. As soon as harmony is obtained or becomes a possibility, tragedy vanishes.' Here the problem we are trying to solve has been grasped at the root. And yet these words contribute to its solution no more than a fairly wide frame of reference, because the statement that tragedy implies insoluble conflict says nothing about the nature of the opposing forces. It will be an imperative task to define this 'conflict' with more precision in every sphere of tragedy, in art as in real life. This proves particularly fruitful in Greek tragedy, where the types of conflict actually found can be briefly indicated. It can either reside within the realm of the gods, or denote a polar tension between god and man; or again it may be a matter of conflicting elements within a man's breast.

Goethe's location of tragedy in a world of radical contradictions provides a helpful approach to the problem, but leaves many questions unanswered. Since our enquiry is directed towards the specific works of art where Greek tragedy is found, we shall only deal with a few aspects of the problem, moving from what has already been clarified or can easily be solved, to more difficult and comprehensive questions. Although throughout these discussions Greek drama is our main concern we hope, in passing, to contribute something to the lively debates of the past years on the subject of tragedy as such.

It is easy to agree about the first prerequisite for tragic effect, namely what might be called the *dignity of the fall.* That was precisely what Aristotle meant when he made *πρᾶξις σπουδαία* part of his definition of tragedy, while Theophrastus' definition, mentioned above, explicitly confines itself to the fate of heroes. For the Greeks this meant that myths were the source of tragic matter, but it also set a standard of social distinction which as the *sine qua non* of tragedy has remained valid until recently. In Chaucer's

Canterbury Tales a monk tells his travelling companions a number of stories, mythical and historical, which he calls tragedies and which he tries to define as a genre. It is clear that he has only the vaguest idea of tragedy as a form of art, but he sticks firmly to its delimitations on social grounds:

> Tragedie is to seyn a certeyn storie,
> As olde bookes maken us memorie,
> Of hym that stood in greet prosperitee,
> And is yfallen out of heigh degree
> Into myserie, and endeth wrecchedly.
> And they ben versified communely,
> Of six feet, which men lepen exametron.
> In prose eek been endited many oon,
> And eek in meetre, in many a sondry wyse.[1]

Only during the last century has the development of middle-class tragedies put an end to the notion that the protagonists of tragic events must be kings, statesmen or heroes. Aristotle's demand for *πρᾶξις σπουδαία*, which he kept in general terms, remains as valid as before; it is just that we no longer interpret it as referring to social status but in a wider human sense. In fact the demand for the tragic hero's high social standing has been replaced by what we might call the *significant depth* of his downfall: a 'tragic' experience involves a fall from an illusory world of security and happiness into the depth of inescapable anguish. This raises another equally important point. Real tragedy depends on a highly dynamic sequence of events. The mere evocation of sorrow, misery and depravity may move us deeply and appeal strongly to our conscience, but for tragedy there is no place here. Aristotle has clearly recognised its link with event when he characterises tragedy not as a portrayal of people but of actions and of life. In this respect he understood the tragedies of his own people better than modern interpreters who so often, with the 'impertinent familiarity' that Nietzsche cautioned against, want to force upon them the categories of modern psychology.

[1] 'A tragedy, as ancient books record for us, is a type of story concerning one who formerly enjoyed great prosperity but, falling from his high estate into misery, comes to a wretched end. Tragedies are commonly composed in verses of six feet, called hexameters. Many also are written in prose, and others in varied meters.' (From the prologue to *The Monk's Tale*; the author is grateful to Maria Wickert for bringing this evidence to his attention.)

A second condition to be fulfilled by whatever we are to acknowledge as tragic, in art or in life, is that it should be *relevant to the world we live in.* The fall must affect us, it should come close to us, change us. Only when we feel that *Nostra res agitur*, when we are deeply stirred, do we experience tragedy. It is, dramatically speaking, of little importance whether the setting in which events take place is familiar to us, or whether a subtle psychological portrayal attempts to bring the figures as close to us as possible. One may appreciate Ibsen highly as a master of dramatic construction and as the genuinely great poet he has shown himself to be in *Peer Gynt*, *Rosmersholm* and other works; and yet one may ask oneself if the fate of the hysterical woman who, disgusted and bored with life, snatches General Gabler's revolver, really affects us – affects *us*, who after the experiences of two world wars must live with the terrifying problem of how to avert the destruction of all life on earth. Sophocles' *Oedipus the King* antedates *Hedda Gabler* and her like by more than two millennia, but the great drama of the defencelessness of human existence has lost none of its tremendous impact.

Our third demand of tragedy is a general one, but it has been particularly well fulfilled in Greek drama. The protagonist of tragedy caught in an inescapable conflict must be *fully aware of his situation*; he must suffer knowingly. There will be no tragic effect when a passive victim, dull and dumb, is led to a place of execution. This is the reason why the 'dramas' of Zacharias Werner and his colleagues, in which destiny plays cat and mouse with unsuspecting people, have nothing whatever to do with tragedy. Tragedy was a product of the Greek way of thinking, and one of its components is the 'need to explain' (*λόγον διδόναι*). That is why the great figures of the Attic stage never tire of expounding, in long uninterrupted speeches, the reasons for their acts, the agony of their decisions and the powers they have to contend with. Jean Anouilh, one of the great modern dramatists, has the same thing in mind when, in his *Antigone*, he makes his leader of the chorus, reflecting on events, say: 'Don't mistake me: I said "shout": I did not say groan, whimper, complain. That you cannot do. But you can shout aloud; you can get all those things said that you . . . never even knew you had it in you to say. And you don't say these things because it will do any good to say them. . . . You say them for their own sake . . . because you learn a lot from them.'[1]

In Greek tragedy rational reflection and wild emotional outbursts are formally and very strictly separated. This sometimes results in what to us are harsh juxtapositions, such as Sophocles' Antigone when she is about to meet her death; it occurs particularly often in Euripidean tragedy.

In fact both the striving for ultimate intellectual clarity and the desire to be consumed in the fire of passionate emotions are profoundly and fundamentally Greek. We now know more about Apollo and Dionysus than it was possible to know in Nietzsche's time, but we may accept as still valid his recognition that certain definite traits in the character of both gods reflect the duality just mentioned. We can only refer in passing to the fact that this polar tension, which was of such immense importance to Greek creativity in general and which touches on the secret of their art, is rooted in origins of the Greek people and the heterogeneous elements from which it was composed.

So far we have only spoken of plainly intelligible matters. Our fourth point, however, touches on a difficult problem, one which particularly concerns Greek drama. To Goethe's remark about an insoluble conflict quoted earlier we can now add another from his *Conversations with Eckermann* which throws it into relief: 'Only a conflict for which there can be no solution is of basic importance, and it may arise from a collision of circumstances of any kind, provided that they are really rooted in nature and are genuinely tragic.' Yet another often quoted passage from a letter to Schiller shows how radical Goethe conceived this conflict to be: 'I certainly do not know myself well enough to be sure if I could write a real tragedy. I am frightened even to undertake it, and am almost convinced that I might destroy myself in the attempt.'

The idea of a conflict from which there is no escape has become the pivot of modern theories and has been called the essential condition of a tragic situation. But this leads to difficulties. There can be no doubt that the *Oresteia* of Aeschylus is one of the greatest of Greek dramas. But the ending of this tremendous poem does

[1] Reprinted from Lewis Galantière's translation of Jean Anouilh's *Antigone*, originally published in the French by *La Table Ronde*, by kind permission of Methuen and Co., Ltd., Random House Inc., and the author.

not leave man broken by the insoluble conflicts which have emerged in the play; it embodies a reconciliation so far-reaching that it embraces the world of the gods as well as man in his suffering. We know little about the trilogies of Aeschylus, but enough to be quite certain that the *Oresteia* was not an exceptional case. Other trilogies, like those of Danaus and Prometheus, had a conciliatory ending. Moreover the later tragedies of Sophocles, the *Electra*, the *Philoctetes* and the *Oedipus at Colonus*, have endings that definitely imply a reconciliation or a harmonious solution. The fact that this even applies to the *Electra* and that Clytaemnestra and Aegisthus find their death as evildoers, not as victims of a tragic entanglement, only confirms our views. Such Euripidean plays as the *Helen* and the *Ion* have a happy ending.

So our provisional definition leads to confusion, for no one would be prepared to support the paradox that the *Oresteia* is not a tragedy or to prove Goethe wrong in his own field. To clear up this confusion, which is usually passed over in silence, we have to start from the word 'tragedy.' Its early history bristles with problems which will be discussed in the next chapter. What matters here is to realise that tragedy can be seen simply as an actual historical phenomenon within the cultural setting that brought it into being. As Wilamowitz put it, in his introduction to the *Heracles* of Euripides: 'An Attic tragedy is part of a heroic saga, rounded off and poetically adapted in a noble style for recital by a chorus of citizens and two or three actors; intended for performance as part of a public festival in the sanctuary of Dionysus.' This definition does justice to historical facts without passing over anything essential. The episodes in question were essentially serious ones, but this does not in any way exclude from Attic tragedy a happy ending with a reconciliation of opposing forces and the rescue of those in peril. But as early as classical times there is a trend which is unmistakable in the passage of the *Poetics* where Euripides is called the most tragic of Attic playwrights because of his catastrophic endings – a trend corroborated by the later meaning of the word τραγικός. The serious episodes chosen as subject for tragedy usually involved suffering. Since this guaranteed what Aristotle considered to be tragedy's specific effect, namely a relief from certain emotions, such events were increasingly regarded as the core of tragedy. Thus an inner logic gradually forced tragedy in the direction of a 'sorrowful drama,' which was definitely not its character at the time when Attic culture was at its height. Recent debates on the idea of tragedy have, however, continued this trend by taking as their starting-point the most radical of dramatic conflicts, thus claiming that the essence of tragedy is its inescapability.

It is quite clear from this account that our modern concept of the tragic is based directly on Greek tragedy, but that the application of the notion we have developed (that of inescapable conflict) to Greek tragedy's earliest fifth-century forms must lead to discrepancies. But the statement that a number of Attic tragedies end in happiness and harmony and are therefore not tragedies in the modern sense was not intended to imply that they did not contain a wealth of tragic motifs. Can one conceive anything more profoundly tragic than the fate of Orestes who had to strike down his mother and was then driven to madness by the Erinyes? Even one of the most serene plays of Sophocles, the *Philoctetes*, is full of tragic situations: an honourable young man hardly able to bear the strain of lying under compulsion, and a suffering hero who, cheated out of hope and faith, sees himself abandoned to destruction. And what bitterness must Oedipus have lived through before he could find peace in the sacred grove at Colonus?

Some formal distinctions may bring order to these complex problems. Let us begin with the most extreme concept of tragedy reached so far: the *totally tragic world view*. This can be provisionally defined as the world conceived as a place where forces and values predestined to come into conflict will inevitably be destroyed; a destruction that remains unexplained by any transcendent purpose.

The second stage in our line of development – or ascent – can be called *total tragic conflict*. Here also there is no escape and the end is destruction. But this conflict, however unalterable its course, does not embrace the whole world. It is only an occurrence within the world, so that what in this special case must end in death and destruction may be part of a transcendent totality, whose laws give it meaning. And if man should learn to recognise such laws and their workings, the conflict would be resolved on a higher level than the one on which it took its deadly course.

The third of these phenomena is the *tragic situation*. Here again we find the same constituent elements: opposing forces poised for battle: man, seeing no escape from perilous conflict, and realising that he is doomed to destruction. But this anguished awareness of the inescapable, which is inherent in the tragic situation, need not be the end. The stormy heavens may break to shed the light of salvation.

These three distinctions raise some profound questions about man's view of the world. These will later be our main concern. At present we shall merely try, on the basis of the distinctions we have formulated, to see how far Greek dramas can be called tragedies when they are not wholly sorrowful and do not fit into Goethe's definition. Let us consider the *Oresteia* by Aeschylus. There can be no doubt of its potent tragic content. Yet only the fate of Agamemnon and Clytaemnestra represents a totally tragic conflict from which complete ruin must result. Orestes, on the other hand, has been forced into a tragic situation which, although it brings him to the abyss of madness, is not beyond ultimate resolution by the interceding grace of the highest god. The final play, and in the light of it the entire trilogy, is incompatible with a totally tragic world view, in which man would have to surrender to such destructive forces as are inherent in existence itself. The conflict in which Orestes becomes involved is unspeakably horrible, but as a conflict it is not totally tragic, since it allows for a reconciliation of opposing forces and thereby for a liberation from suffering and anguish. The fate of Orestes should therefore be considered a *tragic situation*, a stormy phase on the road to harmony. These distinctions can therefore help to answer our initial question. The reason why dramas like the trilogy of Aeschylus, with its conciliatory ending, do not fit into Goethe's definition is that the latter only applies to total tragic conflict. We nevertheless call them tragedies, not only because they belong to a particular type of ancient literature but because their tragic content is apparent in the situations we have discussed.

This distinction may also prove useful when judging the work of a single poet, or a class of literary works. An Attic tragedy, as we saw, may be considered genuinely tragic in so far as it presents a tragic situation, which may however be harmoniously resolved. On the other hand its theme may be a totally tragic conflict ending in death. The final scene of *Oedipus the King* belongs to this category, and here it is particularly important to ask whether we must assume that it reveals a fundamentally tragic world-view or whether the poet leaves open a way to liberation, to enlightened acceptance.

In all three forms under discussion we find ourselves dealing with genuine tragedy, which is ultimately rooted in the actual experience of human sorrows. When these are no longer evident, when a truly tragic situation is replaced by a gaudy spectacle of chance events, and the hero's full awareness of his terrible plight by theatrical gestures and lamentations, we can no longer speak of tragedy. This has a bearing on a later chapter, which will discuss how far the plays of Euripides, e.g. the *Helen*, can be considered tragedies.

The frequently discussed problem of whether tragedy is conceivable within the scope of a Christian view of the world may also be mentioned here. Opinions vary greatly even among Christian thinkers. For some tragedy is the very stigma of true paganism, which Christ has left behind Him. For Bernhardt, Christian salvation has suspended neither the laws of nature nor the form in which historical events occur: 'When one considers the structure of historical events one cannot escape the conclusion that these events obey a tragic law.' Those who theorised on tragedy from a non-religious standpoint have, on the whole, flatly denied the possibility of tragedy within the realm of Christian faith. In the light of our approach the whole question appears capable of a simple solution. There can be no doubt that a totally tragic world view is incompatible with Christianity: the two are diametrically opposed. A tragic *situation*, on the other hand, is equally well conceivable within the Christian world as anywhere else. In fact one might agree with Bernhardt that since the Christian world has acquired an added dimension, the occurrence of tragedy is even more likely. Nor should we exclude the possibility of a total tragic conflict. The type of suffering that culminates in physical annihilation may yet, in a transcendent realm, acquire its true significance and thereby be redeemed.

The suggestion that the essence of tragedy may appear in three different forms enables a number of problems to be clarified. Although these distinctions are phenomenological, they correspond in principle with the view of the historical development of tragedy which distinguishes tragic suffering – more or less comparable to our 'tragic situation' – as it was first symbolically represented in myth, from tragic suffering when it has gained the importance of a central theme for human existence as a whole.

We have dwelt at some length on this aspect of our approach in the hope of throwing light on our final questions. First, however, we should deal with yet another subsidiary question: that of *tragic guilt*. This subject has likewise been under discussion for centuries and could be the subject of an important chapter on the history of Western thought. The notion that tragic guilt necessarily implies moral guilt was already foreshadowed in classical times. The most important and influential feature of Seneca's dramas was the transformation of Attic tragedy from within, the latter being remoulded in the spirit of Stoicism. The tragic theatre became a place where the pattern of human passions was revealed by the Stoic sage – in a spirit of strong disapproval – as the source of all evil. Such figures from ancient myths as Phaedra and Atreus were made to serve as a warning of what may happen when man's violent emotions are not kept within bounds by the strength of his *logos*. Heracles, on the other hand, appears in radiant contrast as the hero of Stoic virtue; and to the horror and distress which tragedy is intended to evoke a new element is added: the admiration which was later to play such an important part in the Baroque theatre. The great Attic dramatists were not responsible for antique drama's great influence on Western Europe in a period of its spiritual decline; it was Seneca whose influence was decisive. With his dramas the moralising trend of Stoicism asserted itself and Kurt von Fritz was able to show how this was bound to coalesce with Christian ideas of guilt-consciousness.

The effect of these combined influences was tremendous. For centuries it was generally accepted that, in the words of Jules de la Mesnardière[1]: 'Le théâtre est le throsne de la Justice.' Even in the posthumous studies on Shakespeare by Otto Ludwig tragic guilt is discussed within the framework of such notions. And not only did these views prevail in the theory of drama, they influenced the interpretation of the great works of the classical Greek theatre with disastrous results. When we discuss the Oedipus plays we shall show how a petty preoccupation with balancing moral accounts

[1] *Poetics* (Paris, 1640).

has for a long time barred the way to the understanding of these and other great tragedies.

The historical influences under which tragedy was turned into a demonstration of moral reckoning, in which crime and punishment would cancel each other out, have been discussed. But in this development a clear statement by Aristotle was either ignored or distorted. In a passage of the 13th chapter of the *Poetics*, mentioned above, Aristotle considers it proper and effective in terms of tragedy, when the hero's fall from status and prosperity is caused by an 'error' (ἁμαρτία). But he protected himself with the greatest possible care against the misinterpretation that what he meant was a moral guilt for in the same sentence he states explicitly that it need not be a moral failure which causes the tragic downfall. And this statement he considers so important that a little later, when he speaks of the necessity of the reversal of prosperity into misfortune, he repeats emphatically that this reversal ought *not* to be caused by moral sin but should be the consequence of a great 'error'. Even if Aristotle had not been so explicit here the trend of his argument would lead us to the conclusion that the error in question was not intended to be a moral one. For according to Aristotle the man who is tragically doomed should be neither morally perfect nor depraved (prophetically, he seems to reject both the moral hero and the evil-doer of stoic moralising dramas); he should be essentially like ourselves, though of somewhat greater stature. Hence Aristotle's much discussed demand for 'average' characters, a notion we find it hard to apply to the protagonists of Attic tragedy, but one which embodies the just claim that it should at all times be possible to relate genuine tragedy to ourselves. In this trend of thought there is no place for the balancing of moral guilt and expiation, and Aristotle says explicitly that we can only experience 'pity' (ἔλεος) if we witness an 'undeserved' (ἀνάξιος) misfortune.

So far all is clear and the contrast between Aristotle's precise statement and the manner in which it was applied in later centuries remains a source of wonder. We must, however, ask what Aristotle meant by 'error' when he so definitely excluded from the term any moral interpretation. It might be assumed that he meant the intellectual failure to grasp what is right, a failure of human insight amidst the confusion of life which surrounds us. This no doubt covers a good deal of his meaning, but there is an important amplification, which Kurt von Fritz has supplied. It is not simply a matter of contrasting *ἁμαρτία* as innocent failure, with the type of wickedness that must be morally condemned. We must assume that for the ancients there existed a type of guilt for which no one was subjectively responsible, but which none the less was objective, was real, a horror in the eyes of gods and men, capable of affecting an entire country like a pestilence. Oedipus is a concrete and thoroughly Greek example. It is within the scope of this type of error of guilt (not sin in the Stoic or Christian sense) that we find tragedy at its most impressive on the Attic stage. How far this type of guilt may also have its origin in a failure of human understanding under the pressure of adverse circumstances we can learn, for instance, from Sophocles' *Women of Trachis*.

This may have touched on the deepest roots of genuine tragedy, but should not be regarded as a magic explanatory formula for the interpretation of all Greek tragedies. It should be emphasised that *moral* guilt may also play an active part in tragedy, especially in Aeschylus. This does not imply that the poet probes no deeper than the mere balance of guilt and punishment, but that moral guilt, in the sense of true culpability, can be an issue for him also.

The potentiality of committing an 'error,' which Aristotle discusses in the passages mentioned, is supposed to be inherent in human existence itself and this appears to confirm our supposition that we have in the *Poetics* a genuine theoretical approach to tragedy – an approach which is admittedly not developed at all in the surviving text.

Closely connected with tragedy's possible role as a moral example is the question of its pedagogic task or intention. Actually this is only part of a much wider range of problems centred on poetry and education, but it is lent importance by the passionate interest and diverse opinions aroused by the discussion of the theatre's role as a moral institution.

The earliest demand that tragic poets should be educators was voiced by Aristophanes in his *Frogs*. In the contest between Aeschylus and Euripides the winner was to be he who made the city profit most by his instruction. This notion, probably originating in Sophist circles, has never since been lost. Plato adopted it most radically in his plan for an ideal State and we might mention in passing Horace's well-known formula 'aut prodesse aut delectare.'[1] For the French classical theatre, and in contemporary theories, the educational value of dramatic poetry was beyond question, and Lessing, though he viewed the matter from an entirely different standpoint, agreed in principle: 'To improve us is the aim of all types of poetry. It is distressing that this should even need to be proved, worse still that there should be poets who themselves doubt it.' But such poets there were, and by no means the least gifted, in complete disagreement with Lessing on this point. In the *Xenien* – Goethe and Schiller had once and for all decided never to discuss the matter of authorship but to let it rest for all eternity – we read in Part 120:

> A poet must improve, improve us! Does this mean the beadle's staff
> May never for a moment rest upon your back?

The poem is certainly Goethe's, but in this case Schiller must have made common cause with him. Not the youthful Schiller who had written a work on the theatre considered as a moral institution, but the same Schiller who, in his study of the reasons why we enjoy tragic themes, complained that the intention to pursue moral virtue – this being the highest aim – produced mediocrity in art, and warped theories on the subject. Goethe began his 49th votive tablet *To the Moralists* as follows:

> Teach then! It suits you well and we approve of the habit.
> However the muse will not permit you to bully her.

Even in a critical work on the *Poetics*, Goethe's attitude towards our problem was extremely negative: 'But music influences morality as little as any other art, and it is always wrong to expect her to do this.' Eight years earlier Grillparzer, in his aphorisms on the character of tragedy, had been in lively agreement with previous opinions of Goethe's: 'The theatre is not an institute for the correction of criminals nor an approved school for adolescents.' It is also worth quoting the words of E. T. A. Hoffmann, one of whose many gifts was a talent for criticism of a high order: 'Generally speaking I date the decline of our contemporary theatre from the time when the moral improvement of man was proclaimed

[1] *Ars Poetica* 333.

to be the highest, indeed the only aim of the theatre, and we wanted to turn it into a house of correction.'

This conflict, which found expression in the works of great poets, kept its importance in some modern studies of tragedy, which supported the opinion that poets were the teachers of their people. But opposition to this point of view has increased recently, and especially in connection with the problem of *catharsis* scholars have gone so far as to deny not only the pedagogic intention but even the moral influence of tragedy.

We entirely agree with Goethe when he rejects the notion of a pedagogic programme for dramatic poets, for all poets in fact. Poetry cannot be shackled by a programme even if the latter is conceived on a far higher level than in the past. Yet we should be careful not to throw out the baby with the bath water, especially where Attic tragedy is concerned. Each of the three great tragedians may at times emerge from the frame of the mythical plot and speak to the Athenians assembled in the theatre of Dionysus in an attempt – whether urged by holy desire (Aeschylus and Sophocles), or by a deep faith in the power of reason (Euripides) – to impart his knowledge of gods and men to others. But this does not mean that the entire work was from the start subordinated to pedagogic intention.

These are difficult and far-reaching problems. When we accept with Goethe that educational purpose and true art are incompatible, do we not imply that great poetry has no pedagogic value? Do we not unthinkingly discard as rubbish one of the few hopeful thoughts that remain in the spiritual desert of our age? And may philology ignore the fact that for centuries the Greeks brought up their youth on the poetry of Homer?

To escape from this dilemma we should distinguish between pedagogic intention and effect. Goethe, who made us face this problem, also shows us where the solution lies. In the 12th book of *Dichtung und Wahrheit* he says: 'For although a good work of art can and will exert a moral influence, to demand a moral purpose from an artist means to interfere with his art.' We should rate the value of this moral influence very high indeed, and the writer is convinced that 'higher' education will defeat itself by ignoring it. Our guess is that the 'moral influence' of great and genuine art depends on its being consistent with a strict order of values, so that the work of art as such bears witness to these values. Such a testimony, moreover, is far more valid than sophistic pedantries on the subject of the true, the good and the beautiful.

We now come to our final problem. This problem, which we must constantly bear in mind when dealing with the poets and their works singly, demands a historical approach.

It was unthinkable that, as long as dramatic poets and theorists of drama looked upon tragedy as a moral example and on poetic justice as the reflection of a great divine order, there should ever arise even the slightest doubt about the meaningfulness of a tragic event. The fact that according to Aristotle genuine tragic suffering was also undeserved suffering was forgotten or deliberately ignored. But once the idea of tragedy was no longer fettered by such notions and the great works of the Attic theatre, on which Aristotle's dictum was based, could be approached in a new way, the question of the meaning of tragedy began to raise its head. In fact the increasing number of attempts to formulate a theory of tragedy, in recent times, made this question the focus of attention. Here we can only pinpoint some arguments which indicate the general trend of thought.

The core of our problem was reached, in the nineteenth century, by the remarkable convergence between a theory of the essence of tragedy and dramatic poetry itself. Three types of tragic drama were distinguished by Schopenhauer: apart from tragedy caused by evil or by a blind decree of fate, we find a third form which he considered of particular importance: a tragedy of circumstance brought about by equal conflicting forces. Schopenhauer naturally found in this tragic possibility a confirmation of his pessimistic world view. Now it so happens that this tragedy of equal opposing forces, inherent in a particular situation, has actually been dramatised by a poet, who only in the course of his writing became aware of a similarity with Schopenhauer's ideas. This was Hebbel, whose work reveals a radically tragic view of existence. He sees, deeply embedded in the world, opposing forces which spell conflict and annihilation to any one who finds himself situated between the two fronts. Since for Hebbel this tragic conflict reaches deep into God's essential nature, those who spoke of his 'pantragic' world view were justified.

Within its horizon a moral emphasis, be it Stoic or Christian, of tragic events has become impossible. When Hebbel speaks of tragic guilt he means something totally different. He has in fact done his utmost to give validity to a concept which in recent times has confused the debate on tragedy with mysticism of a most unclassical kind: 'This guilt is a primeval one, inseparable from the concept Man, barely reaching his consciousness and implied in life itself . . . It is independent of the direction of human will, it accompanies all human action, whether we turn towards good or evil, for we can trespass beyond good measure in either case. It is with this that the highest form of drama has to deal.'

Hebbel's 'pantragic' world view is not identical with absolute pessimism, nor with the view that the tragedy of equal opposing forces should imply that their conflict is senseless. On the contrary, Hebbel sees in the person of the tragic hero the fighter who opposes the world and thus prevents it from stagnating. His defeat is inevitable but by no means senseless. The time in which he lives is not yet ripe for the values for which he fights and dies, but his sacrifice opens the way to a better future. Hegel's triple movement of thesis, antithesis and synthesis is what emerges from this interpretation of tragic events and it is not accidental that Hegel in his exegesis of the *Antigone* has stated that the pattern of tragic conflict is produced by the shock of equivalent opposing forces. It does not concern us here that Hegel's interpretation of the *Antigone* is wrong.

Neither the end of the nineteenth nor the beginning of the twentieth century, however, recognised any longer the dialectic of tragic events, so that, to quote Oskar Walzel, the optimistic pinnacle of Hebbel's all-tragic scheme was removed. In the debates of this period Max Scheler has been particularly influential. Scheler's characterisation of tragedy resembles in many ways what we termed a 'totally tragic world view'. For him the essentials of tragedy are that it is inescapable and that those who are doomed to destruction are morally innocent. For the horror of the catastrophe the cosmos is made responsible, since it either allows or demands destruction in a conflict of values. The awareness of inevitability gives tragic suffering itself a kind of aloofness that is tinged with satisfaction.

Here is a definite concept of tragedy, as inevitable and ultimately senseless, which is influential even today. The pungent observations of the chorus leader from Jean Anouilh's *Antigone* on an essentially tragic situation are in startling agreement with Scheler's characterisation of tragedy: 'Tragedy is clean, it is restful, it is flawless. It has nothing to do with melodrama – with wicked villains, persecuted maidens, avengers, sudden revelations and eleventh-hour repentances. Death, in melodrama, is really horrible because it is never inevitable. . . . In a tragedy, nothing is in doubt and everyone's destiny is known. This makes for tranquillity . . . he who kills is as innocent as he who gets killed: it's all a matter of what part you are playing. Tragedy is restful; and the reason is that hope, that foul, deceitful thing, has no part in it. . . . In melodrama, you argue and struggle in the hope of escape. That is vulgar; it's practical. But in tragedy, where there is no temptation to try to escape, argument is gratuitous: it's kingly.'[1]

This cannot be the final verdict of the great French poet on the suffering of the world. The characters who are so determined to reject the world as they find it are neither branded as senseless throughout, nor do they lack awareness of these great and simple values in which human life may find fulfilment. But this is outside the scope of our problem. If we were to search for an absolute extreme in the range of gradually changing concepts of tragedy, we could not find a more pregnant formulation of it than the one just quoted from *Antigone*. Objections were soon raised to this, however. Behind many of them loomed Nietzsche's conviction that an increasingly bourgeois evaluation of life and the impoverishment of the imagination through rationalism barred the approach to a direct and genuine understanding of tragedy. But a clarification of the different standpoints only ensued when modern theories of tragedy were applied to concrete historical phenomena.

The first question asked was if one could speak of tragedy in connection with Schiller's dramas. The question may appear absurd, but in the light of the attitude which, to a greater extent than Hebbel, regarded tragedy as inevitable and as senseless, it was perfectly valid; for the hero's catastrophe in Schiller's dramas was transcended by the idea of free will, and on a level of experience largely determined by Kantian philosophy, the tragic event appeared as deeply significant. Morality, therefore, prevented the emergence of a totally tragic world view in undiluted form. In this

[1] Anouilh's *Antigone*, op. cit.

context Schiller's idealism was compared with that of the Baroque theatre, although both were rooted in different worlds and the manner in which tragedy was transcended differed in essence. It was argued, however, that there existed a profound similarity in that in both cases the hero's suffering found its justification and reward on a higher level and pure tragedy was therefore suspended. Briefly the problem had narrowed down to this: either the definition of tragedy was too narrow, perhaps altogether wrong, or Schiller could not be considered a tragedian.

When the debate had reached this point Friedrich Sengle joined in, with a full frontal attack against the theory of tragedy of the post-Hebbel period. This saw only a pointless conflict between equivalent forces and values in Hebbel's relativism and tragic sense. Sengle – here in agreement with the earlier opponents mentioned – considered this view to be symptomatic of a more secular, even bourgeois attitude towards tragedy. He is radically opposed to this. Not only does he not exclude transcendent values from the realm of tragedy, he insists that they are essential to it. According to him genuine tragedy only occurs when a tragic conflict finds its solution on a higher level and thus becomes meaningful. The real tragedian must pass through a realm of conflict and catastrophe in order to reach that higher level of understanding where both are reconciled. 'A great tragedy never ends in disharmony and doubt but rather in a statement of triumphant faith, in which the meaning of the fate depicted, as well as the sadness of the world's condition which it reveals, are confirmed.'

We shall pass over the question whether Sengle in his view of tragedy has not separated the realms of conflict and solution too sharply, whether they should not rather be conceived as inseparably interwoven. What matters here is the clear distinction between tragedy bound to the absolute values which give it meaning, and tragedy where this connection is severed, doomed to despair or downcast resignation in the face of meaninglessness.

A number of Karl Jaspers' observations point in the same direction as Sengle's essay. The following sounds like a declaration of war against the nihilism of a completely tragic world-view: 'There exists no tragedy without transcendence. Even in a mere self-assertion, when the battle against gods and fate is lost, there is an element of transcendence, namely an aspiration towards man's genuine being, his true self, experienced at the moment of defeat.' In Jaspers also can be heard the same essential theme that we discern in all those authors who attack a radically nihilistic concept of tragedy: 'Whenever a complete lack of faith seeks to express itself, unredeemed tragedy is apt to serve as a veil to hide the void. Nihilistic man, in his pride, sees tragic grandeur in the pathos of his heroic self-knowledge.'

For Jaspers therefore tragedy as a single occurrence (we would say a tragic situation or a total tragic conflict) has no finality. It occurs in time and is therefore an event in the foreground, beyond which ultimate Being may be perceived. And we would like to add: although, or even because, tragic suffering is so bitterly hard to bear, it is for man a path to self-knowledge.

Our discussion of this last and most important problem concerning tragedy is intended to determine as clearly as possible two conflicting viewpoints. Thus we have kept open the question which will entirely dominate our further enquiry. At least it has become clear by now that opinions on the essence of tragedy represent at the same time a particular view of the world. We have no desire to force our opinion on others whose premises differ from ours, any more than we wish to hide it. The aim of our enquiry is both simpler and more scholarly. There has recently been heated discussion as to whether tragedy presupposes a meaningless world, or whether it allows or even compels us to assume the existence of a higher order which transcends all conflict and suffering. Philosophy and the exponents of modern philology have had much to say on the subject. Those more fully acquainted with antiquity have contributed far less to its solution. This is all the more astonishing since tragedy made its first appearance in ancient Greece and this was the starting point of the entire debate. In dealing with Attic tragedy we shall therefore ask whether the tragic content of each poet, each single work, points to a meaningless void or a higher order.

The clarification of this problem seems of such vital importance that we want to end by summarising the views we expressed earlier on the different stages of tragic awareness.

As we saw, in treating single works we shall have to decide whether their tragic quality consists in a tragic situation or a total tragic conflict. We showed that both may be the case: the horror may be resolved, or have to be endured till the very end. But this raises another urgent question: where we witness the destruction of the sufferer in total tragic conflict, is this all the poet has to show us? Has he no words for us that point beyond the harrowing events towards a higher world of meaning and order? Does he leave us with a crushing sense of defeat, does he perhaps expect us to accept in cool resignation the kind of world in which everything ends in annihilation? Or does he, through a tragic example, uplift us in the awareness that all this occurs in a world of absolute norms and values, a world which allows us to salvage imperishable goods even from tragic affliction?

Each of the three great playwrights will show us tragic situations as well as total tragic conflict. But – this is our main question – does Attic tragedy also contain evidence of the kind of totally tragic world view in which annihilation and suffering do not point beyond themselves but are the culmination of a bitter philosophy?

We have tried to develop this question theoretically to a degree which leaves no doubt of its significance and importance. The answer will emerge from our treatment of the surviving remains of Greek Tragedy. But we hope that the results achieved in the realm of the earliest tragedies may prove fruitful in the wider context of the problem outlined here.

CHAPTER TWO

The Beginnings

EVERY work of art needs to be understood on two levels. Since it faces us as a single inimitable phenomenon its peculiar character can only be grasped if we immerse ourselves in it and thus become aware of the forces that brought it into being, the laws which determined its form. And since every genuine work of art is a cosmos this remains an unending task, at all times, even our own, to be faced anew. But since a living work of art is also subject to historical influences, it is part of a stream of events and cannot be regarded as isolated from the movement of historical changes. The tendency today is to play off one manner of approach against the other, the one concerned with the essence of the single phenomenon, the other with its place in history, the former being strongly favoured. That is understandable as a reaction against a form of historicism which traced its lines of development in complete disregard of its essential character. But this reaction has its dangers, in that it tears apart what should be correlated: a grasp of essentials is impossible without historical knowledge, while the latter cannot hope to elucidate essentials by merely giving a work of art its place in a historical sequence. As methods of approach they are by no means in conflict, in fact their synthesis alone can further our knowledge. To achieve such a synthesis is the task we have set ourselves in the following chapters and for this reason we begin by asking: what were the origins of Greek and therefore of European tragedy?

When during the last century we began to understand the forms of primitive culture it became tempting to connect tragedy – among many other phenomena – with these early strata. In different parts of the world mimes and above all masked dances had been discovered among primitive food gatherers and hunting tribes from their earliest stages, and these could be compared with some very ancient forms of Greek cult. Attempts to find the origins of Greek tragedy here were passionately repudiated. Sentiment rejected the notion that one of the noblest creations of Greek, indeed of human culture, should be connected in any way with the exotic dances of savages, while it was argued more soberly that nowhere had any real form of drama ever emerged from primitive magic practices. The objection is largely valid and forces us to see Attic tragedy in its decisive stages as solely the product of Hellenic culture and of the genius of its great poets. We must add here that in recent times we have come to reject the absurdly exaggerated claims of evolutionist theory. Evolution as we understand it is far more determined by single creative acts than by elusive, quasi-natural, energies which force their way vertically upwards through the different strata of culture. But the material which anthropologists have gathered for comparison from all over the world is by no means valueless. If it cannot throw light on the history of Greek tragedy, it does so on its pre-history. It has rightly been called the hidden foundation of drama.

There is one requisite in particular – the mask – which neither tragedy nor comedy has ever dispensed with, and which goes back to those earliest strata. In primitive culture its uses may vary; most frequently it is a protection, meant to guard man against hostile powers, but a mask may also transfer the power of the daemon it represents to the wearer. The former does not interest us here but the second is most important because it brings in the element of transformation, which is essential to all dramatic representation. The mask was used for such a purpose on Greek soil from very ancient times. Already on Cretan and Mycenaean seals and on one Mycenaean fresco we find figures wearing animal masks. It is important to note that masks were mostly used in the cult of gods of nature and of vegetation and that their use persisted until quite late. At Pheneos in Arcadia the priest of Demeter wore on certain occasions the mask of the goddess; and terracotta figurines of animal-headed women at Lycosura, as well as representations of daemonic dancers of the same type on the mantle of a cult statue of Despoina, point to similar practices. In the cult of Artemis masks played an important part. The most significant pointer to this, after the report of Hesychius concerning the wooden masks of the Italic Cyrittoi in the cult of Artemis Corythalia, are the terracotta masks discovered by British excavations in the sanctuary of Artemis Orthia at Sparta. But masks played their most important part in the cult of the god to whom tragedy was dedicated, namely Dionysus. His own mask hanging on a pole was a cult object, so that he might even be called the God of the Mask. His worshippers, among whom satyrs were the most prominent, were also masked, and satyr masks were brought to his shrine as offerings. We should not forget that the use of masks in tragedy as well as comedy was deeply rooted in the domain of cult and that this in turn goes back to very early superstitious practices. A valuable indication that the magic significance of the mask was still a live experience at the end of the seventh century A.D. is given in a decree of the Trullan Synod: apart from the prohibition of other heathen practices priests were not to wear comic, tragic or satyr masks. And the abominable Dionysus should not be invoked when the wine was casked.

Within the domain of Greek culture there was no lack of practices which appear to have held the seed of drama. Whatever the Eleusinian mysteries consisted of in detail, they must certainly have contained representations from divine legend. The tale of a duel between Xanthos and Melanthos (the Fair and the Dark), connected with the hamlet Eleutherae on the border between Attica and Boeotia, suggests a Greek example of those ritual mock battles which are found almost everywhere. And the surviving customs, noted in Thrace, Thessaly and Epirus by British scholars, in which a wedding was enacted and the bridegroom killed and resuscitated, may well reflect ancient usages, although this cannot be proved. It is understandable that the idea arose that the origin of tragedy should be looked for in such customs, and yet there is no road that leads on from there. It is in the nature of such ritual that it should remain essentially unchanged since only an exact repetition of the act could guarantee the same result. Elsewhere, it is true, the firm structure of liturgical drama may be enlivened by mimic embellishments which then continue to evolve independently, but there is nothing in Greek culture to suggest such a development.

Thus we gain very little from this primitive material for the understanding of the growth of Greek tragedy. Slight as the evidence is, however, it forces us to recognise that ultimately both tragedy and comedy are rooted in the same soil, although in the case of comedy, with its animal choruses, its obscene language and the persistent phallic character of the performance, this is more obvious. To connect Greek tragedy with such matters is not to sin against its spirit. On the contrary, only by doing so can we measure the true greatness of this creation of the Greek spirit, whose inner power overcame what was barbaric and undisciplined to produce such a perfect phenomenon. Is it surprising that we should be so eager to know how this was achieved, when we can only see the end of the road at all clearly; and that tradition should present us with so many problems?

We possess one statement which promises to throw a good deal of light on this process, and its evaluation is obviously a matter of central importance. We read in the 4th chapter of Aristotle's *Poetics* that tragedy originated from the precentors who used to 'lead off' the dithyramb; and a little later in the same text that tragedy evolved from a kind of satyric play (*ἐκ σατυρικοῦ*) by a transformation in which the subject matter was gradually enlarged and the comic element discarded.

By rendering the words of Aristotle in this way, we show where we stand in relation to two aspects of their interpretation. We can take it that *ἐξάρχοντες τὸν διθύραμβον* means 'precentors' and that the term was meant to emphasise that their position was analogous to that of a chorus leader heading a group of respondents. It is true that the general use of the word *ἐξάρχειν* would permit us simply to translate it by 'singer'. However, the argument remains valid that Aristotle would hardly without reason have used the term *ἐξάρχειν* instead of simply *ᾄδειν*. Nor does this question touch on the present assertion that a dithyrambic chorus of singers represented an early stage of tragedy. On the other hand we assume that *σατυρικόν* does not mean here the fully developed satyr play, as Sophocles and Euripides produced it, but an earlier, far more primitive form of this play, though also performed by satyrs.

Obviously the crux of the matter is this: do Aristotle's statements have documentary value, or was it impossible for the founder of the Peripatetics to speak with any authority on the early history of tragedy? Has he used his scholarly prerogatives to fill the gaps in his knowledge with hypotheses, thus joining the ranks of modern scholars who have based their numerous conjectures on cults of the dead, hero worship and the mysteries of Eleusis, so that he is no more credible than they? On this question, which is of decisive importance for our views on the genesis of tragedy, opinions are as sharply divided today as they were formerly. Those who subscribe to Wilamowitz's statement 'the *Poetics* are, and must remain, the basis of our studies' have tried to prove Aristotle's credibility by pointing to the wealth of earlier work on which he could draw. Now it is true that the Greeks began to be conscious of their historical and artistic past in classical times, and that our problem was discussed, above all in the sophist literature of the fifth century; nor should we underrate the importance of oral tradition. But it remains impossible to judge either the quantity or the reliability of such material, so that the authenticity of Aristotle's statement remains probable, but not certain. But however thin the trickle of information may be, apart from the *Poetics*, it is not completely wanting; we also have our own observations on the available dramas. The decisive point, therefore, is whether we can harmonise such deductions concerning the early history of tragedy as we can make from the available evidence with Aristotle's statement. If the fragments in question are compatible with Aristotle's brief sketch, we must probably accept his statements as facts, however much we may disagree with his philosophy, which saw these facts in terms of pure entelechy (inherent, self-guided development), or object to his aesthetics which vitiates for us many of the judgments in the *Poetics*.

We shall soon see that there is evidence of a connection between satyrs and early forms of tragic poetry, and we shall find that the term tragedy itself corroborates Aristotle's assumption that the *σατυρικόν* was an embryonic stage of the tragic play. Many details, however, remain obscure and a different line of argument will lead us to firmer grounds for our conviction that there is a link between *σατυρικόν* and the phenomenon of tragedy which emerged from it. Greek culture, when at its height, knew no virtuosos in the sense of artists skilled in a variety of techniques. An artist remained strictly within the bounds of a particular *γένος*, or literary genre, and did not trespass beyond it. Plato shows us in two important passages how strictly the line was drawn between the two classes of dramatic composition. He makes Socrates speak in the *Republic*

LIBRARY ST. MARY'S COLLEGE

(395A) of the impossibility that one and the same author should be capable of producing good work in both tragedy and comedy. On the other hand, but not less significantly, he forces Agathon and Aristophanes, at the end of the *Symposium*, to agree with him that the same poet ought to be able to write tragedy and comedy. This is a purely theoretical debate and the very reluctance of the two poets, tragedian and comedian, shows how completely this view diverged from tradition and actuality. The combination of the two sharply separated genres in one person was practically unthinkable and information about a certain poet, Timocles, who was supposed to have written both types of drama, was dismissed by scholars. Only if we grasp the significance of the strictly closed literary genre, on the basis of Plato's evidence, can we properly assess the fact that the satyric play was by no means a separate *γένος* and that, precisely because it obeyed to a large extent the laws of tragedy, it was always produced by the same poets, in intimate conjunction with tragedy. This puts it beyond all doubt that, within the scope of Greek literature, satyr play and tragedy are of one class, and that Aristotle was right when he derived tragedy from *σατυρικόν*, since the reverse was unthinkable.

Aristotle, however, also mentions another embryonic form of tragedy, namely the dithyramb. This apparent discrepancy has been used in order to reject, all too hastily, his statements as a whole, and it is certainly strange at first sight that he should not have attempted to harmonise these apparently contradictory assertions. But then his *Poetics* is not a carefully edited book intended for publication; it is best regarded as a collection of notes for his lectures, which makes it understandable that his assertions often seem incomplete and not fully considered. If he was correct in his statement about the origin of tragedy then we must assume that dithyrambs were sometimes sung by satyrs. This assumption would require confirmation from an independent source and this we happen to possess. The dithyramb was a Dionysiac cult song, thought to have been chanted by a chorus and its leader. Its oldest forms are beyond recall, but we find traces of it in Pindar, clearer indications in Bacchylides. When this poet's work was rescued from the Egyptian desert over sixty years ago his Theseus dithyramb with its dialogue form created a considerable stir. It is however more probable, in the case of Pindar, Aeschylus' near contemporary, that fully developed tragedies influenced the dithyramb than that the latter represented a precursor of tragedy. But although we know very little about the development of the dithyramb we do possess an invaluable reference to the work of a choric poet, Arion, whom we find at the turn of the seventh century at the court of the Corinthian ruler Periander. Herodotus tells us (I, 23) that Arion was the first to write, name and sing a dithyramb. This cannot mean that Arion created the dithyramb, which had long existed as a Dionysiac cult song. Presumably Herodotus meant that Arion raised the old religious chants to an artistic form, and that since he named his songs according to their apparently varying content he must have changed their character. The remarks on Arion in the *Suda* (s.v.) have a much wider range: 'he is supposed to be the inventor of the tragic mode (*τραγικοῦ τρόπου*), the first to have established a chorus, to have initiated sung dithyrambs, to have given a name to choric songs and to have introduced satyrs speaking verses.' The affinity between this late statement and that of Herodotus is obvious, and also the significance of what in the *Suda* appears to overshoot the mark. The late compiler was, as Bentley puts it so well, a sheep with a golden fleece and for a long time our attitude towards Aristotle determined which part of the description was stressed. But in 1908 H. Rabe edited a commentary[1] on Hermogenes by John the Deacon, and this contained a passage which provided a valuable justification of the account in the *Suda:* 'The first performance of tragedy (*τῆς δὲ τραγῳδίας πρῶτον δρᾶμα*) was introduced by Arion from Methymna, as Solon taught in his elegies.' Here suddenly a contemporary of Arion appears as witness on an important point, to take the place of the much later *Suda.* Now we shall no longer be able to doubt that in Corinth Arion made members of a chorus, who were masked as satyrs, sing dithyrambs. We therefore have the link between dithyramb and *σατυρικόν*, which we needed to accept Aristotle. Many details still remain obscure. We have no concrete idea of the form or content of these 'tragic' dithyrambs, but the evidence of the *Suda*, now confirmed by Solon, has taught us that they must have represented an important step in the direction of tragedy. Nor should this evidence be invalidated by dividing it up and interpreting it as if Arion was the inventor of

[1] Rhein. Mus. lxiii, 1908, 150.

three different genres, tragedies, dithyrambs and satyr plays. It has also taught us something else. The Peloponnesians always laid claim to the invention of tragic poetry, as we learn from Aristotle.[1] The Athenians denied this, justifiably in so far as tragedy, as we know it, was an Attic creation. In this field too Athens became the centre of intellectual creativity, but the material used came partly from an alien source: from the Peloponnese.

We have found that basically – and that is as far as we can go – Aristotle has been proved correct, but there remain questions which he has not answered directly. One of the most difficult is the one implied in the word *τραγῳδία*, which was as perplexing for the ancients as it is for us. They mainly concentrated on two interpretations, which are still controversial, namely 'A song with a goat as a prize,' for which 'goat-sacrifice song' is a mere variant, and secondly 'goat-song.' Whoever accepts the latter must necessarily connect it with the *σατυρικόν* as a preliminary phase of tragic drama and assume that the singers were those very satyrs whom we met in the early stage of tragic plays. This explanation rests on those parts of the *Poetics* which we have considered so far to be valid. Alexandrian scholars have studied these problems as diligently as we, and they too had to decide on their attitude towards Aristotle. They suddenly discovered a statement which seemed to undermine the Aristotelian structure at a vital point, and which even now is readily brought into play against the *Poetics*. Pratinas of Phlius (early fifth century) was said to have brought the satyr plays to Athens, but not before the form of tragedy had already been fully established. We have no reason to doubt this statement, but after all we have said about tragedy and *σατυρικόν* we can only interpret it as follows: at a time when fully developed tragedies had brought satyr plays into decline Pratinas took the lead and firmly re-established them, thus carrying on Peloponnesian tradition (he hailed from Phlius!). It is possible that the splendid song by Pratinas, which Athenaeus (XIV, 617b) has preserved for us, partly reflects these events that led to the satyrs regaining their ascendancy over the orchestra, and firmly secured them their place after the tragedy in future performances. The Alexandrian scholars, on the other hand, only saw the discrepancy between Pratinas as 'inventor' of the satyr plays and

[1] *Poetics* 1448a.

Aristotle's teaching. They saw no alternative to giving up Aristotle and looking for the origins of tragedy in milieus which particularly interested them. In the hubbub of the vast metropolis of Alexandria, which we may imagine to have been as sterile as most such conurbations, there was an upsurge of longing for the rustic and the simple, and a lively interest in folklore. It is true that a comparison with similar modern phenomena is only superficial. Whereas we have, at least from time to time, experienced a profound awareness of those inexhaustible, life-giving sources from which our people can and must draw, it was more a matter of interest in contrasts which drove Alexandrian poets and scholars towards such phenomena, which they sometimes really understood. Therefore the customs of Attic peasants at their sacrifices or wine harvests, and rustic antics like leaping over wine skins, were affectionately looked upon as worth studying. And since in this setting one came across Dionysus, to whom throughout tragedy was dedicated, and since moreover Thespis, the oldest known tragic poet, was of peasant stock, the origin of tragedy was connected with rustic Greek festivals. Horace, whose *Ars Poetica* is based on Hellenistic teaching, is the best known exponent of this theory (220) that a peasant singer used to compete with a 'tragic' song for the prize of a goat, which contest only later involved a satyr play as well.

By now we have learned to understand the character of Alexandrian scholarship and its particular bias too well to agree with the highly improbable assumption that Hellenistic scholars had more reliable material at their disposal than the much older Aristotle, and to accept their explanations on the strength of it.

The interpretation of the word *τραγῳδία* as a song for which the prize of a goat was offered, or as a song which accompanied the sacrifice of a goat – although we cannot exclude either – is far more forced than that of G. Welcker, who explains it as 'goat song.' If we accept this hypothesis we are bound to connect it with Aristotle's theory of the *σατυρικόν* being an early stage of tragedy: we can only expect to identify the satyrs with goat-singers. But here we have to face new difficulties. In Welcker's day the matter seemed perfectly clear. It was only necessary to look at one of the numerous statues of satyrs, for instance the magnificent flecked faun, to find in his pointed ears and funny little tail the perfect attributes of a goat. But our problems have since been thrown into hopeless confusion by new evidence. In order to understand it we must look more closely at the creatures who became so important to the Attic stage. Erwin Rohde has well said that in contrast with the romantic and musical character of our own perception of nature, that of the ancient Greeks was based on visual reality, with a tendency towards personification. In order to understand this fully we should observe the sunrise depicted on a crater (now in London): on one side Helios emerges with his team of horses, on the other the veiled goddess of the night is fleeing; a splendid winged Eros rushes ahead of the god of light, while the stars, conceived as gay youngsters, boldly dive into the sea.

For the Greeks their whole world was filled with forces that were conceived as persons, tender, loving, terrifying, lascivious or gay. The most wanton of these, simply bursting with vitality, were the satyrs or sileni as they were also called. In a fragment attributed to Hesiod (198) they are called 'good-for-nothing,' and Attic vase paintings show how richly they deserve this epithet, perhaps especially in the uninhibited portrayals of Duris. Here nature's urgent passionate life has found expression in figures which have, for all their mad recklessness, some of her aura of mystery, and in one or two cases even a prophetic quality.

Nearly all Indo-European peoples know similar creatures, though not in such vivid, plastic form. Around Mantua we find the 'wood-demons,' *gente salvatica*, half bestial and with tails, in Hessen the 'wild men' with their fleecy garments, in Graubünden the hairy *Waldfänken* who wear a skin apron. The Swedish *skougman* resembles the satyrs in his lasciviousness and even the *Perchten* from the district round Salzburg can be compared with them since they are vegetation demons with several animal attributes. Such demons who, especially in Northern Europe, closely resemble satyrs are not merely the playful product of a fantasy stirred by the mysteries of nature; they are firmly believed to incorporate the forces of increase and growth, and as such are of the greatest importance to mankind. To imitate them in mimic dances, to wear their masks means to ensure for oneself their sacred power. That is why the dancing *Perchten* jump across the fields. We need hardly emphasise that with these demons of vegetation and their mimic enactment we have regained those primitive strata mentioned earlier, which Greek tragedy alone has left so far behind that there seems to be hardly any connection.

On Greek soil these satyrs are undoubtedly older than Dionysus, but when the god arrived who embodied all the bounty, all the perilous mystery of nature's forces, they joined his *θίασος* ('company') and became his most faithful, inseparable companions.

So much for these creatures who filled the wooded mountains of Greece with life, as they were later to enliven the theatre. We must return to the question of whether we are justified in connecting the goat song with the term tragedy. We have said already that however tempting it may be to link the word with the numerous representations of satyrs with goat attributes, we can no longer do so. Furtwängler has shown us that all these representations are without exception of a later date, and that it was only in Hellenistic times, under the influence of the god Pan, that the daemons assumed short tails, ears and goat horns. We know what the satyrs of earlier periods looked like from a large number of monuments, mostly vase paintings, which show daemons with a powerful horse's tail, horse's ears and in the oldest representations hooves as well. All pictorial evidence from the archaic François vase up to Hellenistic times show us this type of creature. In the great majority of the paintings satyrs are shown dallying with nymphs and maenads, on the wooded mountainside, but even where we see stage satyrs, as on the Pronomus vase at Naples (*c.* 400 B.C.), they have at least horses' tails. Various attempts have been made to avoid the difficulty of connecting goat satyrs, as suggested by the term tragedy, with horse attributes, but none are convincing.

Many attempts have been made to distinguish the Ionic-Attic horse daemons from the caprine creatures who were apparently responsible for both the early form and the name of tragedy. Scholars have tried to find this distinction reflected in their names, and the term *sileni*, as our daemons are sometimes called, was connected with the Attic-Ionic horse-daemons, while the word *satyr* was associated with the hypothetical Peloponnesian goats. But the representational evidence proves unmistakably that satyrs and sileni had the same characteristics, and old Silenus' role in the satyr plays as the father of a band of satyrs is sufficient indication that we have here two names for one genus. The goat satyrs of the Peloponnese are an unproved, unverifiable hypothesis. We do know of goat daemons in that region but then they appear as Pan or Pans. With these we should identify the figures on the so-called Pandora vase in the British Museum, where they are shown with goat horns and hooves dancing round a flautist. Evidence has even been sought in the satyr plays themselves to disqualify the satyrs' horse attributes shown on monuments. But when in the *Ichneutae* (358) by Sophocles Kyllene reproaches the leader of the chorus for showing off with his beard 'like a goat' (ὥς τράγος) she is merely comparing him with a goat, not identifying him with one. Nor can we deduce anything from the goat's skins which the satyrs wear in *The Cyclops* of Euripides, for this is their shepherds' garb, in which they perform the task imposed on them by the Cyclops. More important is a fragment attributed, probably correctly, to *Prometheus the Firebearer* by Aeschylus (frg. 207). For the first time fire has come down to the earth and a silly inquisitive satyr wants to embrace it. Prometheus calls out to him: 'Goat, you'll hurt your beard.' This saying cannot be disposed of as a mere comparison. It is true that it does not prove, against all available evidence, that satyrs had goat form, but the fact that they were addressed as goat because they had certain qualities remains highly significant. We may find a possible solution – but no more – of this difficulty, and of the problem of the term tragedy, in scholarly work from the classical period dealing with this very subject. The *Etymologicum Magnum* (s.v. τραγῳδία) contains in the *résumé* of learned discussions, apart from sheer nonsense, some tentative explanations which bear the stamp of peripatetic literary studies, and are worth considering even today. Even here the discrepancy between the goat element in the term tragedy and the horse attributes of satyrs is not ignored, and a compromise solution is suggested. We need not consider the attempt to deduce the goat name from a peculiar hair style of the chorus; what is important is the explanation of their goat name on account of the hirsute appearance and lascivious sensuality of such wood daemons. Especially in older representations[1] we see their whole body covered with tufts of hair and the tufted garment of Father Silenus, which remained characteristic of him, is a relic of this, like the skin apron of the satyrs on the Pronomus vase which we mentioned earlier. But since goats, not horses, have a

[1] *Myth. Lex.* IV, 456.

tufted coat and a beard as well, we must consider the possibility that satyrs had from the beginning distinct animal attributes, that they were simply wild beasts (Θῆρες), the name by which both Sophocles[1] and Euripides[2] addressed them. But it is conceivable that because of their uninhibited and, for a fertility daemon, very suitable lasciviousness, they were called goats although this did not tally in all details with their attributes; for even in antiquity the goat's lasciviousness was proverbial, as every dictionary will confirm.

Attempts have lately been made to solve the entire question by raking up an old theory. According to this one should distinguish between sileni with horse attributes and the real satyrs which can be identified with a group of fat-bellied, fat-bottomed daemonic dancers. The archaic monuments in which these creatures occur date from the late seventh and the first half of the sixth century and prove that these bloated figures were to be found in large areas of Greece. But there is nothing to indicate that they were called satyrs, since the etymological connection with the word *satur*, which was basic for the old theory, has proved untenable. The entry of these pot-bellied creatures into the early history of tragedy could only be forced by means of complicated theories, so it seems advisable to accept the older hypothesis and to relegate them to the early stages of comedy instead.

Our task has been difficult, and there is no need to repeat that hypotheses are our only guide through the obscurity that hides the initial stages of tragedy. What these theories offer is a more or less plausible picture of its development and the recognition of the greatness of Hellas, since they allow us to see the mature works of art against the foil of such beginnings. The former tower over the latter to such an extent that the connection might be no clearer even if tragedy's origins were plainly perceptible. Yet two fundamental elements, already discernible in the early stages, remain essential for Greek tragedy throughout, namely Dionysus and myth. We shall now consider these.

With the indissoluble connection between tragedy and the cult of Dionysus, we have reached firm ground. The god in whose worship tragedy evolved does not belong to the Olympic circle of Homer's gods. These radiant figures are suffused with the spirit

[1] *Ichneutae* 141, 215. [2] *The Cyclops* 624.

of the aristocratic epic, their blessed concourse reveals the image of a world that was conceived as miraculously, powerfully alive. The gods as higher, more wonderful beings transcend earthly rulers and yet they resemble them in many ways. They live graciously in their Olympian palaces and they assert their will in a most personal manner. They do not carry the responsibility for the eternal laws that rule the universe, nor do they take upon themselves the anguish of mankind in order to redeem it with their own divinity. But they do not remain wholly aloof from mankind: they have friends among humans, favourites, whom they assist when in danger, and gladden with their gifts. They demand respect and yet may be convivial if it suits them. How different, in his relations to mankind, does that other god appear, who has remained an alien in the circle of the Olympians, although – as we know from the Linear B tablets – he was already known to the Greeks in Mycenaean times. Not prayer nor sacrifice alone satisfies Dionysus, man's relationship with him is not the reciprocity of giving and receiving that is often cool and calculating. He demands the whole of man, ravishes him, submits him to fearful ritual, lifts him in ecstasy above the cares of the world. That he should be the god of wine only expresses one aspect of his being, which encompasses all the urgent passionate life of nature, all its creative potencies. In his orgiastic service Nature itself releases man from the problems of existence, draws him into the deepest realms of its mystery, the mystery of life itself, and allows him to gain and experience it anew.

However inadequate this attempt to capture in words the essence of the god, it sets out to make one thing clear: the fundamental aspect of this god is transformation. The human being who is seized by the god and made to enter his domain in a state of ecstasy is different from the one who was caught in his workaday existence. But transformation is also the very root of dramatic art. For this art is not a form of playful imitation, nor does it resemble daemonic impersonation; it is a transmutation of life. The tremendous gulf between the early stages of tragedy and its mature form has repeatedly been pointed out. We could not shirk the laborious effort of wresting from an obscure tradition the history of tragedy's external development, but we must now seek the inner motive power that drove it to final fulfilment. One of its most germinal forces was the god Dionysus and the spirit of Dionysiac religion. The ancients themselves realised this; Aristophanes for instance when he called Aeschylus, in *The Frogs* (1259), our Bacchic lord (*βακχεῖον ἄνακτα*), and when it was later said of the same poet that he wrote in a state of delirium.

That Dionysus was not such a late arrival on Greek soil as had long been thought was finally proved when Mycenaean syllabic writing was deciphered. But this teaches us little about the history of his cult, for we know nothing about this early Dionysus and ideas connected with him as well as his cult may have undergone profound changes in the course of time. Several myths which mention the god's antagonists indicate that the orgiastic cult, based on Dionysiac ecstasy, had to struggle against fierce opposition to gain a foothold in Greece. But we can still clearly distinguish one powerful movement, which in the seventh and far into the sixth century greatly increased the influence of the god. This same movement was of supreme importance for tragedy. We should see it as a convergence of the inner forces of Dionysiac religion and events of a political nature. Aristocratic rule was breaking up, but the transition towards a democratic government was by no means smooth. In several instances a strong personality of noble descent rose against his own class and, supported by the populace, gained despotic power. Such tyrants were mostly innocent of the vices of their later namesakes. What their rule lacked in legitimacy was made good by intelligent and active leadership; they not only relied on the support of the masses, but really governed in their interests. It is therefore not surprising that the god who was not an Olympian aristocrat himself, who appealed to all mankind and to the peasants in particular, came to the fore at that time. We now begin to see the true significance of the fact that it was at the court of Periander of Corinth, the son of the same Cypselus who in the seventh century destroyed the aristocratic rule of the Bacchiads, that Arion became the inventor of the 'tragic mode'. There the satyrs, formerly simple daemons of the woods, chanted the Dionysiac cult song in an improved artistic form, the dithyramb; thus the various elements of the god's cult coalesce. Some highly important evidence from another quarter will soon show that a similar course of events occurred at Sicyon under the rule of Cleisthenes. But by far the most important innovator was Peisistratus of Athens, the greatest of the tyrants. It is highly probable that the most sumptuous of the Dionysiac festivals, the City Dionysia, so called to distinguish them from the rustic festivals, was instituted by him. In any case he was responsible for giving it so magnificent a place within the framework of the state cult. It was not the Ionian Dionysus, generally worshipped at the Lenaea and the Anthesteria, who presided over this spring festival in the month of *Elaphebolion.* The god of this festival, Dionysus Eleuthereus, was brought to Athens from the village Eleutherae, on the borders of Attica and Boeotia. The distinction emphasised earlier between tragedy and comedy enables us to make the further assertion that comedy belonged to Dionysus of the Lenaea, tragedy to Dionysus Eleuthereus of the great or city festival. At this festival under the rule of Peisistratus, between 536 and 533, a tragedy by Thespis was performed for the first time under the auspices of the state. Thenceforward tragic plays remained linked with the City Dionysiac festival, and the following procedure evolved: the days from the 11th to the 13th of *Elaphebolion* were reserved for tragedy and on each day a tetralogy was to be performed consisting of three tragedies followed by a satyr play. When in the fifth century the production of dramatic plays rapidly increased they began, between 436 and 426, to hold a tragic contest during the Lenaea also, which originally had nothing to do with tragedy, just as conversely comedy had already in 486 intruded into the City Dionysia.

The place of acting points to Dionysus as well as the time. Although it is only a possibility that during the sixth century dramatic performances were given in the market place theatre, it is certain that tragedy, from what we know of its production, was intimately connected with the theatre of Dionysus situated on the southern slope of the Acropolis, close to the temple of Eleuthereus. The visitor to this impressive site today finds in the front row the large stone seat which, as the inscription states, was reserved for the priest of Dionysus. It was in this theatre that Aeschylus, Sophocles and Euripides competed on the day of performance and won undying fame. For centuries the theatres of Dionysus remained a setting for drama, until Roman vulgarity degraded it to a circus where gladiators fought and wild beasts were baited.

The actor's costume also points to Dionysus. The mask has

already been discussed. Although this ultimately leads back to the most ancient mimic representations, in tragedy the mask had a special significance since it played a part in the cult of the god of the mask. The gorgeously embroidered sleeved tunic and the soft, fitting high boots, the *cothurni*, which were only in Hellenistic times turned into monstrous stilt-shoes, also provided strong evidence of an origin in the cult of Dionysus.

We said that tragedy was from the start intimately linked with the cult of Dionysus and we tried to solve the mystery of its growth by probing the spirit of Dionysiac religion. But here our road is barred by yet another contradiction. Certainly time, place and actor's costume all point towards Dionysus, but the content of the tragedies leads us, in so far as we know anything definite about the god, in a different direction. Dionysiac myths whose subject is antagonism, namely those which represent the god triumphing over opponents like Lycurgus and Pentheus, were occasionally the subject of tragedy. But they are not a dominant theme and all attempts to ascribe a Dionysiac content to the earliest tragedies, or even to turn Dionysus himself into the earliest actor, are unfounded. Nor should we overlook the fact that the number of Dionysiac myths is so very small in comparison with other mythical cycles that, as tragedy developed, the material they offered would hardly have sufficed. As regards the often noted agony of the god when he was torn to pieces by the Titans, we know far too little about the date of this myth (which played such an important part in Orphic circles) to be justified in connecting it with early tragedy. It is in fact unthinkable that the god who triumphed over his enemies should ever have become the source of tragic content, since tragedy shows us a hero epitomising man's nobility in conflict with the powers of this world, a conflict that leads him to the verge of destruction or beyond. Therefore, although we find in Dionysus one of the living forces which brought the tragic play as a work of art into being, its content had a different source of inspiration: the heroic legend.

The apparent contradiction between tragedy as part of the Dionysiac cult and its non-Dionysiac content was already noticed in antiquity, hence the proverb: 'that has nothing to do with Dionysus' (*οὐδὲν πρὸς τὸν Διόνυσον*). In this connection a passage from Herodotus (V, 67) is significant. In Sicyon there existed from ancient times a cult of the Argive hero Adrastus; Herodotus says explicitly that the inhabitants of Sicyon worshipped not Dionysus but Adrastus, and that they sang tragic choruses (τραγικοῖσι χοροῖσι) to commemorate his suffering, which can only have been that depicted in *Seven Against Thebes*. We can ignore here the old controversy whether Herodotus meant a goat chorus, or a chorus chanting a song with a tragic content, for there is no doubt about the important point: the acts and suffering of a hero from a great cycle of legends formed the content of the song. Then Cleisthenes introduced his reforms and these songs were no longer sung in the worship of the hero Adrastus but in the cult of the new god. There is no indication that their content was changed in favour of Dionysus, for that would have meant a complete innovation, making the relationship with the old Adrastus worship unrecognisable and Herodotus' description untenable. The passage merely reports that the old 'tragic' chorus, which derived its content from heroic songs, now became part of the cult of Dionysus. It is clear that this is another example of the tyrant's policy, which was so significant for the cult of Dionysus and tragedy alike. Although a deep hatred of Argos, whose hero was Adrastus, may have played a part in Cleisthenes' reform, the choruses were still allotted to Dionysus. But the real significance of the passage mentioned is that for once we can see exactly how heroic songs were drawn into the sphere of Dionysiac worship and how Dionysiac tragedy, through its union with the rich heritage of Greek myth, acquired its content. We see how these sagas added a new integrating element to Dionysiac cult, dithyramb and satyrs, and we begin to realise how fruitful was the soil from which the perfect form of tragedy emerged. Tragedy gained through the heroic myth its gravity, its dignity, its poise (ἀπεσεμνύνθη), said Aristotle in the *Poetics* (1449a), and the shameless satyrs were rightly relegated to the end of the tetralogy.

Again we have tried to produce from historical data what can only be a sketch of external development, but now we must realise the immeasurable importance of the legendary content of tragedy for its inner significance. For Greek myths are as miraculous as Dionysus himself. In the course of our study we may see with increasing clarity how much early history they reflect and by comparing them with the sagas of other peoples recognise many of their peculiarities, but their essential meaning does not end here. The full range of Greek myth mirrors human existence itself; it does not reflect a 'world view' which is a mere abstraction of living reality, it reveals a perception of the world so rich, so immediate as to be unequalled. Beyond all those heroes who through their combats set countries free from terrible oppression or heroically succumb to overwhelming forces, who achieve their own deliverance through bold action or clever ruse, we perceive what ultimately determines the life of us all: human existence imperilled and asserted. And when we see that what is at stake here is always man's entire existence, that there is no question of compromise, no evasion of hostile powers, no turning aside of man's unconquerable will, then we have already defined one of the essentials of tragic man, which these figures from Greek myth also epitomise.

Greek myth was important to tragic poets in yet another respect. The legends which inspired them were the common property of their people, they were sacred history, eminently real. We shall in due course see that the art of tragedy was part of the life of the nation and that this was only possible in a community which did not acknowledge a gulf between the populace and the educated classes. The appeal of great poetry to the masses – something that was already lost in Hellenistic times – was largely due to the fact that it was their own heritage of legends which gained a new form in the Dionysiac plays. What did it matter whether the average Athenian could follow word for word the dense, intricate flow of the language? Orestes, who was forced to assume the heavy guilt of murder; Ajax, who valued honour above life; Odysseus, who combined shrewdness with insight; these were as immediately accessible to his feeling as they had been to the poet who infused them with life. It is true that the stories did not tie the poet's hands, in the sense that he would only be allowed to follow tradition; his freedom in the treatment of legend was considerable, as a sensitive observer stated in antiquity.[1] But Euripides was the first who really 'invented,' here as elsewhere, a rebel from classical tradition. This brings us to a different, really essential point. It has already been observed that a poet, in creating figures who represent something of universal validity, must give them the stamp of authenticity by

[1] Scholiast on S.El. 445.

borrowing from traditional sources if the public is to accept them as fully alive. Modern authors either use a historical background or give their figures so many idiosyncrasies that we accept their personality as genuinely alive. Dramatic experiments to bring abstract types like 'the father' or 'the alien' on to the stage have remained experiments. Here also the significance of legend in Greek tragedy is clearly shown. Could the poet be given a more wonderful means to prove the actual existence of every one of his protagonists than this living faith in the heart of the people?

One further point: in legend, as we know it from its epic form, we can already recognise the essence of Greek genius which is so fully expressed in tragedy. Its intellectual discipline moulds chaotic events into form, while artistic creativity – by no means something purely formal or technical – raises this form into the realm of meaning and reveals the forces behind the events. Dionysus and legend, the enchantment of ecstasy and the power of the 'logos' to penetrate to essentials have joined forces in tragedy. There is a vase in the Hermitage at Leningrad on which, in the sacred enclosure at Delphi, Apollo gives his right hand to Dionysus. This is a valuable testimony of the covenant between the priests of Delphi and the new religion. We may, however, also see it as a symbol of those forces from whose union the miracle of Greek tragedy was born.

CHAPTER THREE

The Precursors of the Masters

THE MAIN factors which determined the essence of tragedy and its external feature have now become clear, but our sources were so scanty that it was impossible to link them with any distinct personalities. Even when names become more numerous, at the turn of the sixth century, they are still wrapped in obscurity. Only with Aeschylus do we reach the clarity of Attica's great period in art and history.

Except for the kind of artificially constructed tradition which, for the sake of Peloponnesian claims, brought forward such shadowy figures as Epigenes of Sicyon,[1] the oldest tragedian known to us is Thespis from Icaria in Attica. The place where Dionysus once brought wine to the eponymous Icarus, and which is still called Dionyso, lies in a lovely valley at the foot of the Pentelicon. We mentioned earlier that Alexandrian scholars wished to derive tragedy from rustic festivities in this region. When against this we acknowledged, with Aristotle, the part played by the Peloponnese, we did not mean to exclude the possibility that Thespis followed many of the usages of his homeland when preparing the ground for tragedy. It is true that Horace's 'wagon of Thespis'[2] is probably pure fiction. The Alexandrians may have invented it on the basis of cart processions in Attic carnivals.

Thespis produced a tragedy for the first time at the great state-sponsored Dionysiac festival between 536 and 533. This, of course, does not exclude the possibility that he wrote plays long before that official occasion, and modern scholars are inclined to accept the historical validity of an anecdote by Plutarch.[3] According to this story the ageing Solon (d. 560), in a discussion with Thespis, had turned against the increasingly popular tragedy – in which he was interested, as we have already noticed in connection with

[1] *Suda*, s.v. Thespis.
[2] *Ars Poetica* 276.
[3] Plutarch, *Solon* 29.

Arion – because he considered it a play of deception (we called it transformation).

How gladly would we exchange the herm, found not far from Tivoli, which mentions that Themon was the father of Thespis, for some further knowledge of his work, or even for a fragment of the peripatetic scholar Chamaeleon's writings about it. The few verses which tradition has handed down in his name are useless, since it has been recorded[1] that the peripatetic scholar Aristoxenus accused the Platonist Heracleides Ponticus of publishing his own tragedies under the name of Thespis. The fragments themselves confirm this, so that even the surviving titles, among them a *Pentheus*, have become unreliable.

But it should now be possible to bring one vital aspect of Thespis' great significance in Attic Tragedy into sharper focus. A most important question has been omitted from what has so far been said about the origins and development of tragedy. We spoke at length about choruses and looked for a union between dithyramb and *satyricon*. We then tried to understand how legend affected the content. But all this was a matter of choric songs that were chanted, rather than the one element on which a dramatic play as such depends, namely the actor. Where did he come from? Here we find two opposing views in support of two possible solutions. It has often been assumed that dialogue might already have developed within the scope of the choric song and that such a dialogue, later spoken in verse, might have led to the actor's speaking part being separated from the song of the chorus. It is possible, however, that the actor's role as speaker did not develop organically out of the choric song, but was introduced from outside. Many considerations strengthen this view: the language of actor and chorus are tinged with different dialects. The latter's lyrics are more or less Doric, the former's Attic iambics show many Ionic affinities. They also have different themes to express: the choric song has an emotional content, the actor's speech serves to develop and explain the action. The union, already shown to exist in tragedy, between a Dionysiac dithyrambic element and a treatment of myth that is controlled by reason, now reveals itself in a new aspect.

But we need not confine ourselves to conjecture. Themistius[2]

[1] Diog. Laert, V, 92. [2] *Oration* 26, p. 316 Dindorf.

has handed on a statement by Aristotle that it was Thespis who added prologue and speech to the original choric song. The highly cultured Themistius knew his Aristotle well and paraphrased certain of his writings. Since the statements given in the *Poetics* are bound to be fragmentary because of the nature of the work, and it is evident from *Poetics* (1449b) that Aristotle knew about the introduction of actor and prologue, we need not be so sceptical as to disregard Themistius' valuable information. Moreover it suggests a perfectly plausible form of development. As the choric song grew richer in content and poets dug deeper into the inexhaustible store of legends, it became imperative to make the audience acquainted with the situation which the theme presupposed. For this purpose the iambus, already commonly used in Athens and very close to speech (*μέτρον λεκτικόν*), was the most suitable medium. At the beginning of the play an actor, in the earlier stages the poet himself, appeared before the audience and explained whatever was needed for the understanding of the song. We shall see in connection with Phrynichus how this was done. But the actor could also clarify transitions by inserting such explanations into the song itself, or impart new information to provide a theme for new lyrics, as in *The Suppliant Maidens* of Aeschylus.

According to Aristotle (*Poetics* 1449a) the transition from trochaic tetrameter to iambic trimeter coincides with the development of the speaking part. We are unable to check this statement; in the oldest fragments accessible to us the iambic trimeter prevails on the whole, but the trochaic tetrameter was never entirely abandoned in tragedy.

But tragedy at this stage had not discovered its full potential of conjuring up, through the interaction of its protagonists, the great forces that rule existence. A second actor had to join the first, and tradition credits Thespis with having taken one of the most significant steps in this direction. One may doubt whether his name was more than a mere symbol by which to indicate the early stages of tragedy, but his definite place, in antiquity, at the head of the list of tragedians, strengthens the assumption that he was the first poet actor. This also explains the statement[1] that he was the inventor of the mask. It is true that the mask was of very

[1] *Suda*, s.v. Thespis.

ancient origin and antedates tragedy, but when actors were introduced the old half-bestial satyr mask had to be replaced by a purely human one. If it was Thespis who introduced the actor, such an innovation with the mask must also be attributed to him. Did he also make the chorus discard their satyr costume? We do not know. But since for Phrynichus, his alleged pupil, satyrs had no place in tragedy, it is likely that Thespis had already given the chorus a human form.

A valuable inscription[1] has preserved part of a list of prize-winning tragedians. In the missing first part about eight tragedians must have preceded Aeschylus, who won his first victory in 484. We can partly fill this gap by a few names which have come down to us from different sources. But it is rarely possible to say anything about their personality and their work. Choerilus, for instance, who came to the fore in 525, remains a very shadowy figure although, according to none too reliable late lexicographers, he wrote 160 plays. At least we have some sidelights on the work of Phrynichus, mentioned as the pupil of Thespis. He won his first victory between 511 and 508 and remained a figure of importance on the Attic stage well into the fifth century. The most interesting of the plays attributed to him are those whose themes were also used by later tragedians. He dealt with the Danaids (*Αἰγύπτιοι* and *Δαναίδες*), as did Aeschylus, and his *Alcestis* was a forerunner of the Euripidean play of the same name. But the most significant information we possess about his work is that he used historical events as a theme for tragedy. In his *Fall of Miletus* (*Μιλήτου ἅλωσις*) he made Athenians witness the terrible fate of the town, which the Persians conquered in 494. And his description of the suffering of the inhabitants, who were related by kinship to the Athenians, was so eloquent that the latter, in sorrow and anger, made him pay a large fine and forbade him ever to produce the play again.[2] A poet who wished to speak to his people from the stage had to submit his play to the Archon of the year who was responsible for the theatre, and everything points to the probability that Phrynichus handed his play in 493–2 to Themistocles, the future victor at Salamis. He may have wanted to see that the Athenians were reminded of past defeat and warned of danger to come.

[1] IG II/III,[2] 2325.

[2] Herodotus VI, 21.

On one other occasion Phrynichus used contemporary events on the stage. It is highly probable that his victory in 476 was won with his drama *The Phoenician Women*. Among the titles of his plays mentioned in the Suda we also find *The Persians*. It is possible that this was an alternative title for *The Phoenician Women*. As in *The Persians* by Aeschylus its subject was the terrible impact of the naval victory at Salamis on the Persian palace. Perhaps Phoenician women at the Persian court formed the chorus and gave their name to the play. Its introduction was in the archaic manner, which we discussed in connection with Thespis: a eunuch preparing the seats for an impending council meeting informed the spectators in a spoken prologue of the defeat of Xerxes, where it took place and what led up to it. Themistocles had a hand in this play also. For when a poet had submitted a play to the Archon and it had been accepted, a *choregus* (producer) had to be appointed, who defrayed the cost of the production. It cannot be accidental that we meet as choregus for *The Phoenician Women* the same man who in all probability had, as Archon, accepted the tragedy of *The Fall of Miletus*.

The step which Phrynichus took in staging historical events may appear rather more momentous than it actually was. For us myth or legend and history are different categories; not so for the Greeks, for whom myth itself meant a kind of history. There was no clear dividing line which Phrynichus would have had to cross. And yet this historical tragedy which borrowed its subject matter from contemporary events remained a mere episode within the range of classical drama; an episode to which *The Persians* by Aeschylus also belonged. The reason for this will become clear when we consider the nature of epic and dramatic art in general. An essential feature of both is the contrast between the immediacy and passion with which the poet brings his characters to life, and the gulf that still separates them from us. This is precisely what brings their true greatness, their authentic humanity, into view. The presentation of great qualities is far more difficult to achieve when the subject matter has contemporary associations than when it is remote from us. We cannot see the contours of a giant mountain as long as we are painfully negotiating its stony slopes; only from a distance will its majesty reveal itself! Here again we recognise the significance of myth for Greek tragedy: it implied the remoteness of its figures by which triviality was transcended and greatness could come into view.

The curtailment of historical drama's development may have saved tragedy from a dangerous possibility. We have already denied that the link between Phrynichus' historical dramas and Themistocles was accidental. And although we are not justified, on the strength of this, in considering these plays tendentious, we can see here a potential development which would have led away from the deep, genuine bond between tragedy and city-state which existed in the case of Aeschylus.

We have already mentioned Pratinas and discussed the statement that he invented the satyr play. He also wrote tragedies, and if the record that he wrote approximately 32 satyr plays and 18 tragedies is reliable we may conclude that he was mainly concerned with the satyr play which he reinstated. It is very probable that the poet who restored the satyrs to their rightful place campaigned for the satyr plays to be given more prominence, before their evolution gained them their fixed place after the trilogy.

In the case of Phrynichus and Pratinas we have evidence that their sons Polyphrasmon and Aristias continued their fathers' work. We shall observe the same continuity in the case of the great tragedians, and may conclude that tradition within the family bond was here, as in other branches of ancient art, of great importance.

CHAPTER FOUR

Aeschylus

We have now emerged from the realm of pieces of evidence that needed to be interpreted and correlated and are faced with actual works. These reveal from the very beginning such power and depth that we must confess at once that all our efforts to understand and interpret them remain wholly inadequate. Here an urgent question arises, which the interpreter must always ask himself anew and which has often been used to cast doubt on the value of literary criticism as such. What are we actually doing when we analyse a work of art? Can we hope, in our desperate effort at comprehension, to achieve more than a dissection which obscures the meaning of the work as a whole? Must our search be explained as an effort to follow in the tracks of the poet, as he organises and constructs his work from a number of elements? And when we have clearly separated these elements and have shown what holds them together, have we then understood the poet and his work, so that we can say complacently: 'Now we know how he has done it'? We need not emphasise the absurdity of such a notion, nor our profound misgivings about claims to understand the workings of the poet's mind, and the nature of his artistic creations. Here modern 'Gestalt' psychology, which is mainly concerned with our perception of form, has given us fresh insight. It has taught us to see a work of art not as the result of calculation and deliberate construction but as a whole of which the conceptual form exists prior to its parts. Not the outlines of the picture nor the stones of the building are the primary data, but the image of the whole as it appears to the artist's imagination, in a manner which resembles ordinary human perception though it is more intense and creative. It is of course undeniable that there are stages in the creation of a work of art when various parts have to be deliberately smoothed down, exchanged or joined up by the artist. But since he always does this with the entire work in view, the latter has priority and is not the result of elements previously assembled. Our task will be to comprehend and describe this *Gestalt* or form, as if it were an organism, charged with life. This does necessitate an examination of its parts, but not as primary elements into which the work can be dissolved again; we have to examine its structure as a creation of the human spirit rather than a technical achievement. And since 'form' is not born in a vacuum the problem of the poet's personality and environment, the sources of its mysterious creation, are highly relevant. It is with such problems in mind that we turn to Aeschylus.

The year of his birth – he was born in 525–4 at Eleusis, the son of Euphorion, an aristocrat and landed proprietor – indicates the greatness of the period in which he grew to manhood. At the time of his birth the terrible upheavals, which accompanied the dissolution and transformation of the old aristocratic society, were by no means over in Athens. He was already on the brink of maturity when in 510 the rule of the tyrants came to an end, a period which had never brought a final solution of the conflicts although peace had reigned for a long time and the city had prospered. Cleisthenes, a man of noble birth, became the leader of the populace and established the kind of order which for a long time fostered a vigorous growth. The Attic *polis* was unique, like every historical phenomenon, and to call it a democracy merely leads to a superficial conception of it. Least of all should we associate it with the kind of democracy in which Cleon was later to play a leading part, when Athens' worst enemy, demagogy, led her from greatness to ruin. The kind of order which Cleisthenes established guaranteed that every citizen was equal before the law, but up to the time of Pericles did not prevent outstanding men of established noble families from putting their knowledge and ability at the service of the community as acknowledged leaders. It was one of those blessed periods in the history of a people when the individual knows himself to be part of a great and significant whole. Did this spirit enable the town to survive her terrible crises, or was it born under their pressure? We shall not be far wrong if we point to the interaction between personalities and circumstances which has shaped most great events in history.

When Aeschylus was an *ephebe* it looked as if the newly established state was already doomed to destruction. The kings of

Sparta campaigned against Athens and conquered, among others, the town of the poet's birth. The Boeotians crossed Cithaeron and the Chalcidians, attacking Athens in the rear, laid waste the coast land of the Euripus. Who could fail to see that the gods protected Athens when at the eleventh hour a quarrel between the Spartan kings frustrated the Peloponnesian attack, enabling Athens to enlarge her territory as well as to defeat her other enemies?

The divine protection of Attic soil was even more wonderfully revealed in Aeschylus' manhood. A certain type of historiography, which aims at reducing the alarming magnitude of some events to the measure of mediocrity, has fastened on the undoubtedly exaggerated traditional figures concerning the number of troops involved in the Persian wars, in order to reduce the latter to the size of minor expeditions, which the great Persian Empire undertook against a small border state. We will merely point out how strange it would be for a great king to lead such an expedition himself, for all that matters to us is the significance of these wars for Athens. A great historian, Ulrich Wilcken, has reaffirmed a view which has often been ridiculed as the brainchild of over-enthusiastic humanists. Of the decisive phase of the struggle, he rightly said: 'Now that Hellas was to become a satrapy of the Persian Empire, ultimate values were at stake: the question was whether the Greek people would develop their own potentialities in complete freedom, or whether under the pressure of an Eastern world power they were doomed to become orientalised through lack of intellectual freedom under priestly rule.' Here is the essential point: the threat to Greece, if she should willingly submit, was not harsh tyranny, which on the whole was not characteristic of Persian rule over subjected peoples, nor the destruction of the Greek economy, which would not have fared badly in a great empire; what was at stake was the kind of freedom which alone could safeguard Greece's intellectual life in centuries to come.

These well-known facts had to be mentioned because the crisis of this period is of twofold importance for our subject. In the unqualified finality of the decision with which Athens, facing destruction, pitted her strength against the attacking power of a vast state, in the absolute singlemindedness with which she accepted even the necessity of sacrificing her capital city, we recognise the attitude of heroic man as he moved on the Attic stage in the following decade, heroic man with his unshakeable resolve that knows of no compromise whether the outcome be triumph or disaster. The parallel is not fortuitous. It shows us that tragedy was perfected when the genius of Aeschylus and the greatness of Athens coincided. Moreover the Persian wars were a decisive chapter in the life of Aeschylus. This is most impressively worded in the epitaph he wrote for his own tombstone. There he does not proclaim: *exegi monumentum aere perennius*; what he wants posterity to know is that he was there when the battle of Marathon was fought. That was the great glory of his life.

Well into the lifetime of Aristophanes the generation that fought at Marathon epitomised for the Greeks the manliness that had stood the test of critical years in their struggle for freedom. At Marathon the poet's brother Cynegeirus was killed; at Salamis he himself fought again when fate hung in the balance. We can grasp the importance of all this for Aeschylus in the light of what it meant to others who experienced it. To them it was not as if distant gods had influenced the course of events from afar; they knew that the divine powers of their homeland had taken part. What we call legends and anecdotes reveal here, as so often, a deeper meaning. When the messenger sent by Athens to Sparta to beg for assistance hastened through the lonely Parthenian hills above Tegea, Pan appeared to him and ordered him to assure the harassed Athenians that he was their friend and would come to their aid. He kept his word and they, in gratitude, dedicated a sanctuary to him.[1] At Marathon a man in peasant garb suddenly appeared who mowed down the Persians with a ploughshare; it was the hero Echetlus – whose name contains the word for plough handle – risen from the sacred soil of his homeland.[2] And at Salamis an onlooker saw at the critical moment mysterious flames rising from Eleusis, where the secret rites were performed, while from Aegina, to whose heroes, the Aeakids, the Greeks had appealed for help,[3] gigantic armed figures held their protecting hands over the Greek ships.[4] Could the Athenians have felt differently from Themistocles who, according to Herodotus (VIII,

[1] Herodotus, VI, 105.
[2] Pausanias I, 32.
[3] Herodotus, VIII, 64.
[4] Plut., *Them.* 15.

109), declared: 'It is not we who have achieved this, but gods and heroes'?

Here lie the roots of Aeschylus' realisation that human events are interwoven with the divine. This knowledge is basic to his tragedies as nothing else is. Here, too, is that significant interplay between community and individual which we discussed earlier. It was from within the *polis*, in which gods and men live and operate, that the poet's own quest began, his search for the meaning and justification of the divine in the world; it was here that he reached his insight into the unity of Zeus, *δίκη* (what is right; justice) and fate. All this we shall find clearly expressed in his work, especially in the *Oresteia*.

Since the period in which he lived shows us so much of what greatly mattered to the poet, we hardly regret the scarcity of other data and the insolubility of a number of individual problems. The poet hailed from Eleusis and there has always been a tendency to connect him with the mysteries of Demeter. Nothing is known about this. The validity of the story that he was involved in a lawsuit because he had profaned the mysteries of Eleusis appears doubtful, since not even ancient sources mention what play had given offence. In case the story was well founded, we should add that Aeschylus was acquitted since he had not been initiated and had offended unwittingly. There is nothing whatsoever in the surviving plays which would make a closer link between the poet and the Mysteries plausible. His religious thought and feeling do not, as we shall see, point to Eleusis.

A few years after Salamis Aeschylus obeyed a call to Syracuse from the tyrant Hiero, where he celebrated the founding of Aetne with a festival play. We cannot be sure if the title was *The Women of Aetne* or *The Aetnaeae*. Among the newly discovered papyri which have a bearing on Aeschylus there is one fragment[1] which belonged probably to this play. This suggests that it consisted of five parts, each acted in a different setting. Another fragment from the new finds[2] that is certainly Aeschylean and contains a speech by *Δίκη* has recently been attributed, with great probability, to the same play. There is admittedly an element of uncertainty here due to the fact that the manuscript catalogue of Aeschylus contains a genuine and a spurious play called *The Aetnaeae*, but

[1] POxy 20/No. 2257, frg. 1. [2] POxy 20/No. 2256, frg. 9.

LIBRARY ST. MARY'S COLLEGE

we may assume that the newly discovered fragment belongs to the genuine play.

It is possible that Aeschylus also produced his *Persians* again in Sicily. In the year 468 we find him in Athens, where he was defeated by Sophocles in the tragic contest.

The court at Syracuse was, like that of other tyrants such as Periander who patronised Arion, a centre of the arts. We can well understand that Aeschylus honoured it with a visit. But it remains a problem why the ageing poet left Athens again and spent the last years of his life at Gela in Sicily, where he died in 456–5 far from the homeland for which he had fought, the people for whom he had written. In the ancient world a number of foolish conjectures were made and the Mysteries were mentioned again, but nothing is known for certain. Had the poet's ideals for which he fought at Marathon and Salamis not been fulfilled in the political development of his time? Did his audience no longer understand him? Aristophanes hints at this in *The Frogs* (807). We can offer no more than guesses.

In the dating of the Aeschylean tragedies, which for long seemed firmly established, a small scrap of papyrus[1] has brought about a veritable revolution. It is the remnant of a list of the poets who took part in a certain competition and of the plays with which they contested. The minute fragment of this *didaskalia* poses a number of very difficult problems, which we can ignore here because what matters most is beyond any doubt. This is the mention of a contest in which Aeschylus gained first prize with his Danaid trilogy and his satyr play *Amymone*. The second prize was granted to Sophocles and the third to Mesatus, for us a shadowy figure but one whose existence at any rate has been confirmed by this find.

The first part of this Danaid trilogy was the *Ἱκέτιδες* or *Suppliant Maidens*, the drama which was almost unanimously considered to be the oldest we possess. It seemed practically certain that it could be dated before Salamis and a few scholars even dated it before Marathon. The reason for this was that certain of its features were clearly archaic in character. This will be examined when we discuss the play. This early dating of the play, however, has become untenable for one simple reason: the papyrus

[1] POxy 20/No. 2256, frg. 3.

fragment shows that *The Danaids* was performed at the same time as plays by Sophocles. Now we know that Sophocles produced his first play in 468, which gained him his first victory. The Danaid trilogy therefore cannot have been staged before 468, nor even in that year because Aeschylus won first prize with it. The same holds good for the year 467 when Aeschylus produced the Theban trilogy. We must therefore date the Danaid trilogy, which contained *The Suppliant Maidens*, between 467 and 458 when he produced the *Oresteia*. If the remnants of a few letters on the papyrus could be restored to form the name of the archon Archedemides, 463 could be fixed as its date.

We cannot hide the fact that some scholars of standing, among them Max Pohlenz and Gilbert Murray, have refused to accept these implications of the find, but the manner in which they are evaded is either hard to follow or very questionable. It is of course well known that the Athenians were prepared, after the death of the poet, to produce his plays again, but this would have been mentioned in the notes on the play, while our *didaskalia* can only refer to a first performance during the lifetime of Aeschylus. The son of the poet, Euphorion, gained four victories with his father's posthumous plays, but on those occasions Euphorion was victorious in his own name, and besides, we have to think, as in the similar cases of Sophocles and Euripides, of tragedies from Aeschylus' last years, which he did not live to produce. The theory that he had written the trilogy at a very early stage of his career and had left it lying about, to be produced much later either by himself or his heirs, is entirely unfounded. Nor does it fit in with what we imagine to be the connection between the amazing productivity of the tragedians and the urgent need of the Dionysia for the work of first-class poets.

And have these evasive theories any purpose? Are we really justified in dating the surviving plays according to our idea of a linear chronological development of Aeschylus' creative output? The development of great artists is more often spasmodic than smoothly progressive. And even if we disregard this basically important point, does the former dating really suggest a gradual upward movement? Does not the *Seven Against Thebes*, firmly dated at 467, with its seven great matched speeches, seem a strikingly archaic composition, almost without parallel?

All we can do is to change our ideas about the chronology of *The Suppliant Maidens*, which is what the present writer has done in this new edition of his book. It would then appear that the oldest known play is *The Persians*, which according to tradition was first performed in 472. This has important implications. We have to accept the fact that we do not possess any play by Aeschylus from the earliest period of his writing, just as they are lacking in the case of the two other poets. But whereas until recently the image of his early work was dominated by *The Suppliant Maidens*, we are now free to fill a gap. More weight may be given to Aristotle's account in the *Poetics* that it was Aeschylus who introduced the second actor, who reduced the part played by the chorus and attached primary importance to the spoken word. The change from *The Persians* in 472 to the *Oresteia* with its three actors in 458 means an unparalleled advance in dramatic expressiveness. Now there is an account that Aeschylus entered the arena with Pratinas and Choerilus in the 70th Olympiad (499–496), which means that his dramatic output began a quarter of a century before *The Persians*. It may be assumed that these early plays were quite unlike *The Persians* or *The Suppliant Maidens*, being far more primitive and more like choric songs. Gilbert Murray in his fine book on Aeschylus[1] has called him in the sub-title *Creator of Tragedy*. Only our new insight into the dating of the plays gives us a historical basis for the achievement implied in this honorific title.

One of the greatest artistic inventions is the trilogy of three plays linked in theme, of which the *Oresteia* is a superb example. Later tragedians abandoned this powerful structure and their reasons will be considered later. But we cannot say when and by whom the content of three tragedies which were to be performed together was made to form a most impressive unity. *The Persians* was performed in 472 as the second of three plays, the others being the *Phineus* and the *Glaucus Potnieus*, followed by a satyr play *Prometheus the Firebearer*. Various attempts have been made to establish a plausible link between the content of the plays, with completely negative results. *The Persians*, therefore, now considered the oldest of the known Aeschylean dramas, is not part of a thematically linked trilogy. The obvious explanation is that at the

[1] *Aeschylus, the Creator of Tragedy* (Oxford, 1940).

time of its being written the trilogy was not yet the normal type of construction, and that Aeschylus himself developed it.

We can deal with this play – for which Pericles trained the chorus – rather briefly because we have already discussed the historical drama, Phrynichus' position as precursor, and above all the historical events on which the work was based.

The first part of the play explains the situation. It begins, unlike the work of Phrynichus, with a choral procession of Persian councillors, whose song not only evokes the magnitude of the army despatched to Greece but also the concern felt for it by those who stayed behind. When the queen mother Atossa tells of her dream in which she saw a proud woman who refused to be harnessed to Xerxes' chariot, anxiety deepens, until a messenger, who had hurried ahead of the defeated army, brings definite news of the catastrophe. After the lament of the chorus the spirit of the dead king Darius is conjured up, with whose name the grandeur of the empire is linked. He emerges from his mausoleum – we must imagine a replica of this on the stage – and reveals the meaning of what has occurred: *hybris*, the presumptuousness that oversteps the range of justice, has led Xerxes against Hellas. Never again must Persian weapons be raised against a country which is denied to them. Only in the last scene is the defeated king himself brought on to the stage, and the play ends with the wild strains of Asiatic keening.

Aeschylus himself fought in the battle which is the focal point of *The Persians*, experiencing the anguish and horror, the deliverance and the exultation. Yet he treated this subject as he did the others derived from legend or myth, entirely in its relation to the realm of the divine, thereby revealing the grandeur of his religious concepts. It is true that the speech of the messenger – in which we are made to share the struggle of the Hellenes for the liberty of their women and children, for the sanctuaries of their gods and the graves of their forefathers – is the finest imaginable monument to a people in their hour of greatness; but what informs it is not triumphant chauvinism but a deep faith in the divine powers which so directly influenced these events also.

We now understand why individuals are kept in the background and no Greek hero is mentioned by name: it was the community which had triumphed and the divine powers which sustained it.

We need only think of the manner in which modern historical dramas and novels concentrate, sometimes exclusively, on the motives of individuals to see clearly what distinguishes the art of Aeschylus: its being rooted in a community.

But we also understand why no word of contempt is uttered against the defeated army in a drama which depicts in bold outlines tragic guilt and divine retribution. Darius describes the expedition against Greece, the chaining of the Hellespont, as *hybris*, odious to the gods, but much earlier in the play the chorus prepares us for this view. With a truly Hellenic, and especially Aeschylean, ascent from concrete happening to insight into universal truths, the chorus (93) sings of ἄτη, the terrible delusion which seizes men in her toils and brings about their ruin. Here is a concept which is basic in Aeschylus and which occurs again and again in his work. Human existence is constantly threatened from the realm of the gods, for man, when tempted to acts of *hybris*, will be overcome by *ate*, the most terrifying form of delusion. We can sense here the poet's struggle with the ultimate problems of guilt and fate, since he does not suggest that the gods send disaster without reason, but allows disaster to develop out of sin, previously committed. Such sin is fated for man, but not in such a way that he is absolved of responsibility; he himself has committed the act, even if a god is actively involved in his delusion. Darius states this:

739 Alas! that prophecy was quick to act!
Zeus hurled against my son its lightning-end,
While I expected after many years
The gods would make an end; but when a man's
Willing and eager, god joins in.

When a divine power is called συλλήπτωρ ('partner')[1] we must take the meaning of the word quite literally if we want to understand Aeschylus' view of the part played by god and by man in the anguish of human guilt. But the poet's thoughts probe deeper, they are not satisfied with a concept of gods capable of leading man to destruction through guilt and delusion. The suffering which ensues has a deeper significance; it is the road which leads man to

[1] *Ag.* 1508.

recognition of the eternal validity of divine decrees. To learn, to gain understanding through this suffering, is also the road which Xerxes must follow in *The Persians*, and here a thought begins to take shape which so clearly and impressively dominates the *Oresteia*.

Something else has emerged from *The Persians* which is equally striking in the other Aeschylean tragedies: the tragic event is brought about by gods as well as men. Man's inordinate desires come into conflict with a great, essentially divine order, which reveals to man his own limitation and gives meaning to his downfall, since his very ruin testifies to the existence of such an order. All this should be seen in the light of the questions considered in the introductory chapter.

Aeschylus has dealt with the cycle of the Theban legends in the form of a tetralogy, which gained him a victory in 467. The *Laius*, the *Oedipus* and the *Seven Against Thebes* formed a trilogy, which was followed by the satyr play *Sphinx*. The motif of all three tragedies is a family curse, which pursues the house of Laius until it is utterly destroyed. Aeschylus reveals yet another aspect of his ethical world view in his concept of the real meaning of such a curse. Solon had already assumed that its relentless force was due to the gods seeking to punish the guilty in their children and grandchildren. This must have seemed particularly appropriate to the Greeks who conceived the family through all its generations as a unit. And it must have been such beliefs, still held, that inspired the image which Aeschylus uses in the *Choephoroe* (506): the living members of a family act as the floats which prevent a net from sinking. But Aeschylus has given a new depth to the idea of a curse resting on a whole family. The curse does not manifest itself in successive generations without reason, fortuitously driving innocents to destruction; instead it reveals itself time and again in connection with sinful acts, which are expiated by disaster.

Here also the *Oresteia* will show the outcome of such thoughts in a perfected form, but their trend is already unmistakable in the Theban trilogy. Guilt looms from the beginning over the Theban royal house and its dreadful fate. Three times Apollo warns Laius not to beget children, since only by this renunciation can he safeguard the town. Laius, deluded, begets a son and exposes him, only to be ultimately slain by his hand. This must in essence have been the subject of the first tragedy, and through a recent find[1] we now have evidence that it was Laius who recited the prologue. The second part (*Oedipus*) revealed the son of Laius to be the murderer of his father and the husband of his mother. Unfortunately we have no means of comparing this play with the drama of Sophocles; only one thing is certain: Oedipus' curse that his sons shall divide their inheritance by the sword. We find this conflict at its height in the only surviving drama. Thebes is surrounded by the Seven, Polyneices and his comrades, while the position of Eteocles appears ambiguous: he is the shield of the invested town, a responsible king, a succour in distress, but he is also the cursed son of Oedipus, destined to ruin. The play should be seen under the aspect of this duality, for as an account of Thebes in peril and her deliverance the play is rounded off, complete, a drama full of warlike spirit (Ἄρεως μεστόν) as Aristophanes calls it.[2] As the tragedy of Eteocles it is only part of a larger whole. The construction of the play is such that his personal fate only gradually detaches itself, in solitary grandeur, from the larger canvas of the city's peril.

The play begins with a kind of prologue in which Eteocles speaks to his soldiers of their peril and their duty. It is again the man who fought at Marathon and Salamis who makes Eteocles call their homeland Mother and demand that for its sake they shall pledge all. Then a scout announces that the storm is upon them and wild with terror the chorus of women swarms round the statues of the gods, in a scene evocative of distress and danger. Here as in *The Persians* a structure was erected, but in this case, as in *The Suppliant Maidens*, it was a large altar dedicated to several gods. Eteocles cannot endure such an unrestrained display of grief and directs the women to pray to the gods.

The central part of the play consists of seven matched speeches, separated by short choral interludes, between the king and the scout, in which the scout describes the aggressor stationed at each of the seven gates, and Eteocles sets up against each a Theban warrior. This is a potent means of drawing us into the beleaguered town, whose plight has gradually been unfolded in earlier speeches and songs. But when the scout announces that Polyneices is

[1] POxy 20/No. 2256 frg. 2. [2] *The Frogs* 1021.

stationed outside the seventh gate, the accursed fate of both the sons of Oedipus stands out sharply from the smooth narrative. The reply of Eteocles is not that of a man who is carefully considering the protection of his town, his first reaction is a lament for the fate of his wretched stock, detested by the gods. He knows this fate cannot be evaded, in fact – and here we recognise the Aeschylean notion of how the curse operates – he wilfully goes out to meet it and now desires the fratricidal combat. This dual motivation of the act, objectively by the curse, subjectively through personal desire, is typical of Aeschylus. Again we meet the *δαίμων συλλήπτωρ* but in a more compelling form, because the urge, which Eteocles feels, to commit the inexpiable crime of fratricide is here combined with the appallingly clear knowledge of the meaning of what is going to happen: the final fulfilment of the curse.

We see the actors changing parts: in one passage where the king replies in a speech to the song of the chorus (in epirrhematic form) the latter warns the king and tries to restrain him. The maidens who were silenced with harsh words when they cried out in terror now oppose his violence and speak to him in motherly fashion:

686 Chorus:
What do you long for, child?
Let not the frantic lust
for battle, filling the heart
carry you away. Expel
the evil passion at its birth.

Eteocles:
It is the god that drives this matter on.
Since it is so – on, on with favoring wind
this wave of hell that has engulfed for its share
all kin of Laius, whom Phoebus has so hated.

Chorus:
Bitter-biting indeed
is the passion that urges you
to accomplish manslaying,
bitter in fruit,
where the blood to be shed is unlawful.

Eteocles:
Yes, for the hateful black
curse of my father loved
sits on my dry and tearless eyes
and tells me first of gain and then of death.

And when the chorus suggests a pious offering to allay the anger of the gods and avert the threat of disaster, Eteocles bitterly rejects it because he knows the gods have abandoned him:

702 We are already past the care of Gods.
For them our death is the admirable offering.
Why then delay, fawning upon our doom?

In our introduction we claimed for genuine tragedy that the doomed hero should be fully aware of his fate, however terrible. The figure of Eteocles exemplifies this as do few others.

'If gods give ill, no man may shun their giving' (719); these are his last words and with them he rises to tragic grandeur, for he conquers the inevitable by identifying it with his own will.

After an anxious song by the chorus a messenger announces the liberation of Thebes and the death of the brothers. The two themes of the drama – the plight of the town and the fate of the royal family – have found contrasting solutions and the lament for the death of the brothers, by which their race is wiped out, forms the end of the play and the end of the trilogy. This conclusion, in which a total tragic conflict ends with the death of the protagonists, is so significant that the ending of the traditional version is quite unbearable. In it a herald of a council of deputies (such as never existed in Athens until after 417) announces that the burial of Polyneices has been prohibited; against this Antigone passionately protests. Part of the chorus supports her and criticises the decrees of the state. Philological considerations, though not decisive in themselves, also support the view that this is a rewritten ending for a later production. Inscriptions show that such a revival of an old play (παλαιά) was quite a common occurrence, and Sophocles' *Antigone* and Euripides' *Phoenician Women* would have provided a pretext for the addition of the burial theme whose natural ending was the destruction of the accursed line.

The Suppliant Maidens, whose dating has already been discussed, begins, like *The Persians* but unlike the *Seven*, with an entrance-march of the chorus. It consists of strangely attired young girls, the daughters of Danaus, who, in order to escape from marriage with their cousins, the sons of Aegyptus, have fled from the banks of the Nile and across the sea to Argos. There, at one time, their ancestress Io had been the beloved of Zeus, but Hera's wrath had pursued her across half the world until she found refuge in Egypt. The maidens now hope that Io's homeland will give them protection; they describe their plight in the very first verses of the play.

It is of symbolical significance that the first word used is 'Zeus'. For thus we meet at the start the god who has become the deepest expression of the poet's religious faith, the god who for him rises high above the Olympian, but very human, father god of the epic, to become the upholder of justice, the focal point of the universe. In the song which follows we see, as so often with Aeschylus, how in the words of the maidens' prayer the poet's own feeling breaks through:

96 From towered hopes
He casts, men destructive,
No violence
He armors.
All providence
Is effortless: throned,
Holy and motionless
His will is accomplished.

The girls' father Danaus has accompanied them. In comparison with the chorus he is inconspicuous. To his daughters he speaks words of advice or exhortation, but his main contribution consists in providing material for songs by imparting news, as is shown very clearly at 600 ff. For instance he announces after the first choric song that the king of the region approaches and tells the girls to draw nearer in prayer to the gods, whose images are placed together on a great altar (*κοινοβωμία*). The king, with his attendants, enters and in a long dialogue, which the girls later transform into song, learns the reason for their arrival and of their request for protection from Argos. This scene, presented on an ample scale, is important for two reasons. To begin with, we experience for the first time in the person of Pelasgus the tragic plight of decision. It is hard to turn away the girls, since they appeal to Zeus, the guide of those who seek protection. But it is equally hard to take them in, since that may mean war for the city. The maidens' supplication becomes more and more urgent, while decision becomes increasingly difficult for the king. He conjures up his terrible dilemma in an image of true Aeschylean forcefulness:

407 We need profound, preserving care, that plunges
Like a diver deep in troubled seas,
Keen and unblurred his eye, to make the end
Without disaster for us and for the city;
That neither strife may bring reprisals, nor,
If we should give you back, seated thus
On seats of gods, we settle the god, destructive
Alastor, in this land, who even in Hades
Never frees the dead. Seem we not
To need preserving counsel?

Finally the chorus gains its victory by the horrible threat to hang themselves from the statues of the gods, which must bring a dreadful pollution on the community.

Secondly, the scene lays bare the poet's political views. The king is the ruler of his country but he shares his responsibility with the people; his decisions must be theirs. This concept of a leader who wants to make sure that his actions have the support of his people represents the political ideal which was a distinctive factor in Athens at that time. It also left its mark on conditions in Argos. It is therefore not a firm pledge which the king makes, but he promises to plead the Danaids' case before the Assembly in such a way that the issue cannot be in doubt.

Next the chorus sings of Io's wanderings and again the praise of the highest god soars triumphantly in the chorus's words. Danaus announces that all is well. The people of Argos have decided to accept the fugitives and now the flowing song becomes a wonderful benediction for Argos. But soon Danaus indicates a fresh danger. The Egyptians have landed, the herald of the sons of Aegyptus comes with his helpers to seize the girls, who have meanwhile fled in terror to the altar of the gods. But the king arrives at the crucial moment, drives back the emissaries of the Egyptians and allows the girls to form an orderly procession into the town.

The song of the chorus as it leaves the stage has one remarkable feature which gives a clue to the meaning of the whole trilogy, of which we only have the first part. Each of the Danaids was throughout escorted by a servant girl. So far this subsidiary chorus has remained silent but now it begins to chant. It confesses that it knows how to honour Aphrodite, who governs the bonds of human love and is almost equal in power to Zeus. Differing here from the chorus of the Danaids, who apart from Zeus like to appeal to the virgin Artemis (150, 1031), these servants honour the goddess who has by her side *Pothos* and *Peitho*, Desire and Persuasion:

1035 But careless not of Cypris this gracious song:
With power equal to Hera nearest to Zeus,
Honored the goddess sly-intent
In rites sacred and solemn;
Which share with a fond mother
Desire and, to whom no denial,
Persuasion; and Aphrodite
A province to Concord bestowed,
And Eros whispering wanton.

This raises a question: are the Danaids justified in their headlong flight from marriage with the sons of Aegyptus, and why do they shun them so? The king put this question in the first dialogue, but does not get a clear answer. And so there has long been a controversy over whether the Danaids merely flee from union with the sons of Aegyptus, who desire it so fervently, or whether they recoil from a union with any man. Verse 8 mentions their *αὐτογενὴς φυξανορία*. These words, convincingly restored from a corrupt text, have been interpreted in very different ways. They might indicate a congenital aversion to men, but they may simply mean the free decision of the girls to escape from their lovers. In the course of the play we sometimes get the impression that they simply fled from brutal suitors, whereas other passages suggest a basic general aversion to the marriage bond. Yet it is this discrepancy which alone explains the sequence and the conclusion of the trilogy. At the end of the first drama the servants state explicitly that a woman's fulfilment is in union with a man; to scorn Aphrodite is *hybris*, the goddess is too powerful.

The second play, *The Egyptians*, brought the chorus of suitors on the stage. Only its main outlines can be conjectured, but it is certain that the suitors, by force or through negotiation, compel the Danaids to marry them. The wedding becomes a massacre. All the young men are murdered by their brides, with the exception of one: Hypermestra spares her husband, Lynceus. The third play, *The Danaids*, may have dealt with her fate. She was accused of having acted against her father's will and that of her sisters. But now a goddess comes to her aid, one whose name appears at the end of the surviving fragment from *The Danaids*.[1] In words which have fortunately been preserved the goddess proclaims her power:

> Holy heaven yearns to violate earth,
> And desire seizes earth to share in marriage;
> And rain, fallen from streaming heaven,
> Impregnates earth; and she brings forth for mortals
> The food of herds and Demeter's grain.
> And by watery union the season for trees
> is perfected. Of these things I am cause.[2]

It is also the power of the goddess which vindicates Hypermestra. There cannot have been any question here of a formal judicial procedure, for Aeschylus, until he introduced the third actor, could not implement it. We may accept it as highly probable that Aphrodite also exonerated the other Danaids and ordained that they should enter into a new marriage bond. The legend that Danaus offered his daughters in marriage as a prize in a running match may fit in here. In any case the trilogy ended with a reconciliation of conflicting forces in a new order, decreed by the gods for mankind.

The importance of the verses spoken by Aphrodite cannot be overrated because they disclose how artists of this time conceived Eros. Aeschylus does not focus on individual passion, with that leaning towards the pathological which so fascinated Euripides. Eros is seen as a natural cosmic force; when it manifests itself in

[1] Aeschylus, frg. 44N².
[2] Translation by William M. Calder III © 1964.

man this power does not differ essentially from the one which sustains life the world over. This Eros is perceived as an impersonal force and we may imagine what upheavals had to take place before Euripides could bring on stage a Phaedra who, with the flames in her own heart, could set on fire a whole royal house. Therefore we must not believe that the relationship between Hypermestra and Lynceus was depicted in terms of erotic passion between individuals. It is hardly even necessary to refer to a passage in the *Prometheus* (865) which mentions that Hypermestra spared Lynceus because she felt a woman's desire for children.

The satyr play *Amymone* represented at the end of the tetralogy one of the daughters of Danaus in love with Poseidon.

There are still two subjects to be considered, namely Aeschylean tragedy in general and the peculiar character of this play.

In *The Suppliant Maidens* the elements of action, in the narrow sense of the word, are unevenly spread and crowded together in the last part of the play: the Egyptians have landed, the herald arrives, the girls are to be snatched away from their asylum, the king and his warriors come to their aid. Such concentrated action differs strikingly from the leisured movement of the songs and dialogues in the earlier part where only the girls' threat to commit suicide has any dramatic effect as we understand it. A division between reflection, lyrical description and prayer on the one hand, and action on the other, recurs in other Aeschylean dramas, especially in the first two parts of the *Oresteia*. We are justified in calling this archaic – however little the term in itself will help us to understand Aeschylus – and must conclude that there is a dissociation between action and *logos*, the kind of *logos* which lays bare the inner motivation of action. Here we may already point to the classical perfection of the plays of Sophocles, in which an interpenetration of action and *logos* has been achieved with consummate skill.

The predominance of impressive choric songs in the first half of the play is particularly striking in the *Agamemnon*. This is the only play, apart from *The Suppliant Maidens*, which can definitely be said to be the first part of a trilogy. In both cases this peculiarly Aeschylean composition is influenced by the fact that these songs have to expound the religious significance, not only of the play but of the entire trilogy. For *The Suppliant Maidens* it must also be remembered that the chorus is in the exceptional position of being the protagonist as well. This explains the mainly choric character of the play, which as an extremely archaic feature was long used as the main argument for dating it early.

This very early dating made it understandable that the statement by Pollux (4, 110) that the tragic choruses originally consisted of 50 singers was believed to apply. The legend itself mentions 50 daughters of Danaus and although there is nothing in the play to suggest such a number, the Danaids themselves do speak once (321) of the 50 sons of Aegyptus. There is no need to disbelieve Pollux's statement entirely, for the old cyclic choruses, which sang the dithyrambs, had 50 members. But it cannot possibly have any bearing on *The Suppliant Maidens* since we now know the date of the performance. It is much more likely that the chorus numbered 12, as in other Aeschylean plays. In the *Oresteia* we have clear evidence of this in the scene where Agamemnon is being murdered within the palace (1346). Sophocles increased the number to 15.

But although we need not presuppose an unusually lavish display of stage figures in *The Suppliant Maidens*, there must have been very lively group movement. In the final scene (957) the servant girls are instructed each to stand next to her mistress, so we must assume that the subsidiary chorus was the same size as that of the Danaids. Moreover neither the king nor the herald arrived unattended on the scene. The latter had sufficient followers to drag the girls away, while the former arrived with enough warriors to prevent the assault. In general, this play shows a particularly full use of supernumeraries, who must also have been present in *The Persians* and the *Seven*.

The stage, on the other hand, was quite simple: the orchestra had no fixed backdrop as yet, only a slightly raised structure, which in this case represented the altar of a group of gods, adorned with statues or symbols. Several passages containing stage directions suggest that this dais was accessible to the chorus, since the girls are instructed to place themselves on the altar or to move from there to the orchestra (189, 508, 730).

Aeschylus found the form he needed for his plays only in the trilogy, for here he could reach beyond the single, incomplete event and view it in the larger context, which alone would disclose its full meaning. It is therefore only in the *Oresteia*, consisting of the tragedies of *Agamemnon*, *The Choephoroe* and *The Eumenides*, with the lost satyr play *Proteus*, that we begin fully to understand the poet's intentions. This trilogy gained a victory in 458, and it will remain supreme as long as we allow its greatness to move us.

We shall start with a completely external bit of information, namely the number of verses in each of the three dramas: 1673, 1076, 1048. This shows that in the first play – just as we assumed to be the case in *The Suppliant Maidens* – an exposition of the entire trilogy was given.

The stage itself has changed: for the first time we find a solid backdrop, which remained a temporary wooden structure throughout the period of classical drama. In this case it represented the palace of the Atreidae in Argos. A watchman is lying on the roof and complains about the hardship of his vigil. It is imposed on him by Clytaemnestra, to watch for the fire signal that will be passed from one mountain top to another to announce in Argos the fall of Troy. But the night watch is not his only complaint; he is oppressed by the thought that in the palace of his king former decencies have given way to corruption. Suddenly he starts up: the beacon flares over the mountains, proclaiming victory. He jumps for joy. But in an instant his sense of triumph collapses: however gratifying the thought of seizing his master's hand again, fear and anxiety cling to the palace walls, which harbour guilt and crime. A reason has already been given for considering the watchman's speech a legacy of the prologue which at an earlier stage explained the situation before the chorus appeared. But how far removed from this simple means of exposition is the poetry of Aeschylus! The beginning of *The Phoenician Women* by Phrynichus shows up the immense gulf between them. Not only is the prologue of the *Agamemnon* an essential commentary, an integral part of the play, but these few verses evoke the entire mood of the drama, especially those abrupt transitions in which recurring jubilation over the fall of Troy is stifled in the terror exuded by the very walls of the accursed palace.

We notice the same thing in the songs of the chorus of Argive elders, which now appears on the stage. It is true that the verses deal mainly with Paris who by his rape of Helen trampled on the laws of hospitality and could not escape ruin; but when they mention the Erinyes, who strike late but unfailingly (58), the thought of guilt and retribution, which is a basic motif of the entire trilogy, comes to the surface. The next song, with its compelling strophic form, starts with the omen of the eagles devouring the hare. This had predicted ultimate victory to the army in Aulis, which was ready to sail, but also the sacrifice of Iphigeneia exacted by Artemis. The goddess in fact prevented the fleet from sailing and Agamemnon was faced with a terrible decision: he had to sacrifice either his own child or the glory and the purpose of the expedition. Again Aeschylus shows us a man in a fateful crisis, but bearing the full burden of individual responsibility. The Atreidae thrust their sceptres into the ground and their eyes fill with tears at this plight imposed by the yoke of Necessity. But the decision remains with Agamemnon. Here again Aeschylus interprets events in human life as an interplay between the forces of destiny and personal will: he says of Agamemnon that he accepted the yoke of destiny and planned the crime (218). We are not spared the sight of the girl, pleading to deaf ears for her life. But this passage far exceeds the significance of a mere lyrical description such as Euripides inserts as an ornament. A link in the dreadful chain of sin and retribution has been forged: Iphigeneia has been sacrificed, the fleet can sail, but Clytaemnestra's hatred and revenge smoulder in the palace of the Atreidae (155). The vague hints in the watchman's prologue have thus gained depth.

This great choric song is divided into three parts, as is often the case with Aeschylus. Inserted between the fearful prophecy of the eagle and its fulfilment in Iphigeneia's sacrifice we find, significantly, the glorious hymn to Zeus, which soars above all anguish into a realm of freedom. We must pause for a moment to consider this most impressive testimony of Aeschylean religion:

160 Zeus: whatever he may be, if this name
pleases him in invocation,
thus I call upon him.
I have pondered everything
yet I cannot find a way,
only Zeus, to cast this dead weight of ignorance
finally from out my brain.

Here the ancient cult form of the invocation has been used. It is rooted in the universally accepted magic power of names: he who really wants to be heard by the god must call him by the right name, and if the god has several they must all be pronounced. But what depth of meaning this ancient form has acquired here! When Aeschylus begins with *Ζεὺς ὅστις ποτ᾽ ἐστίν*, then this 'whatever he may be' does not express a sophist's doubt about the possibility of his being known at all, but the poet's feeling, who in the fullness of his heart finds no words with which to express his god. It has already been briefly indicated that Greek religion could not find satisfaction in the world of Homer's Olympians. We saw that the experience of ecstasy led in the direction of various mystery cults – not only that of Bacchus – while an entirely different path led to Greek philosophy. Neither case represented a further development within the tradition of Homeric religion. This occurred in a third form, of which Aeschylus is the greatest exponent. Pindar had already criticised the traditional myths on ethical grounds, hence his rejection of the Pelops legend in its usual form in the first Olympian Ode and of the quarrel about the tripod between Apollo and Heracles in the ninth. But whereas the reason for his rejection is simply the ethical inadequacy of the story, Aeschylus probes deeper. For him the figure of Zeus begins to transcend all other gods; justice rests in his hands and it is he who causes it to prevail among men. The rule of justice is so interwoven with earthly existence that it becomes the bearer of its essential meaning. As the poet says in the hymn of the *Agamemnon*:

176 Zeus, who guided men to think,
who has laid it down that wisdom
comes alone through suffering.
Still there drips in sleep against the heart
grief of memory; against
our pleasure we are temperate.
From the gods who sit in grandeur
grace comes somehow violent.

Wisdom through suffering; here, as elsewhere in the trilogy, this is put forward as the meaning of life – or part of the meaning, for we only grasp the whole truth when we add this: 'Who acts, shall endure. So speaks the voice of the age-old wisdom' (*Choeph.* 313). Action brings guilt, all guilt finds its retribution in suffering; but suffering leads to understanding and wisdom. This is the god-directed path through life, as Aeschylus saw it.

In Zeus the conflict between the coercion of fate, which may appear in the form of a family curse, and man's free will is resolved. Zeus and fate are one, assert the final verses of the *Oresteia*, but it is also Zeus who leads man on the difficult path through action and suffering to wisdom. Zeus is in all things: 'For what thing without Zeus is done among mortals? What here is without God's blessing?' (Ag.1486.)

After the choric song Clytaemnestra appears on the stage and explains to the elders the glorious message of the beacons, whose flames pass the news from mountain to mountain till it reaches Argos. She stands in front of the elders, a strong, a domineering woman: we feel that these are not the only men she rules. The next song is not one of jubilation, for the fall of Troy only reveals the will of Zeus and his inexorable judgment. Soon the song turns again to the wider theme of guilt and retribution, now intensified because there is mention of a revenge which may affect succeeding generations (374). This does not refer to Paris but to the house in front of which the chorus is chanting. Then, when Helen is named (402), this leads to the curse that rests on a struggle in which a people must suffer for the sake of a woman. Whatever the beginning of each choric song, an inner necessity urges it on to the burden of guilt which lies on the Atreidae. The fact that the transition towards such thoughts is independent of the strophic form is a formal manifestation of this inner necessity.

In the meantime the army has landed and we realise that the passage of time has no relevance to the form of Aeschylean poetry. The rationalist explanation, that the intervening choric song suggests an indefinite period of time, is clearly invalidated in the chorus's final words (475), when they announce in parentheses that the fire-signal's message is spreading through the town, and that it will soon be confirmed or denied.

A herald arrives; we hear of his joy in having regained his homeland, of the hardship suffered by the expedition, of the tempest which destroyed part of the fleet and drove Menelaus off course. This forms the link with the satyr play *Proteus*, which is based on the *Odyssey* (4, 364). With subtle artistry the poet places this simple man's thoughts and feelings in the midst of all the oppressive horror and shows him to be touchingly unaffected by it. The same happens with the nurse in *The Choephoroe*.

Again Clytaemnestra appears and triumphantly dispels the doubts of the chorus about the signal. We now know that she will receive with hypocritical submissiveness the husband whom she hates and whom she has long deceived with Aegisthus.

The third choric song starts with Helen, the real cause of Troy's destruction, but it soon returns to an attempt at understanding the meaning of it all, and we are made to probe deeper. There is a strong note of personal conviction in the attack the poet makes on contemporary belief that the gods destroy man's all too good fortune through malicious envy:

750 It has been made long since and grown old among men,
this saying: human wealth
grown to fulness of stature
breeds again nor dies without issue.
From high good fortune in the blood
blossoms the quenchless agony.
Far from others I hold my own
mind; only the act of evil
breeds others to follow,
young sins in its own likeness.
Houses clear in their right are given
children in all loveliness.

Here is a clear statement of what could already be conjectured from the Theban trilogy: a family curse, the greatest disaster that sin can breed, is fulfilled in the recurring guilt, and subsequent disaster, that afflict succeeding generations. Not that the *Oresteia* should be seen as a moral tract in which sin and retribution cancel each other out; but we are shown the inexorable link between fate and crime which determines the essential form of the trilogy.

We have now reached the end of the first half of the drama and critics who subscribe to Aristotelian or modern categorisation will be pleased to note that so far there has been no action. We can now understand this peculiarity of Aeschylean drama: external events have so little general significance that there is no room for their meaning to be explained. With incredible skill Aeschylus allows the storm clouds to gather round the accursed palace of the Atreidae. At any moment lightning may strike; we are waiting for it to happen almost as a release from tension. Then Agamemnon, coming home, appears on the stage. His words make it clear that he feels no joy over his victory, he views his own action with horror. 'We who fenced within our toils of wrath the city; and, because one woman strayed, the beast of Argos broke them' (823). Clytaemnestra casts her net of hypocrisy over the king – the horror of her real act is still to come. She is delighted when he finally accepts her invitation to walk – to his doom – on the purple carpet she has spread for him in front of the palace. There is a terrible double meaning in her cry to Zeus, the Accomplisher, when she enters the house at the end of this tense scene.

The chorus has watched the return of the victor full of foreboding. Then Clytaemnestra comes out of the house again. A stranger has come with Agamemnon: Cassandra, the daughter of Priam, whom he has brought home to his wife. Clytaemnestra, planning to kill her also, graciously invites her in. Silence is her reply, and never has a poet used silence so skilfully as a means of expression. As soon as Clytaemnestra has left her Cassandra lets out a wild shriek. Apollo, the god who has forced her into his dreadful, thankless service as a prophetess, has taken possession of her and reveals the gruesome past of the house before her.

The song of the chorus has told us much of guilt and retribution, and of Iphigeneia's murder as a link in this chain. But now the prophetess tears the veil and we can look back into the accursed history of the house of Atreus. It is a human slaughter house, its steps running with blood; there are the whimpering children whom Atreus killed to serve as a meal to his brother Thyestes. A crowd of Erinyes, drunk with human blood, clings to the palace. And so crime will be committed again. Inside Agamemnon will find his death and for Cassandra too there is no escape. No analysis can lay bare the poetic genius which created Cassandra, who after the wild ecstasy of her lyrics is made to speak with inexorable clarity of her thoughts of fate and crime, which are turned to reality in the history of the Atreidae. Twice the stream of words is interrupted by the terse dialogue form of the *stichomythia*. Each time she is again overcome by visions. When she goes to meet her death in the palace she gains tragic stature. Knowingly she accepts the inevitable doom – a figure strongly reminiscent of Eteocles, who left the stage having gained the same insight. And we must admire Aeschylus' humanity as well as his greatness when, in a final upsurge of youthful will to live, she recoils from the reek of blood that meets her at the palace gate before surrendering to her fate.

The double murder has been committed, the timid chorus have proved quite helpless; suddenly the wide palace door opens and we see Clytaemnestra standing by the two corpses with the blood-stained axe. Our imagination longs to re-create such scenes and their effect on the antique stage. But here we are always coming up against the limits of our knowledge. We can only presume that in this and similar cases a wide central door was opened; it is unlikely that by this period the *ekkyklema* was used, a device on rollers that could bring scenes, previously prepared within, to the front of the stage.

The deed is done, but Clytaemnestra is still absorbed with it. Wildly she praises the bloodstain on her forehead as a blessing from heaven, a moistening of the seed bed. Then begins a long hard struggle with the chorus, who point out the appalling nature of her deed. But the masterful woman knows no repentance, no change of heart. That would be alien to the drama of this period. She does, however, realise something else. The act, accomplished in hot passion, reveals itself to her as a link in the dreadful chain of events that encompass the house of Atreus. The double meaning of the act begins to dawn on her; it is determined both by fate and by will, the two forces which in Aeschylus always converge catastrophically. Through her the daemon of the house has acted and will act again. She would like to bargain with him, buy him off with her treasures, but both chorus and spectators know that her effort will be in vain: action brings suffering. With Aegisthus her cowardly lover, who brags about what has happened, she enters the palace. He had nearly come to blows with the indignant elders, but Clytaemnestra pacified them. Enough has happened, her bloodthirsty intoxication has passed away and has left only disgust. The elders must now go home in peace before they too get involved in action and suffering. Again the ominous, almost symbolical words are used: παθειν ἕρξαντας (1658).

We only possess fragments of the prologue of the second play, which was spoken by Orestes at his father's tomb, but here too the emotional content must have been strong. Orestes has come home from afar and stands in prayer at the tomb of Agamemnon, which forms the centre of the second play, *The Choephoroe*. He is innocent but the house of Atreus will involve him in the curse also, for he bears Apollo's command to take revenge on his mother for his father's murder. A group of women approaches, Choephoroe, bearers of libations to the tomb. Electra leads them. Ominous dreams have caused Clytaemnestra to send the gifts to pacify the dead. But Electra cannot pray for her mother, she prays for the return of Orestes and for revenge as she pours the libation. Already a lock of hair and a footprint have betrayed her brother's presence, although he has gone into hiding. He now emerges and reveals his identity to his sister, who greets in him a father, a brother and a king. Orestes speaks of Apollo's inexorable command and now follows that magnificent passage in which the chorus, Orestes and Electra, their lyrics wonderfully intertwined, join in a commos, or funeral song. Again and again Agamemnon's aid is invoked; in true archaic fashion the dead man is imagined as a powerfully effective daemon, and is conjured up with all the magic of tomb ritual. And yet the commos is not intended for him alone. It would, admittedly, be quite wrong to say that it was the description of the outrage upon his father and Electra's anguish which made Orestes decide to kill his mother, for he had already taken that decision when he appeared on the stage. But we should remember that in human acts both divinely ordained destiny and human will participate. Elsewhere we have seen the daemon as *συλλήπτωρ*, as assisting human passion. Apollo's command, however, made the act of Orestes one that was largely forced on him from outside. This will ultimately prove the reason for his acquittal. But to make this act fateful for him initially, it must be entirely integrated with his own will. This is expressed in the commos where he cries: 'Shall she not pay for this dishonor' (435). Here he is no longer aware of Apollo, in fact Apollo is only mentioned by his friend Pylades in a brief reminder (900) and at the end of the play. The *δαίμονες* of verse 436 are those powers of the underworld with which the commos is exclusively concerned (475). Nor does Orestes think of the god's protection – he will only do so much later. All he wants is revenge, even at the cost of his life (438).

The leader of the chorus now relates Clytaemnestra's dream, in which she gave birth to a dragon which sucked blood from her breast. Then the ruse is discussed by which Orestes shall approach the palace. Once again we are half way through the play before real action begins. Orestes goes to meet Clytaemnestra, disguised as a traveller from Phocis, and tells her of her son's death in a far country. There is no hypocrisy in her few words of grief. She must have wished for the death of Orestes and yet she believes that he too is involved in the fate of their house, of which she has become so clearly aware. She invites Orestes to enter and sends for Aegisthus. This spells terrible danger, for if he comes with armed men all is lost. Clytaemnestra has sent Orestes' nurse with the message. This simple woman, quite unaffected by the anguish and depravity of the house, mourns in a moving speech the child she has tended with all the usual care and anxiety. When the chorus suggests that all may yet be well she is soon ready to tell Aegisthus he may come without armed men.

After a choric song in which the powers of the underworld are again invoked, Aegisthus appears and is soon killed by Orestes' hand. Clytaemnestra rushes from the women's quarter; the words of her servant, 'The dead slay the living,' have thrown a sudden cruel light on what has happened. Orestes has already reached her. In mortal terror she tries to rouse his filial affection, again and again she uses the word *τέκνον* ('dear child'), while Orestes avoids the term 'mother.' When she bares her breast his will-power collapses and Pylades, who only speaks at this point in the play, must force him to obey the god's command. He leads Clytaemnestra off to her death.

In a clear parallel to the *Agamemnon* this play prepares the way slowly and leads up to the act by several stages. And in both dramas its accomplishment reveals its double significance. The chorus praises the liberation of Argos but qualifies the murder as both criminal and as determined by fate. Already Cassandra had prophesied a crowning act of evil (Ag. 1283) and after the commos the chorus had predicted (466) that the house would be cursed by matricide. Again, as in the *Agamemnon*, the palace door opens, the murderer is standing near his two victims. In his last moments of sanity Orestes struggles to justify himself. He clings to Apollo's command. In this scene, which is hardly equalled on the tragic stage, the power and richness of Aeschylean imagery reaches a climax. Even the best translation is a mere shadow of the original:

1021 I would have you know, I see not how this thing will end.
I am a charioteer whose course is wrenched outside
the track, for I am beaten, my rebellious senses
bolt with me headlong and the fear against my heart
is ready for the singing and dance of wrath. But while
I hold some grip still on my wits, I say publicly
to my friends: I killed my mother not without some right.
My father's murder stained her, and the gods' disgust.
As for the spells that charmed me to such daring, I
give you in chief the seer of Pytho, Loxias. He
declared I could do this and not be charged with wrong.
Of my evasion's punishment I will not speak:
no archery could hit such height of agony.
And look upon me now, how I go armored in
leafed branch and garland on my way to the centrestone
and sanctuary, and Apollo's level place,
the shining of the fabulous fire that never dies,
to escape this blood that is my own. Loxias ordained
that I should turn me to no other shrine than this.
To all men of Argos in time to come I say
they shall be witness, how these evil things were done.
I go, an outcast wanderer from this land, and leave
behind, in life, in death, the name of what I did.

He struggles in vain; gruesome figures emerge, visible to him alone: the Erinyes:

1048 No!
Women who serve this house, they come like gorgons, they
wear robes of black, and they are wreathed in a tangle
of snakes. I can no longer stay.

Lashed by madness he rushes off.

The Eumenides, the third play, opens in the tranquil scenery of the Delphic mountains. The priestess of Apollo enters the temple in prayer, but she rushes out with all the signs of horror. Near the sacred stone of the god, which marks the hub of the world, sits Orestes with his bloodstained sword. Round him is a band of Erinyes, asleep. Then the temple is opened to reveal what is inside. Apollo himself has come to Orestes, he offers his services and will not desert him. Since it is the shade of Clytaemnestra which drives the Erinyes in hot pursuit, he, the god of Light, expels the daughters of Darkness from his temple. He had already sent Orestes with Hermes to Athens:

79 Never fail
until you come at last to Pallas' citadel.
Kneel there, and clasp the ancient idol in your arms,
and there we shall find those who will judge this case, and words
to say that will have magic in their figures. Thus
you will be rid of your afflictions, once for all.
For it was I who made you strike your mother down.

According to an older legend, still known to us, it was Apollo alone – since he commanded the murder – who absolved Orestes from his crime. But the idea that human blood could be washed away by animal blood did not satisfy the poet's intellect. While retaining the old notion that murder should be expiated, he added the solution which his heart dictated: Orestes goes to Athens where the local goddess Athena herself places justice in the hands of human beings by founding the Areopagus. They can now pass judgment according to its decrees in cases where formerly magic purificatory rites were needed.

The scene changes. In Athens Orestes is seated near the statue of the goddess of the city. Soon the Erinyes find him and dancing around him sing the song of bondage (*ὕμνος δέσμιος*). But they are not wholly horrifying; they render the poet's own thoughts when they proclaim that awe is a blessing and wholesome for mankind; without it the life of the community would disintegrate:

389 Is there a man who does not fear
this, does not shrink to hear
how my place has been ordained,
granted and given by destiny
and god, absolute? Privilege
primeval yet is mine, nor am I without place
though it be underneath the ground
and in no sunlight and in gloom that I must stand.

Athena appoints a court of citizens and a trial begins, in which Apollo himself appears before the judges and defends Orestes against the Erinyes. But the poet has already made it clear that the blood of murder cannot be washed away, and that a crime once committed will always breed crime again. How can Orestes be acquitted? His case cannot be decided by argument (470), that is obvious from the unsatisfactory bickering in the judgment scene and above all from the parity of votes. But the highest god, who rules the world according to eternal laws, also knows χάρις, the mercy which can solve the apparently insoluble. His most beloved daughter Athena has decreed that parity of votes means acquittal. Man cannot by his own power break away from the bondage of crime and destiny which encircles him, but the χάρις of the gods, in whose hands he is, can release him. That is the poet's message when in the closing scenes he brings the gods themselves on to the stage. Orestes can go back to his homeland in the joy of liberation and his Argos will always remain the most loyal ally of Athens. This was said at a time when the alliance with Argos, directed against Sparta, was of decisive importance for Athens.

The Erinyes are still angry and threaten in malignant songs to bring disaster to the land of Athena. The goddess contends with them calmly (this great passage with its alternate song and speech is composed epirrhematically) until the spirits of vengeance are soothed with the promise that, as Eumenides, they will enjoy a cult at Athens. They, in turn, promise rich blessing on the country of the goddess. For they have always been infernal daemons by nature, who have risen from the earth, and that means in Greek religion that they embody not only the horror of the underworld but also the powers of blessing that slumber in the depths of the earth. As Aeschylus sees them they have not been conquered, not rejected by the world, but form part of it. The fear they inspire is a blessing, a wholesome awe, and according to pious belief they send up their gifts from below.

The third part of the *Oresteia* shows with particular clarity one highly important characteristic of Attic tragedy. The play began at the palace of the Atreidae in Argos, continued at Delphi and found its final solution on Athenian soil. Thus all the questions which the trilogy raised became integrated with the life of the Athenian community. Those who interpreted this as an attempt to give topicality to the myth on a festive occasion lacked real understanding of Attic tragedy. For what we have here is not a grafting of ideas on to a given theme in order to force it into conformity with life. In its poetic form the play discloses a genuine religious awareness of the Attic homeland's sanctity.

The court in whose hands Athena herself has placed the care of justice, which derives from Zeus, is the Areopagus. A few years before the performance of the *Oresteia* took place, its powers were the subject of fierce controversy. At that time the administration of the city, which had survived the terrible crisis of the Persian wars, began to yield to the radical pressure of democracy and Ephialtes succeeded in depriving the high court of the Areopagus, a stronghold of tradition, of all its judicial powers except in cases of murder. Aeschylus does not register any protest against this in his *Eumenides*, which has no political bias. In it the Areopagus, founded by Athena, only deals with a crime of murder, exactly as it did at the time of the performance. But the poet views the trend of the new development with misgiving and it is his own ethical ideal which he expresses in Athena's inaugural speech:

696 No anarchy, no rule of a single master. Thus
I advise my citizens to govern and to grace,
and not to cast fear utterly from your city. What
man who fears nothing at all is ever righteous?

Here again there is no question of topicality being foisted on to the play, as occasionally happens with Euripidean attacks on Sparta. Aeschylus remains entirely within the spirit of the play when he makes Athena say what the Erinyes have proclaimed earlier. His tragedy is political in the noblest sense of the word, edification is not the purpose of the work – this invariably spoils a work of art; it results from its inherent living power.

In the introduction we discussed our attitude towards the problem of whether a pedagogic intention was compatible with a great work of art and should be required of a poet. We agreed with Goethe rather than Lessing, but did not by any means condemn those scenes of the Attic stage, where the tragic poet speaks directly to his public. The most magnificent example of how this can be done without breaking the spell of the play occurs in *The Eumenides*. The passage just quoted comes from the solemn speech of Athena in which she announces, before the counting of the votes, that the Areopagus must remain at all times the shield of justice for Athens. She begins with the words 'If it please you, men of Attica, hear my decree' (681). This raises a question of stage management: to whom did Athena speak in the actual performance?

The answer to this is instructive. Rationalists are tempted to assume that apart from the two contesting parties and the judges there must have been a silent group on the stage representing 'the people of Attica.' We need only observe the significance of the passage to recognise that the simplest solution is the correct one. Aeschylus' goddess spoke to none other than the townspeople themselves, assembled in the theatre. The exposed staging in the semi-circular orchestra made it easy to turn to the audience, a form of participation in the work of art by the community such as we can hardly imagine. The kind of unity in cultural life that we ourselves so deeply desire has been historically realised in that tragedy which, having grown out of the *polis*, could address itself to it again.

As soon as art breaks away from the nourishing soil of a shared culture it is in danger of becoming more and more remote from the community, a development which ends in the senselessness of *l'art pour l'art* whose products are anaemic and ephemeral. Like all genuine art Attic tragedy offers the greatest possible contrast to such aesthetic isolation, in that it not only feeds on the life of the nation but is wholly part of it. A tragedy by Aeschylus or Sophocles was not for the cultural enjoyment of an élite but meant a festive occasion for the entire populace. Admittedly this did not include slaves, who in any case were mostly not Greeks, but the *demos*, which was united by its equality before the law, was also at one in its attitude towards a work of art. Sceptical scholars have denied this and suggested that ultimately the tragedians were only understood by part of the public, while they remained cut off to the rest. We need not counter this with generalisations, history itself refutes it. The full-blooded comedies of Aristophanes that mirror Athenian life are full of allusions, quotations, parodies, which refer back to the early period of mature tragedy. Aristophanes could never have conquered the comic stage in Athens so completely if all these allusions were a mere literary patchwork, instead of being material with which he could hit straight at the cultural life of his city. Attic tragedy has many great characteristics, and one of its greatest was its intimate bond with the life and thought of the people. This made it a communal art in the best sense of the word.

There is one drama as yet unconsidered: the *Prometheus Bound*.

It leads us into a rugged landscape where, by command of Zeus, Hephaestus and his helpers Kratos and Bia have fettered the Titan to a rock. The rule of Zeus is young and cruel. Prometheus, himself a Titan, had stood by him when he hurled the race of Titans into darkness and ascended the throne of the world. But Prometheus stole fire and thus saved mankind, which Zeus wanted to destroy. Now the new god is angry and has meted out immoderate punishment to Prometheus. The chorus in this play are the Oceanids who rise up from the deep to approach the sufferer at the edge of the world, to hear about his fate and to bear him company while expressing their thoughts and feelings in speech and song. The play is kept moving – we can hardly speak of action until the end – through the entry of various persons who come to see the fettered man. Oceanus himself arrives, but his cautious advice to be more yielding and conciliatory has no effect on the stubborn pride of Prometheus. Io arrives, herself brought to a terrible plight by Zeus. She had aroused the passion of the king of gods, but Hera's jealousy pursues her throughout the world. She tells Prometheus of her wretchedness and learns from him that her road through lonely lands will be immeasurably long but that she will ultimately be redeemed by the god in Egypt. And since it is Zeus who, controlling the fates of both, is the significant link between them, Io's future redemption points to that of the Titan, which is to occur in a later part of the trilogy. Heracles, a descendant of Io, is to bring release and conciliation.

A third person to appear at the end of the play is Hermes, the messenger of Zeus. Prometheus, as the son of Themis, who once possessed the oracle at Delphi, has a profound insight into future events. The highest power rests with *ἀνάγκη* ('Necessity'), who is guided by the Moirai and the Erinyes of unfailing memory (516). Just as Zeus overthrew his predecessor so may he in turn be brought down, and his fall is in fact certain since he is ignorant of a secret which Prometheus knows: the union of Zeus with Thetis, from which a son with greater strength and more powerful weapons will grow to overthrow him. In his own bitter humiliation Prometheus can savour the one that awaits his divine enemy. But Zeus has heard of the secret and sends Hermes to wrest it from him. The Titan nevertheless refuses to give it away, and would prefer the lightning of Zeus to strike him so that he and the

Oceanids who stand by him would be hurled into the depths from the shattered mountain.

We do not underrate the greatness of the poem but cannot disregard its doubtful authenticity. Even today opinions are divided and the fact that outstanding scholars are to be found in either camp shows how difficult the problem is. Language and metre, especially a simplicity of speech which comes close to that of daily life, are unusual in many respects. But it is certain at present that these considerations do not in themselves exclude an Aeschylean origin. And the same holds good for the clumsiness in the sequence of scenes in a play with a unique setting, or for that extraordinary bickering about what Prometheus ought to tell or should not repeat because it has been told already (615, 621, 631).

The problem clearly centres on the question of whether the play's content fits into the work of Aeschylus. From the earliest known play to the *Oresteia* we are given an image of Zeus that gradually deepens but remains in essence unaltered. Zeus epitomises justice and the meaning of the world, he is one with fate, as is stated at the end of the *Oresteia*. In the *Prometheus* he is a tyrant, new to mastery, who inflicts exorbitant punishment on one who has committed a crime – for the theft of fire was undoubtedly a crime against world order – forgetting the wrongdoer's past assistance. The rule of Zeus is not established for ever, fate may ruin him, for the Moirai are more powerful than he is. However much this and other things may shock us we must never forget that of the ninety plays which the *Suda* credits to Aeschylus, and the seventy-nine of which we know the titles, we possess only six with which to compare the *Prometheus*. This is not very reassuring in view of the unity which exists between these six, but the *Prometheus*, if Aeschylus was the author, was probably part of a trilogy. *Prometheus the Firekindler*, the satyr play which followed the trilogy of which we only have *The Persians*, did not belong to it. But a play called *Prometheus Unbound*, which depicted the liberation of the sufferer and his reconciliation with Zeus, definitely existed. The surviving *Prometheus Bound* alludes to this and to the shooting of the liver-devouring eagle by Heracles, and this link is one of the strongest arguments in favour of the authenticity of the play. In the place of the wanderings of Io the *Prometheus Unbound* gave the journey of Heracles to fetch the apples of the Hesperides, and the chorus consisted of Titans whom Zeus had released from Tartarus. The position of a third play, *Prometheus the Firebearer*, remains problematic. Pohlenz in particular has argued that it should be placed first in the trilogy, that is before the *Prometheus Bound*. But it may still have been the last play. In that case its content would have to be the reconciliation of conflicting divine powers and the rehabilitation of Prometheus, which fits in well with the structure of other Aeschylean trilogies. The problem can hardly be definitely solved, but the sequence of the trilogy might have clarified a great deal in this play, especially the image of Zeus.

We count the *Prometheus* among the plays of Aeschylus but do not share the opinion that a Prometheus problem as such has ceased to exist. It remains most difficult to account for the shift of the emphasis from the theme of the theft of fire. In the surviving play it has receded into the background and in the long story told by Prometheus to the Oceanids (436) it has given way completely to an extensive account of his activities as creator or, as the ancients put it, as the inventor of practically all man's cultural achievements: architecture, the domestication of animals, metallurgy, the art of healing, the interpretation of omens. All of these he gave to man, and thus lifted him from a dull, bestial existence to a worthy life. It is impossible to divorce this account from the questions which preoccupied the sophists about the origin of human culture – questions which we find discussed in Plato's *Protagoras*. But here again it is impossible to say how far Aeschylus was aware of these new problems. We allowed for our ignorance on this point when we accepted the Aeschylean authorship of the *Prometheus Bound*, but all doubts cannot be suppressed.

We had believed for a long time that, apart from some scholarly interest in Aeschylus, the late classical period hardly knew him any longer. The lack of papyrus finds seemed to confirm this, since they threw so much light on Euripides, and a Sophoclean satyr play, as well as other fragments, had been found. But arguments based on a lack of evidence are always uncertain, and so it happened that in 1932 some Aeschylean material came to light in Egypt. A few verses are from the *Niobe*. In our opinion – but it has been contested – they are from a speech by the heroine. After long and silent torment she speaks of her suffering and gives it a true

Aeschylean interpretation: 'God plants guilt in mortals, whenever he wants to destroy a house.' We find in these words, which we quoted earlier from Plato (Rep. 2, 380a), a fundamental Aeschylean concept. Some other verses derive from *The Myrmidons*, the first part of a trilogy in which Aeschylus dramatised the *Iliad*. This part dealt with the wrath of Achilles and the death of Patroclus, then followed *The Nereids*, with the fate of Hector, and finally *The Phrygians*, when his body is retrieved.

The publication of the Aeschylean texts in the 18th (1941) and the 20th (1952) volume of the Oxyrhynchus Papyri was no less remarkable than the Italian finds. We now have fragments, admittedly very small ones, of quite a number of Aeschylean tragedies and valuable notes on the plays. What we said in the biography of the poet about his festival play for the people of Aetne and in connection with the chronology of *The Suppliant Maidens* shows how important the finds were. It is particularly gratifying that they allow us to revise a statement made in the first edition of this book. In it we regretted that the Italian finds gave us such pitifully small fragments of a satyr play, the *Diktyoulkoi* ('The Net Drawers'), since they did not enable us to get acquainted with that aspect of the poet's work. This was all the more unfortunate because in classical sources Aeschylus gained the highest praise for satyr plays. Today we possess just enough to understand this estimate of them, and to admire the fresh gaiety of the satyr plays, as well as the tremendous stature of the tragedies, with the same awed astonishment that we accord to Sophocles.

Apart from the Florentine papyrus (PSI 1209) we now have for the *Diktyoulkoi* a large fragment from the Oxyrhynchus Papyri (18, No. 2161) which according to the line-number θ (=800) comes from a later part of the play. This enables us to reconstruct the plot in general outline and to form an idea of the style.

The setting of the play is the island of Seriphos and the Florentine papyrus gives us an idea of the beginning. Two fishermen are trying to bring to the surface a mysterious heavy object which they have caught in their net. In the end they have to call for help in their arduous work. Here we must restore the plot and assume that the satyrs led by Father Silenus rush to their aid and manage to drag ashore a large chest. But they hear strange noises emerging from it, as if a woman were calling and a child whimpering. We may imagine that the cowardly satyrs ran away from the uncanny object, just as they did in the *Ichneutae* of Sophocles, when they heard the mysterious sounds of a lyre. But when a most beautiful woman emerged from the chest with an infant – Danae, whom her father had consigned to the deep with the child Perseus – they came closer again and inquisitively gathered round the strange newcomers. Probably one of the fishermen, called Dictys, went to the town to inform his half-brother, the local king Polydectes, not realising in what an awkward situation he had left Danae. For she soon roused the desire of the lustful Silenus and he, to her horror, began to press her with proposals and promises of all the delights of a life together. This is precisely the content of the second, larger fragment of the play. It is delightful to see how the old reprobate Silenus tries to make use of the baby Perseus to further his far from platonic designs. We give here the verses in which he attempts to befriend the child in order to win the mother. No less charming are the anapaests of the satyr chorus in which they explain the averted face of the desperate Danae, as the shy longing of a woman who missed a husband on her long sea voyage.

786 Silenus:
See, the baby's looking, laughing
at my red and shining pate!
(six lines missing)
There is in the young one's looks
a lover of the tool!
(four lines missing)
Damn Dictys, who has robbed me
of such a quarry as this!
Phinton, here, come here!
(smacking the lips)
Cheer up, baby! Why the whimper?
Come, let's go and join the boys!
A father's nursing arms you'll find,
my darling – let's be friends!
You shall have delightful playmates, –
weasels, fawns and little piglets,
children of their bristling mothers.
You shall sleep as thirdsman with us,
with your mother and your father –

that is me, of course!
And your father will provide you,
when you're small, all sorts of fun,
and a healthy rearing so that
by your rearing he may rest
his own feet in quiet comfort,
some day in the hills, at last, –
he need hunt the deer no more.

You will seize the quarry bravely,
You will bring it to your mother,
You will bring it for our supper,
just like all your kinsmen you'll be
just like them in manners, too.

Chorus:
Come, friends, come, let us hasten along,
hasten along to the marriage.
The perfect occasion dictates our words –
though it's true, you can't hear its voice!
And here I can see right before me the bride
and she's mighty keen, too, to content our love
No wonder at all! She's been long aboard,
sea-tossed and manless, in misery.
But now she has a look of joy in her eye
as she sees us young fellows and feels like a bride
with joy in the torches that shine
at Aphrodite's feast.[1]

It was a long time before modern readers found their way to Aeschylus, for there is no quick, easy response to the poet's language or the world of his thoughts. Goethe, who read the *Agamemnon* in W. von Humboldt's translation (1816), recognised the greatness of the work even through this medium. Today we consider Aeschylus the most vitally forceful of Greek tragedians and, in his compelling verse and the compass of his thought, one of the greatest in world literature. Some important conclusions can, however, be drawn from our survey about the way in which the tragic element appears in his work. In *The Danaids* as well as in the *Oresteia* we found tragic situations in which divine dispensation

[1] Translation by David Grene © 1964.

showed the way to a solution. If we are right in our interpretation of the Prometheus trilogy, the same holds good there, and a close examination of other fragments makes it at least probable with trilogies now lost. But total tragic conflict is also not foreign to Aeschylus. The sombre ending of the *Seven Against Thebes* shows how a terrible chain of crime and fate in the history of one family leads it to destruction. But nowhere in Aeschylus do we find the merest suggestion of a totally tragic world view, in which the nature of the universe would make tragic fall inevitable and suffering senseless as an ultimate state. Aeschylus' work is diametrically opposed to such a secularised, relativistic idea of the tragic. In its final climax in the *Oresteia* it points to a theodicy, born of profound religious speculation. Aeschylean tragedy shows faith in a sublime and just world order, and is in fact inconceivable without it. Man follows his difficult, often terrible path through guilt and suffering, but it is the path ordained by god which leads to knowledge of his laws. All comes from his will:

> All providence
> Is effortless: throned,
> Holy and motionless,
> His will is accomplished. (*Supp.* 100)

In god rests the meaning of the world, in the knowledge of him all wisdom is contained:

> Cry aloud without fear the victory of Zeus,
> you will not have failed the truth. (*Ag.* 174)

CHAPTER FIVE

Sophocles

SOPHOCLES was not much more than a quarter of a century younger than Aeschylus, for the Parian chronicle, not to mention other sources, makes 497–6 the most probable date of his birth. But even this means a great deal in the extraordinary progress of the fifth century, and there is a deeper significance in the old tradition that after the battle of Salamis, in which Aeschylus fought as a mature man, Sophocles led the boys' chorus that sang the paean of victory. The period of his formative years differed from that in which Aeschylus grew to manhood. Sophocles was a child on the day of Marathon; he never knew the terrible danger, nor the miracle of the deliverance by the gods. The youth's horror in seeing his native city burning was wiped away by the glorious song of victory.

But like Aeschylus he also reached maturity at a time when Athens was great, though this greatness differed from that of the years of the Persian war. They were not years of crisis and divine intervention, but of the rich rewards of pride and power. What the gods had not allowed the Hellenes to achieve by themselves, had now apparently come into being. The founding of the Confederacy of Delos in 478–7 linked together widely separated colonies, the still rather loose confederation gradually took on a more definite form, and in many innovations, such as uniformity of legal procedure and coinage, the outline of an Attic empire could already be discerned. The lustre of this new political vision manifested itself in the embassies sent by the dependent allies to the official celebrations of the Great Dionysia. The whole trend pointed to one ultimate but feasible conclusion: Athens as the mistress of the Greek world. When Sophocles was a fully mature man the Acropolis was being embellished with works that are the glory of Greek art, and under the guidance of Pericles democracy had apparently gained lasting and valid form.

The development had been impetuous, it was also fraught with danger. At the time of the Persian wars military weakness and external pressure had brought the community to the brink of destruction, from which only civic virtues and divine assistance had rescued it. The road uphill had been steep, but as greater heights were reached dangers increased, arising from the immoderate claims made by those whose life had now become fuller and richer. The spirit of Marathon became a legend, and a new mental attitude conceived an image of the world in which the gods who had fought for them there were absent. The firmness of the political structure was actually dependent on the one man who was its leader, but already those forces could be discerned which were to destroy it when he retired. And over it all hung the threat of inevitable conflict with Sparta, the second great power in Hellas, a conflict that could only be solved by complete victory or utter defeat.

Sophocles shared in the life of this period, full of greatness and danger. Despite expansion it remained firmly rooted in the *polis*. His work reveals that he was aware of its two aspects: the uncurbed pride of human will and the powers that lie in wait to destroy man's *hybris*. For only thus can we explain how the man whose good fortune was proverbial in Athens, whose serenity is reflected in the charming account given by his contemporary Ion in his *Epidemiae*,[1] and whose charm won him the love of all men (*Vita* 10), could depict the most terrible suffering in his plays and create the most tragic figures of the Attic stage.

We can observe in three different ways, in his work, his administrative functions and his connection with religious cult, that a close link must have existed between Sophocles and his city, which was the reason why, unlike Aeschylus and Euripides, he never obeyed the summons of princes abroad. He was not yet thirty when he won a victory in 468 with a tetralogy, which contained the *Triptolemus*. If Plutarch's account is reliable (*Cimon* 8) then his first performance won him his first victory. The circumstances of this victory were unusual. The impression made by the work was so strong that the archon in charge of the theatre left the judgment, usually made by self-elected judges, to the council of generals under Cimon. Although we know little of the *Triptolemus*

[1] Frg. 8 Blumenthal from Athenaeus 13, 603e.

there appear, in the speech with which Demeter sends the young hero on his mission to bring her blessings to the world, to be traces of Aeschylus in the rich geographical detail with which the journey is described. This tallies with the poet's own confession[1] that he was in the beginning strongly influenced by Aeschylus, with whom his own work overlapped for a considerable period, and that only later did he move from Aeschylean harshness and artificiality to his own more natural, relaxed style. We possess only works belonging to Sophocles' maturity and old age, but we believe that there are traces of his earlier style in the *Ajax*.

At first Sophocles also acted, as did Aeschylus at the beginning of his career. This was usual at the time. Tradition has preserved[2] the story of his ball game when he acted as Nausicaa in the *Plyntriae* ('Washerwomen'), and his lyre-playing in the *Thamyris*, the tragedy of the Thracian who challenges the Muses and is punished with blindness. When tradition also reports that his voice was not good enough, then this may just mean an effort to give an explanation at any price. We must reckon with the possibility that increasingly exacting standards made poet and actor play separate roles.

His creativity as a poet continued until a ripe age, and the report that Alexandrian scholars knew of 123 plays in his name, of which 114 titles have come down to us, shows how prolific he was. In contrast with Aeschylus[3] he had no complaint against his Athenian audience. It frequently awarded him through its judges a first, but never a third prize in the tragic contest.

The achievement of Sophocles, as we shall see, was rooted in tradition, but it reveals the spirit of a new age when we find that he was preoccupied with the theoretical problems of his work. The ancients knew of a composition of his in prose, *On the Chorus*, and we may assume that in it he discussed the increase in the number of members from twelve to fifteen. He also introduced the third actor in tragedy. Aeschylus used a third in the *Oresteia*.

Sophocles was prominent in political life: in 443–2, when the districts for the payment of tribute were being readjusted, he was treasurer of the Delian confederacy[4] and shortly afterwards, in the

[1] Plut., *de prof. in virt.*, 7.
[2] E.g. Athenaeus I. 20 f.
[3] Aristophanes, *The Frogs* 807.
[4] *IG* I.² 202. 36.

revolt of Samos (441–439), he was, with Pericles, one of the generals, a function he probably fulfilled again in 428 in the war against the Anaeans. He certainly never won fame either as a military commander or a statesman, but he possessed all the civic virtues of a good Athenian, as was said by Ion of Chios.[1] It is not surprising therefore that we find him a member of the Council of ten *Probouloi*, who after the Sicilian catastrophe (413) were to use their authority to bolster up the now decaying democracy, without being able to prevent its downfall. There seems to be no reason to assume that the Sophocles whom Aristotle mentions[2] was not our poet.

That he was closely connected with religious cult in his homeland is exemplified by the fact that he was a priest of Halon, a minor Attic divinity of healing. When finds on the west slope of the Acropolis brought to light a sanctuary of the healing god Amynos, scholars were inclined to alter Halon's traditional name. But later research has confirmed it. When in 420 Epidaurus' great god of healing Aesculapius was adopted for the state cult, Sophocles sheltered the god – for whom he wrote a paean, – until he acquired a sanctuary of his own. For this reason Sophocles himself became after his death a *heros*, a bringer of blessing, under the name of Dexion and was thus incorporated in the religious life of Athens. That is how he was looked upon by his people, this man in whom a good daemon lived and was active, one who was in truth εὐδαίμων. That is how we see him too, taking his *Oedipus at Colonus* as a testimony to the rich vitality of his old age. The rumours of a lawsuit brought against him by his son Iophon, because Sophocles had favoured an illegitimate branch of the family, can only be regarded as one of those touches of comedy that, as in the case of Euripides, found its way into the biographical writing of people like Satyrus. We cannot discover if there was any truth in it and it is hardly worth knowing.

Fate was merciful when, in the autumn of 406, it allowed the old man to die before witnessing the catastrophe of his native city, for which he had lived and written his poetry.

The entire structure of the *Ajax*, as well as technical and metrical details, leave no doubt that it is the oldest of the seven surviving tragedies, a predecessor of the *Antigone* which can be dated with

[1] Epid. Frg. 8 Blumenthal (Stuttgart, 1939). [2] *Rhet.* 3, 1419a.

LIBRARY ST. MARY'S COLLEGE

fair certainty at 442. At the very beginning of the play – and that means the beginning of all known Sophoclean tragedies – there occurs a scene which reveals as few others the poet's view of the world.

Ajax is one of the greatest heroes fighting against Troy and after the death of Achilles it is he who expects to acquire the dead man's glorious arms, forged by divine hands. But the judgment of the Achaeans goes against him and the arms are allotted to Odysseus. The terrible effect of this decision on Ajax can only be understood in the light of that spirit of Homeric heroism which did not yet admit of any distinction between outward recognition and intrinsic worth. Ajax is not a Stoic philosopher, but a warrior, a hero, whose reputation for valour is indelibly stained by this slight. Embittered beyond all measure he wants to avenge his honour with the sword. But he is struck with madness and instead of attacking the Achaean princes he slaughters the herds of the Greeks. At the beginning of the play he is in his tent and, drunk with blood, believes that he has triumphed over his enemies. Odysseus is searching for him to find out what he is doing when the voice of his divine guardian, Athena, tells him what has happened. She has averted the raving man's sword from the Greek princes by driving him mad. Now she summons Ajax from his tent, elicits, in cruel scorn, his own account of his madness and exposes his degradation to Odysseus. At the end of the scene (127) she clearly states its meaning from the divine point of view. Compared with the power of the gods human dignity and human greatness are as nothing; in a single day man can be brought low. Pride does not avail a man when fortune has blessed him, only a proper awareness of his ephemeral frailty and humility in the face of the immeasurable power of the gods.

Here we must ask a question that is of central importance: Has Sophocles conceived the god-directed path through the world as Aeschylus did, in the form of an ever-renewed balance between guilt and retribution with wisdom as the ultimate aim? Is his Ajax a guilty man doing penance? True, he planned murder before madness assailed him, but his honour had already been affronted – we have tried to show how serious this was – and there is nothing in this scene to indicate that his dreadful fate was a matter of guilt and retribution. As Athena herself says:

119 Who was more full of foresight than this man,
Or abler, do you think, to act with judgment?

Later, in the messenger's report (762), Calchas is said to have spoken of the *hybris* of Ajax, which has disastrously antagonised the gods, especially Athena. But this is not a revelation of the ultimate, essential meaning of the event, such as Cassandra revealed in the *Agamemnon*. The statement by Calchas is, admittedly, reminiscent of Aeschylean interpretations, but it remains peripheral and does not penetrate to the heart of the matter. Since this guilt-motif is absent in later plays, as is notably proved by the innocence of Oedipus, who is most cruelly struck by fate, we are justified in considering it a remnant of Aeschylean theodicy, which is already beginning to be replaced by a different concept.

This argument introduced by the *Ajax* shows that Sophoclean tragedy views the guilt-motif in an entirely different light from Aeschylus. Sophocles' world too is full of gods. All events come from the gods. When in *The Women of Trachis* a loving wife, in her anxiety for her husband, brings about his appallingly painful death through her own loving care; when a hero, who has liberated many lands from plagues, dies in terrible agony, then the final words of the drama are: 'There is nothing here which is not Zeus.' Aeschylus ends the *Oresteia* also with the acceptance that Destiny and Zeus are one, and yet the words of Sophocles have a different meaning. We saw that for Aeschylus this fate decreed by Zeus implies that crime demands retribution, that mankind is brought to wisdom through suffering, but that mercy (*χάρις*) is not excluded. Sophocles, however, does not reach beyond the events themselves towards their ultimate meaning. All that happens is god-given; Zeus and all the other gods are immanent in this world, but the significance of their activity is not revealed to man. He should not probe impertinently into the secret of divine decrees, nor revolt against the terrible burden which their fulfilment may impose on man. Good sense, which knows its own limitations, is what the gods value in man – as Athena says.

But the true greatness of the *Ajax* prologue, which is one of the most beautiful scenes in Sophoclean drama, resides in something else, namely in the attitude of Odysseus. Athena is here not only the exalted goddess who expounds divine doctrine, in character she is very close to the Homeric goddess who has her favourites among the heroes, and who watches over them with the very personal concern of friendship. And although the main purport of the scene is the serious warning with which it ends, we also see that she wishes to delight Odysseus, whom she values above all others, with the spectacle of his enemy in defeat. 'But to laugh at your enemies – what sweeter laughter can there be than that?' she calls out to Odysseus (79). But here we feel that the man is greater than the goddess. He does not utter a word of delight or triumph and when Athena asks him if he knew a single hero who was greater than Ajax – to measure the depth of his fall – he answers, deeply moved:

121 None that I know of. Yet I pity
His wretchedness, though he is my enemy,
For the terrible yoke of blindness that is on him.
I think of him, yet also of myself;
For I see the true state of all of us that live –
We are dim shapes, no more, and weightless shadow.

This great poet can reveal his own thoughts from within the play. His Odysseus draws the spectator right into the play and the words 'I think of him, yet also of myself,' show us how we should approach this and other Sophoclean tragedies. The spectacle of man's wit, man's efforts and, entirely beyond his grasp, the ruling power of the gods, this is the kind of insoluble conflict in which Goethe saw the essence of all tragedy. In recognising it we have established contact with a fundamental element in Sophoclean drama. It is a form of tragedy that differs profoundly from that of Aeschylus, but is likewise not enacted against a godless background. The awareness of the tension which constantly threatens existence does not produce in a man like Odysseus an attitude of resignation. The transcendent powers which he has to face may end his life at any moment, but he will not be perplexed once he has realised the limitations of his existence and has made this knowledge his very own. In this calm, truly heroic acceptance lies the secret of the Sophoclean serenity of which Hölderlin speaks:

Many attempted in vain, with joy to express the most joyful,
Here at last it is said, here in sadness to me.

But what we have considered so far only gives us the framework in which the tragic heroes appear. In their acts they do not show the calm wisdom of Odysseus, the very excess of their energy makes them collide with the unforeseeable; it throws their lives into a confusion from which only death can release them. The characteristics of Sophoclean heroes can be seen more clearly in other plays, so can be discussed later. But even in the *Ajax* we know from the start – and without raising the problem of guilt – that for this warrior whose most lofty sense of honour suffered the deepest humiliation there will be no escape from his desperate fate except in death. In the first and major part of the play we see Ajax taking this road.

A chorus of sailors from Salamis enters. They have heard dark rumours and learn from Tecmessa what has happened. Then they see Ajax himself, roused from his madness to the gruesome reality, who now sees only death ahead of him. Tecmessa, whom he gained as booty and who is wife and servant to him, tries to deter him from his decision, but this is so much an expression of his whole character that he does not waver for an instant. Ajax's words of farewell to his little son are the last he will ever speak to his child. Tecmessa remains entirely in the background, as is fitting in her position and also in the masculine society for whom Sophocles wrote. The chorus can do no more than sing of the inevitable. Suddenly Ajax reappears from the tent, with the words of a changed man. He has realised that the weaker must give way to the stronger and he will not relinquish wife and child. He would rather be cleansed by the sea and bury the fatal sword – he owes it to Hector – in a safe place. He is prepared to learn that one must give way to the gods and even to the Atreidae, since they are the commanders of the army.

After his exit the chorus is jubilant and wants to dance for joy. Sophocles likes to insert a relaxed, happy song just before a catastrophe, and it is not only the artist in him who uses such contrasts: their tragic irony emphasises the horrible dissonance between human illusion and divine decree. No wonder that the jubilation of the chorus suddenly changes when a messenger arrives, sent by the anxious Teucer, brother of Ajax. Calchas has prophesied that on this very day Athena's anger threatens Ajax with destruction. (We have already spoken of the general significance of this motif in Sophocles' work.) The chorus hastily goes off with Tecmessa to look for Ajax. It is one of those rare occasions when the stage is quite empty during a play and as in *The Eumenides* of Aeschylus this indicates a change of scene, for the unity of place was not a binding law for early tragedy. The stage now represents a lonely place, away from the camp, and we may assume that a few bushes sufficed to indicate this.

Ajax appears and delivers his last soliloquy. In it he commends to Zeus the care of his dead body, and asks Hermes, who guides the dead, for his gracious escort. But in the middle of his speech he asks the Erinyes, in terms that have a certain binding magic, to wreak vengeance on the hated Atreidae. Because man was then aware that his life was part of Nature, he refers in his last words to sunlight and water, to the soil of his homeland and the fields of Troy. Then he falls on his sword.

In his first speech, after he had regained perfect sanity, Ajax had proclaimed (479) that for him there was no middle way, such as exists for puny souls, between a great life and a great death. In his death scene these words become reality. Coming between these two is the deceptive speech with which he lulls the anxiety of Tecmessa and the chorus, so that they may let him go. Lately there have been repeated attempts to foist another meaning on to this speech – apart from the obvious one that Ajax wishes to be free to seek his death – which would make him at least understand the ties whose severance he must atone with death. This is invalidated by the passion with which Ajax, in his final soliloquy, unleashes his fury against the Atreidae, to whom in his supposed change of heart he had promised to yield. Just as the sword which he held in his hand during this speech will end his plight in a manner different from the one suggested, so the other words he used merely served a purpose he could only fulfil through a feint. If the words of Ajax should hide a deeper significance, beyond their dramatic function, then it could only be this, that the hero critically surveys modes of possible behaviour which are alien to his nature and to which he cannot become reconciled. However, the length of the speech and its startling insertion reveal the true dramatist who wants us really to share the deception of the chorus and their joy.

The drama does not end with the death of Ajax. The chorus and Tecmessa find the body, Teucer arrives and there is loud lamentation. Then Menelaus wants to withhold from the dead hero the last honour of funeral rites and Agamemnon arrives on the scene to support him with his authority. Odysseus interferes and reveals the same nobility of attitude as in the first scene. When Agamemnon, bewildered, asks him: 'Do you, Odysseus, take his part against me?' then Odysseus replies: 'I do. I hated him while it was fair to hate.'

Here, significantly, an idea has been introduced which is prominent in the *Antigone*. Hatred, the dreadful embroiler of human affairs, is to be kept within bounds. It would be intemperate and evil to dishonour the body of the greatest hero after Achilles. Thus the dead man gains his rights, the quarrel is ended and through his death Ajax has not only restored his honour but also the equilibrium which his action had disturbed.

As a tragedy the *Ajax* stands by itself. It is true that a few years ago a didaskalic inscription[1] was found at Aexonae which mentions a *Telepheia*, which was apparently a trilogy, but generally speaking – and the *Suda* (s.v. Sophocles) confirms this – Sophocles gave up composing trilogies. After the vigorous pace of the action in the first two plays of the *Oresteia* there was a slackening off in the third, and something similar may be assumed for *The Danaids*. But in Sophocles this rhythmic curve may be entirely contained within one play. In such a case the hero's catastrophe occurs not far beyond the middle and the last part ends on a note of serenity or, as in the *Antigone*, with a conflict resolved. In these plays, which in our opinion belong to the earlier group of those we possess, the disturbed world-order regains its equilibrium.

One path only was open to Ajax, the one irrevocably determined by his character; and the same applies to Antigone. In this play, probably dating from 442, the events described in Aeschylus' *Seven Against Thebes* belong to the past. Thebes has been freed from the danger that threatened her, the male offspring of the accursed line has perished in fratricide. But Eteocles fell as the defender of his homeland, Polyneices as the aggressor. Therefore his body is to remain exposed, a prey to dogs and birds. This order issued by Creon, the new ruler of the city, lacks moderation; not in the sense of some noble excess that seeks self-realisation and

[1] *IG* II² 3091; see Sir Arthur Pickard-Cambridge, *The Dramatic Festivals of Athens* (Oxford, 1953), pp. 52–54.

cannot exist in the general framework of life, but as a sin against the divine command that the dead shall be honoured, upheld by Odysseus in the *Ajax*. Therefore Antigone has no reservations, she appears on the scene determined to bury her brother. Her character and her decision are in striking contrast to the attitude of her sister Ismene, who does not condone Creon's prohibition but submits to it. It is true that the poet wanted to create an effective contrast, but that does not exhaust the meaning of the confrontation, which is repeated in the *Electra*. The comparison conjures up the image of the Sophoclean hero, with his uncompromising determination, for whom a readiness to bargain, to calculate and to evade not only acts as a foil but may even appear as the temptation which cannot lure him. And when in the course of this scene Ismene turns away from her sister and Antigone is left to act entirely by herself, then we witness the loneliness that characterises all great Sophoclean figures, and all that is great in the world.

Haemon, Creon's son and the betrothed of Antigone, remains entirely in the background in the first part of the play, and there is in the entire drama not a single scene in which the pair appear together on the stage. There is certainly no place for Eros as a subjective experience in Sophoclean tragedy; but apart from that a scene between Haemon and Antigone would be incompatible with her loneliness.

In the song of gratitude and praise by the chorus of Theban elders is a note of rejoicing over the liberation of the town. Then Creon announces his prohibition and immediately one of the guards, placed near the body of Polyneices, reports that the order has been flouted: an unknown person has covered the body with a layer of dust to ensure, by symbolic burial, that the dead man's soul will find peace in the Underworld. Creon is furious about this infringement, he suspects betrayal and bribery and threatens the guards with terrible punishment unless they find the culprit. Glad to escape at least for the present from his master's anger, the guard leaves the stage. Sophocles has given a delightful sketch of a sly, garrulous old man of low birth and mean intelligence.

Then follows an ode about the dangers of man's greatness. Scholars have often tried to connect this with some particular part of the action. This is in fact one of those passages in which the Attic tragedian speaks from the stage of the theatre of Dionysus to the Athens of his day, warning, entreating it. At the time when the *Antigone* was performed the movement to destroy the very roots of the νόμος, the respect for law in all spheres of life, was already articulate. What had seemed unshakeable since time immemorial, sanctified by tradition and never doubted by any sane person, now had its validity submitted to a rational examination. Reason alone was to judge what was out of date and should be discarded, reason was to be the architect of a new era, when man would rid himself of the shackles of tradition and go forward on the road to perfection. We shall have more to say about the programme of the sophists in connection with Euripides. It was typical of a time when the emergence of Athens to proud and formidable greatness raised the question of where this development might lead.

It was then that Sophocles composed his ode about man's uncanny gift for widening the range of his power over nature and for spreading the symbols of his rule to the ends of the earth. Such a restless desire for power amazed and alarmed him. The last strophe is clearly aimed against the sophists who subjected even faith in the gods, and in the values they upheld, to their destructive criticism. This final strophe is one of the greatest testimonies of faith in absolute, as against relative, values. Is it still necessary to say that the validity of these words reaches beyond fifth-century Athenians to touch all mankind? We let the poet speak in his own words, hoping that the English rendering does justice to the Sophoclean verse:

332 Many the wonders but nothing walks stranger than man.
This thing crosses the sea in the winter's storm,
making his path through the roaring waves.
And she, the greatest of gods, the earth –
ageless she is, and unwearied – he wears her away
as the ploughs go up and down from year to year
and his mules turn up the soil.

Gay nations of birds he snares and leads,
wild beast tribes and the salty brood of the sea,
with the twisted mesh of his nets, this clever man.
He controls with craft the beasts of the open air,
walkers on hills. The horse with his shaggy mane
he holds and harnesses, yoked about the neck,
and the strong bull of the mountains.

Language, and thought like the wind
and the feelings that make the town,
he has taught himself, and shelter against the cold,
refuge from rain. He can always help himself.
He faces no future helpless. There's only death
that he cannot find an escape from. He has contrived
refuge from illnesses once beyond all cure.

Clever beyond all dreams
the inventive craft that he has
which may drive him one time or another to well or ill.
When he honors the laws of the land and the gods' sworn right
high indeed is his city; but stateless the man
who dares to dwell with dishonor. Not by my fire,
never to share my thoughts, who does these things.

Again the guard appears on the scene and brings with him Antigone, whom he has surprised in a second attempt at burial. Twice she went to her brother's body, and the first time she succeeded in what she set out to do. Now she must bear the consequences. Here we must admire the technique of Sophocles – Tycho von Wilamowitz has pointed out this mastery in many other passages – but it is not the kind of technique which merely serves dramatic effect and proves the artistry of the poet; its undoubted purpose is to bring out the heart of the play.

Creon and Antigone confront each other in irreconcilable conflict. Sophocles uses a large canvas. Antigone explains what she fights and suffers for: the great unwritten laws of the gods, which put to shame any statute that makes a mockery of them. Again these words disclose a profound conception of timeless validity and we need not emphasise the relevance for our time of this protest against the omnipotence of the state and ethical conformity; it sounds as if they were spoken today:

450 For me it was not Zeus who made that order.
Nor did that Justice who lives with the gods below
mark out such laws to hold among mankind.
Nor did I think your orders were so strong
that you, a mortal man, could over-run
the gods' unwritten and unfailing laws.

> Not now, nor yesterday's, they always live,
> and no one knows their origin in time.
> So not through fear of any man's proud spirit
> would I be likely to neglect these laws.

This great battle scene contains yet another passage that seems to represent the poet speaking. Again he points out that hatred, the enemy of all that is human, should be kept within bounds, but more emphatically and in more general terms than he makes Odysseus use in the *Ajax*, for it is a woman who speaks:

523 I cannot share in hatred, but in love.

It throws a curious light on recent cultural history that scholars have tried very hard to limit the significance of this saying to Polyneices and to deny it the wider human application which we consider so typically Sophoclean.

But power rests with the new ruler and Antigone must die. With Ismene, who has now joined her, she is led into the palace. Not until this moment does Haemon interfere, but neither entreaty, nor reproach, nor an appeal to the opinion of the whole Theban people can shake the determination of the tyrant. What drives Haemon to speak is his love for Antigone, but he does not mention this: the Sophoclean stage ruled out such subjective display. And when the chorus catches an echo of this scene in a song to Eros, then it is the cosmic Eros, who has power over man and beast, even over gods, and who holds sway throughout the world. It is the same Eros that we met in Aeschylus.

Antigone is led to her death: she will be buried alive. And now begins the flow of her lament. In a long dirge she bewails with the chorus her life whose fulfilment in marriage has been denied. It is the same Antigone who was so resolute on the point of action, but only now can we gauge the real greatness of her act. It was not prompted by an obstinate clinging to principles, nor by a masculine aggressiveness that was eager to fight the power of the state; Antigone is a woman like Ismene, like every other Theban woman she has the hopes and expectations of womanhood. Only in this commos does she appear completely human, revealing the extent of her sacrifice. But she does not regret her action, and follows up her lyrical lament with a closely argued justification. Her argument that fate might have made good the loss of a husband and children, never of a brother, we must think, like Goethe, strange. It is probable that Herodotus, with whom Sophocles was in touch, influenced him with his story of the wife of Intaphernes (3, 119). But apart from this we should not underrate the value, for Greek minds, of this rational exposition of the significance of sisterly love.

Ever since Hegel tried to find in the *Antigone* an objective conflict between two valid claims, that of the state and of the family, similar explanations have often appeared. But the complete rejection of Creon in the next passage shows that they are refuted by the actual text. What Antigone really fights for are the unwritten laws of the gods; the laws with which, as she puts it, the *polis* ought never to be in conflict. But Creon does not act as the representative of the *polis*, which is unanimously in favour of Antigone (733); his decision is arrogant and evil. The very first scene after Antigone has gone to her death leaves no doubt about this. Teiresias, the seer, arrives and announces that Creon, by prohibiting the funeral, has polluted himself and his city with dreadful guilt. The gods themselves speak through him, but even now Creon refuses to yield: 'Not if the very eagles tear their food from him, and leave it at the throne of Zeus. I wouldn't give him up for burial' (1039). Only under the threat of a personal disaster does he hastily, but in vain, reverse his decision. Antigone shall be set free, but already she has hanged herself and Haemon commits suicide near the body of his bride. Eurydice, Creon's wife, dies when the news reaches her and Creon is left a mere shadow, whose physical survival means nothing since his mental ruin is complete. The eternal laws are confirmed by the sacrifice of Antigone, who staked her life on them, and by the collapse of Creon, who fought against them.

The subject of *The Women of Trachis* is the reversal of human schemes by powers that are beyond man's comprehension. Deianeira, the wife of Heracles, confesses in a prologue her anxiety for his fate since he has stayed abroad for the last fifteen months. Hyllus her son, who knows that Heracles has planned a campaign against Oechalia, is to inquire about his father. When Heracles went away he left a prophecy behind that a campaign against Euboea would entail either death or happiness and peace. Deianeira's anxiety deepens when she learns of an attack on Eurytus and when the chorus enters–consisting of women from Trachis, a town in the Oetean mountains where the action takes place – they are unable to allay her fears. But suddenly there is good news. A messenger arrives, who has gone ahead of Lichas, the herald of Heracles. He announces that the hero has gained a victory and is on his way to Trachis. Lichas is already approaching with a procession of captive women, among them Iole, the beautiful young daughter of the king of Oechalia. Lichas does not tell Deianeira that Iole is intended to appear and share the house as the concubine of Heracles, with his ageing wife. But the messenger who brought the first news discloses the truth. Thus instead of being merely told the facts, we are given a sequence of scenes full of tension, which makes us fully realise the shock Deianeira suffers. She hides her feelings from Lichas, as she would have hidden them from Heracles. She speaks of the overwhelming power of love, which Heracles also must obey, and of her willingness to do as he wishes. But to the women of the chorus she speaks of her deep sorrow and of the only remedy which she, a weak woman, has at her disposal. When the centaur Nessus was dying he gave her his blood as an infallible charm if ever Heracles' love for her should waver. She has therefore steeped a garment in it and will now send it as a victory gift to her beloved husband. She is convinced that she is not doing anything wrong. In her innocence she cannot see the grave risk and is not, as she says: 'a woman who tries to be bad and bold. I hate women who are' (582). But after a short choric song – the relaxed and happy Sophoclean song before a catastrophe – she comes on to the stage deeply perturbed. The wool with which she rubbed the blood on the garment has dissolved into bloody foam in the sunlight, and now Hyllus arrives wildly cursing his mother for making his father die maddened by pain. Without a word Deianeira goes to her death, like Eurydice in the *Antigone*. A servant girl who has witnessed the suicide tells the story.

Heracles is brought on to the stage asleep, in a state of exhaustion. Soon he starts up, in a renewed attack of pain. He, the Doric ideal of strong inflexible manhood, is helplessly writhing in agony. All that remains to him after a life of heroic effort is a fierce desire for revenge on Deianeira. But when he hears that she caused his death unintentionally, through the poisonous blood of the centaur, he recognises the hand of destiny. An old prophecy that a dead man would kill him has been fulfilled. All that remains now is to arrange his passing. Hyllus must, reluctantly, do his father's bidding: he is to erect the funeral pyre on Mount Oeta and to make Iole his wife. The procession that will conduct Heracles to his fiery grave leaves the stage. In his terrible grief Hyllus accuses the gods (1272) for allowing this outrage upon their greatest hero. He puts the gods to shame in terms which scarcely occur elsewhere in Sophocles. But this outburst is immediately offset by the significant final words of the play: 'There is nothing here which is not Zeus.' This terrible happening, which the poet does not mitigate by the promise of future bliss for Heracles in the realm of the gods, stands for the world, and the world is Zeus.

There is no denying that the influence of Sophocles' younger rival Euripides is very noticeable in *The Women of Trachis*. There is the prologue in which Deianeira reveals her character and tells us much that anticipates the action, but we should not overlook what is Sophoclean even if the characterisation reminds us of Euripides. The latter's influence is also to be detected in the greater softness of the female portraiture. It is most moving to see how Deianeira reveals her feminine sensitivity when, having asked Lichas to convey her loving greetings to Heracles, she suddenly draws back because she does not know if her longing is reciprocated (630). Nevertheless the Euripidean character of the play has been overrated, for scholars have failed to appreciate how far it exemplifies all the features of Sophoclean tragedy. The catastrophe does not originate in the type of passion that ravages Phaedra, but in the typically Sophoclean conflict between human desires – which in the case of Deianeira are understandable and pure – and destiny in general as an incomprehensible transcendent power. This power plays a significant part in tragedy by means of prophecies, and the fact that prophecies are justified by inevitable fulfilment – as often happens in Sophocles – has a more than superficial similarity to the ideas of Herodotus.

The overrated influence of Euripides cannot provide the information on dating which was hoped for. In particular it has proved impossible to maintain the long held assumption that the sleeping scene in *The Women of Trachis* imitated the *Heracles* of

Euripides, implying a late date. The intellectual content of the play, its division into two parts, its sparing use of the third actor, and many metrical details assign it to the plays of the older group, although we do not dare date it with greater precision. Yet it is very likely that the account of Deianeira's farewell to her house and her marriage bed (900) had as its prototype the servant-girl's description of Alcestis' departure (E. *Alc.* 152) in Euripides' play of that name which was produced in 438. The similarities are too striking to be accidental and the motif can definitely be derived from the *Alcestis* because of the significance which Euripides gives to his heroine's sacrificial death.

The dating of the Sophoclean plays which we have accepted as the most probable means that *Oedipus the King* comes somewhere in the middle of the series. This is symbolical for a play which represents the core of Sophocles' tragic poetry.

The decisive events, the killing of Laius by Oedipus, his marriage with his mother, precede by a few years the beginning of the tragedy. The play itself gives the 'tragic analysis' (Schiller) of a situation in which Oedipus becomes fatally aware of the meaning of these acts. We see him in the prologue as ruler, at his most impressive, and Sophocles shows this not by the extent of his power but by his profound human qualities. Thebes is being destroyed by a plague and the description of it may well owe much to the dreadful epidemic in Athens at the beginning of the Peloponnesian War (430). The people, seeking aid, communicate through a priest their horror and anxiety to the king, who once before acted as their saviour when the Sphinx oppressed the town. And the king longs to help them. He speaks to the suppliants with all the concern of a father, calls them 'poor children.' He had already sent his brother-in-law, Creon, to Delphi and he has just returned with the information that the plague would be halted as soon as the pollution was removed which had affected the land since the murder of Laius.

After the first processional song of the chorus of Theban citizens, praying and lamenting, the struggle begins to expose the crime on which the god has placed his curse. Oedipus, who solved the riddle of the Sphinx, announces his inflexible determination to find the murderer of Laius. The seer Teiresias is first called in. It is the most brilliant feature of the construction of the play, the most dramatically effective in the literature of the world, that the whole truth is unequivocally exposed at the very beginning of the play. At first Teiresias does not want to speak, but Oedipus extracts the truth from him: that the king himself is the murderer and is living in an incestuous relationship. This revelation is so monstrous that the reaction of king and chorus is anything but the fear that it may be true. Only slowly, step by step, is this early revelation confirmed. Oedipus is soon ready with his conclusion: Teiresias is the tool of Creon who wants to be king himself. Startled and indignant, Creon defends himself, but only Jocasta's interference saves him from a judgment that has already been pronounced. It was the revelation of Teiresias which caused the quarrel. She would therefore like to deprive Oedipus of his reverence for oracles: had not oracles prophesied that Laius would be killed by his son, instead of which he was killed by robbers at a crossroads? But instead of reassuring Oedipus she achieves the opposite. In a fit of anger Oedipus had once at a crossroads hit an old man, who had beaten him first, with his staff and killed him. Now for the first time a deep uneasiness begins to stir in him. But the servant of Laius who had managed to escape and who, since Oedipus became king, has lived far from the city, did say that there had been brigands. This still leaves some hope. He must be fetched to clear the matter up.

In the following passages Sophocles shows his mastery in the use of contrast. Jocasta's doubt about the validity of prophecy incites the chorus to sing of the greatness of the gods. Again the poet contemplates the eternal unwritten laws, for which his Antigone died and which the insolent cleverness of his age wished to rob of their high honour:

863 May destiny ever find me
pious in word and deed
prescribed by the laws that live on high:
laws begotten in the clear air of heaven,
whose only father is Olympus;
no mortal nature brought them to birth,
no forgetfulness shall lull them to sleep;
for God is great in them and grows not old.

The next scene, however, brings a messenger from Corinth, who seems finally to refute the prophecy that Oedipus would kill his father. King Polybus of Corinth, at whose court Oedipus grew up and whom he called father, had died a natural death. Now Oedipus is only worried about the second part of the prophecy, about marriage with his mother, for Merope the wife of Polybus is still alive. The messenger from Corinth believes that he can reassure him, but the opposite happens: Polybus and Merope are not the parents of Oedipus at all. The messenger himself, when he was a shepherd, took him over from another – a servant of Laius – on Cithaeron where the helpless infant was found with his ankles pierced. Now the veil is torn for Jocasta. She still attempts to hold Oedipus back from further questioning, and seeing that her effort is in vain, as he sends for the shepherd, she rushes off into the palace to kill herself. But the strains of the chorus, still in doubt, as is Oedipus, rise hopefully again, only to make the depth of the fall more appalling: perhaps a god has begotten Oedipus on Cithaeron, one of those who roam the mountain meadows and woods – Pan or Apollo or Dionysus.

Sophocles has, by a stroke of genius, combined various dramatic functions in one person and thus achieved an astonishingly concentrated action. Just as the messenger from Corinth is the same man who rescued the condemned child on Cithaeron, so the Theban shepherd who handed it over was the same who accompanied Laius on his way to Delphi. He witnessed the killing and fled to the country with his knowledge of the new king's secret. When he now appears by order of the king, he first refuses to speak, as Teiresias did, but again Oedipus forces him to tell the truth: he, the king, is the son of Laius who, alarmed by the prophecy that his son would kill him, had exposed his child on Cithaeron. Oedipus is an incestuous parricide. With this knowledge he rushes into the palace.

The chorus in their ode plumb the depth of the catastrophe: then a messenger enters and announces what has happened in the palace. Jocasta has hanged herself and Oedipus has blinded himself with a brooch from her robe. He appears on the stage in fearful agony, he who at the beginning of the play was a beloved king, a helper of others. Now he begs Creon to banish him and for permission to say farewell to his children. Creon – very different from the tyrant in the *Antigone* – orders them to be fetched, and once again the father embraces his daughters. Then he enters the palace to wait for the verdict of Apollo, which Creon wishes to obtain before he takes further action.

Even the shortest *résumé* of the drama will show its marvellous construction, and the Sophoclean antithesis between the human will and the workings of destiny is immediately evident. The tragic irony with which Oedipus in the beginning curses the murderer and undertakes to avenge Laius as if he were his own father (264), the irony which turns every reassuring statement into its opposite, becomes an indication of this irreconcilable antithesis. But to say that Fate is a protagonist is almost as much of a misinterpretation of the play as the absurd, but recently repeated, assertion that it is a detective story. The protagonist, the hero of the tragedy, is man himself when he faces this 'fate'. In Aeschylean tragedy, which is so predominantly concerned with divine rule, we could hardly apply this concept to Eteocles and certainly not in the *Oresteia*; but it is perfectly valid in Sophoclean tragedy. We must also try to analyse its essential features.

Destiny as an unaccountable power which man must accept has produced in dramatic art the kind of 'tragedy of fate' which in German literature has rightly earned a bad reputation ever since Werner wrote his naïvely melodramatic *The 24th of February*. But real tragedy evolves where there is a tension between the dark unpredictable forces to which man is exposed and his determination to struggle against them. This is usually a pointless struggle; it may involve the hero in still greater suffering, and often lead to his death. But man must fight it out, he may not give up. The tragic hero stands out against a background of those who yield or avoid a decisive choice, his absolute determination is pitted against an overwhelming power; but in him the dignity of a great human being remains intact in defeat.

We have seen in the *Ajax* how Sophocles keeps the problem of guilt in the background, and to bring it up in connection with *Oedipus the King* is a gross misinterpretation of the main figure, which has bedevilled our reading of the play for quite long enough! The main characteristic of Oedipus, which he shares with Ajax, Antigone and Electra, is superlative energy and an unbending resolve in action. Fate is closing in on him, the net is being drawn tighter and tighter, but he can still avoid catastrophe at the last moment if he lowers the veil which he himself has lifted. So he could if he was not Oedipus, the tragic hero for whom nothing is impossible but this feeble compromise for the sake of a token of peace, for the sake of mere existence. He becomes a hero because his will is inexorable, even when it leads to destruction, attaining a tragic stature which perhaps reaches its summit in the antithesis portrayed in verse 1169 ff. Just before the final revelation the shepherd cries:

> O God, I am on the brink of frightful speech.

and Oedipus answers:

> And I of frightful hearing. But I must hear.

When, blinded, he has entered the dark realm of suffering he may have wished that Cithaeron had kept the child, but it would be unthinkable for him to wish that the truth had remained hidden, as it had for so long. By the side of the great tragic figures, who take up the fight and whose concern is human dignity, not mere existence, we find, as the embodiment of temptation, those average persons who want to be secure and to stay alive at all costs. Tecmessa throws herself and her child in the path of Ajax, the only path open to him. Ismene is to Antigone what Chrysothemis is to Electra. Beside Oedipus we see Jocasta. She has much to say (e.g. 857) against prophecies, but this does not mean that she is a blasphemous rationalist; we see her even praying to Apollo (911). What she says is prompted by her wish to avoid the threat, not like Oedipus to meet it. Even at the last moment she begs him (1060) not to question any further. But his course cannot be checked.

Aeschylus shows us man as part of the divine world order, which fulfils itself through him in terms of action and suffering, and wisdom through suffering. With him it is man through whom this order is not only realised, but justified also. The Sophocles of the older plays sees man otherwise in an irreconcilable conflict with powers which rule events in a world that is for him also divine. His religious sense is not less profound but totally different from that of Aeschylus. It comes closer to the precept of the Delphic oracle: 'know thyself,' which shows man his human limits. Sophocles is prevented from probing into the manifestations of the divine in the world, as Aeschylus did, by that religious awe which is the finest feature of classical Greek religion. In Goethe's poem *Natürliche Tochter* ('Illegitimate Daughter') we find in a completely different context verses which beautifully render the thoughts of Sophocles on the irrationality of divinely ordained events:

> That which on high in vastnesses unmeasured
> Moves here and there, tremendous and erratic,
> Kills or revives un-reasoning, un-judging,
> Perhaps obeys a different calculation
> Whose measure and whose number
> Remain unknown to us.

Sophocles himself says it quite clearly in the verses of a lost drama (frg. 833 N^2): 'It is impossible to grasp what is divine, when the gods themselves hide it from us, even if the search follows every path.' What God ordains for man may be terrible and one can understand that this had led to the assertion that tragedy implies cruelty of the gods. Hoffmansthal, in his *Oedipus and the Sphinx*, has elaborated the theme in this sense. His Oedipus hurls indictments at the gods:

> Gods, Gods!
> sitting on golden seats above,
> gloating because now he is caught
> whom you have hounded day and night.
>
> (sombrely and impressively)
> The whole world is your net
> and so is life. And all our actions
> expose us naked to your wakeful eyes
> that look upon us through the meshes.

These dark and passionate words are great poetry, but they are no more Sophoclean than is *La machine infernale*. The assumption of a recent critic that Sophocles was passing through a religious crisis when he wrote this tragedy rests on a serious misunderstanding. The contrary is true: throughout the horror of this truly total tragic conflict that ends in destruction, the poet's deep faith in the greatness and the wisdom of his gods remains unshaken. In the same drama which depicts the tragic fall of the hero there occurs the choric song, quoted earlier, in praise of the eternal laws that are to be revered with awe. Neither Sophocles nor Aeschylus conjures up the image of a world deserted by the gods, in which tragedy would be senseless.

The figure of the tragic hero in Sophocles is subjected to terrible tensions. But because he can only take up the fight against the powers of life if he relies on his own inner strength, the hero becomes a character and the man as a tragic figure is depicted as entirely self-sufficient.

We can now understand the deeper meaning of the fact that Sophocles had given up the form of the trilogy. No longer is it the generations of a family which are the object of divine dispensation, but an individual personality. This is why *Oedipus the King* has been lifted from the context of Aeschylus' Theban trilogy and why in Sophocles a single drama, the *Electra*, corresponds to *The Choephoroe*, which is merely a part of the *Oresteia*. For the same reason Aeschylus' central theme, the family curse, has been kept almost entirely in the background in the *Oedipus* and the *Electra*. Man no longer acts with his daemon as a partner (συλλήπτωϱ). Whatever he does is prompted entirely by his own will, although the outcome is outside his control.

If we are to understand the *Electra* of Sophocles we should note that both Aeschylus and Sophocles show Electra's grief and anxiety and later her jubilation when she recognises her brother. But in Aeschylus the respective scenes follow each other immediately, while Sophocles separates them widely so that they occur at the beginning and the end of the play. If we take these scenes as the firm border-lines of a self-contained structure and move nearer the middle of the play we shall find two parallel scenes between Electra and Chrysothemis, which both take their tone from the conflict between Antigone and Ismene. In the first Electra's character, her awareness of the disgrace of the house and demand for revenge make a striking contrast to Chrysothemis, who knows the meaning of absolute integrity but prefers an easy compromise with those at the head of the house, Clytaemnestra and Aegisthus. In the second scene Electra is under the impact of her brother's death. She has to reject as groundless the hope raised by the offering of a lock of hair and is now determined upon an extreme course. She herself will perform the act of revenge which should have been the task of Orestes. The shy withdrawal of Chrysothemis again throws into relief the loneliness in which all Sophoclean heroes must plan their great deeds and carry them out.

Transferring our attention to the centre of the play, we reach by way of lyrical passages of roughly the same length (the stasimon 472–515 and the commos 823–870) the scenes in which the two opposing forces in the drama, Clytaemnestra and Electra, are in actual conflict. In a violent quarrel between mother and daughter, the latter unmasks her father's murderess: it was not, she says, the wish to avenge Iphigeneia which guided Clytaemnestra's hand, but a criminal passion for Aegisthus with whom she lives in the palace. Electra emerges victorious and as if to confirm her accusations Clytaemnestra now prays that she may keep the chattels she has acquired through her crime and that her secret wish may be fulfilled. This can only refer to the death of Orestes.

Again here tragic irony plays its part, although in the later plays it is overshadowed by the emphasis laid on the link between the action and the characters of the protagonists. No sooner has Clytaemnestra uttered the last words of her prayer than the pedagogue, who came with Orestes, enters with a false announcement of his death to prepare the way for revenge: Orestes, he says, has been killed by a fall in the chariot race at Delphi. The poet evokes the scene with such impressive reality that the unprejudiced spectator's knowledge that it is only fiction is suspended by the impact it has on the other actors. After a brief stirring of maternal feeling Clytaemnestra gives vent to the joy so long denied to her by anxiety. But Electra, now that all her hopes have vanished, feels drained of purpose, and only in the second scene with Chrysothemis does she find herself again in the decision to act alone.

Thus the great centre part of the drama – in which its motive forces are caught as in a burning lens – is enclosed by a concentric arrangement of scenes, closely related to it through Chrysothemis' confrontation of Electra in one case, and in another through the contrast between Electra's mourning and her ecstasy in her brother's arms. In the whole of this superb dramatic construction there is not a single scene, after the dialogue between the two men at the tomb, in which Electra is not on the stage. This differs from Aeschylus, who after the first part of *The Choephoroe* allows her to disappear from the stage for good.

The structure of the play suggests what the portrayal of Electra's character confirms: that she is the main figure in the drama, all events being focused on what she feels, thinks and plans. While in Aeschylus an episode in the history of the house of Atreus served to reveal the working of divine justice, this is the drama of a human soul whose courage leads her from anguish and despair to liberation.

The poet presents this liberation in one of his most beautiful scenes: Electra has already decided to act alone when Orestes approaches, unrecognised, carrying the urn which contains his ashes, according to the false information which is to deceive Clytaemnestra and Aegisthus. He does not recognise Electra either. Only when she takes the urn from his hands and reveals in her lament how deeply she loved her brother, now presumed dead, does he recognise her and lifts her from deepest gloom to ecstatic joy.

The question of a family curse's effect on later generations is never mentioned, but the poet had to show Orestes' revenge. That is why he brings him on to the stage at the beginning of the play, with the pedagogue who accompanies the young man to his homeland and watches over his action. The brief final scenes show the deed performed. Clytaemnestra is killed first, and then Aegisthus. But although the matricide is not of such central importance as in Aeschylus, the question of whether it was justified is not simply ignored. The subject of the quarrel, which forms the hub of the play, connects these peripheral scenes to the whole. Here Electra so completely condemns Clytaemnestra, the adulteress who killed her husband and banished her children, that death is her rightful punishment. We now understand why for this Orestes no Erinyes rise up from the earth at the end of the play; the way is open to a serene future.

The formal aspects of *Electra* have been emphasised in this discussion, because this play best shows Sophoclean tragedy as a classical work of art, rightly belonging to the time when the Parthenon was built. Classical art as a unique historical phenomenon as in fifth-century Greece, certainly cannot be understood by applying purely formal aesthetic criteria. Such an approach, which isolates the formal element as something self-sufficient, is doomed to failure from the start. Correlation of form and content, reaching the level of organic unity, should of course be regarded as a basic characteristic of such classical art. Harmony of form then becomes the fitting expression of the living forces embodied in the work of art. In this case the correlation between Electra's dominant position and the construction of the play should help us to understand such classical forms as the Parthenon sculptures.

The discussion of the *Electra* should remind us of the work of K. Reinhardt, who has contributed so much to our understanding of Sophocles. Through him we have gained a deeper insight into the developing structure of the tragedies that we possess. In the older dramas, especially the *Ajax*, the image of the great legendary figures has a fairly fixed outline; their character does not develop in ever-changing relationships with other protagonists, but emerges in reaction to external fateful events. The great speeches of Ajax (430, 815) should be seen in this light, and it is significant that the deception by which he gains the freedom to seek his death does not occur in a lively interplay of forces, but in a single long speech by the hero (646), flanked by two choric songs, which is not a reply and does not solicit one. Reinhardt used a striking phrase borrowed from syntax for the juxtaposition of single scenes which each disclose an important idea: he calls it a paratactic arrangement. The *Electra*, on the other hand, shows how in the later plays characters develop in dramatic confrontations and how the dynamics of single scenes become more lively, e.g. in the Creon-Teiresias scene in *Oedipus the King*, where the situation is completely reversed. The significance of this phenomenon, which has so far only been considered stylistically, is connected with the increasing emphasis on human personality. The conflict between a solitary man and fate is replaced by a struggle between an individual and those around him. *Oedipus the King* is still entirely concerned with the former relationship, but the excitement of its plot-development suggests that it belongs to a period of transition.

The *Philoctetes*, performed in 409, provides the clearest example of the mobile dynamics of a play that is entirely dominated by the character of the protagonists. The drama involves three people. Philoctetes himself had been abandoned by the Greeks on their way to Troy on the island of Lemnos, suffering from a foul, incurable wound due to a snake bite. The poet represents the island as uninhabited. There he lives, bearing his suffering with fortitude, but filled with a deep hatred against those who left him in this distress. Round Troy the endless struggle for the capture of the town continues and Philoctetes appears to be forgotten. But suddenly a prophecy by the captured Trojan seer Helenus turns him into a person of decisive importance. Only his miraculous bow, a gift from Heracles, can bring victory to the Greek army. But the difficulty is to get hold of it. The wonderful weapon itself is a protection against force and the hero, embittered by suffering, would never yield to persuasion. Two very different persons have accepted the difficult assignment. Odysseus is exactly the man we know from the epic. At once energetic and cautious, he has but one aim and the cunning of which he is a master provides the means. He may remind us of the sophists in some of his arguments (e.g. 98), but this is not inconsistent with the Sophoclean image of him. We shall see later that for his companion, Neoptolemus, he may bring temptations to self-betrayal, but this does not altogether condemn him. What Odysseus represents is the will of the army's council, and this he serves faithfully. Neoptolemus is the son of Achilles who, also on the strength of the prophecy of Helenus, has been fetched from the island of Scyros to the theatre of war to help put an end to it. Here Sophocles has introduced some innovations, for the 52nd discourse of Dio Chrysostom[1] gives one or two important clues to Aeschylus' and Euripides' treatment of the theme. In Aeschylus it was Odysseus alone who deceived Philoctetes and stole the bow. A new fragment[2] seemed to suggest that Neoptolemus also figures in the Aeschylean play, but a different reconstruction is quite possible. Euripides, who produced his drama in 431 at the same time as *The Medea*, focused it on the conflict between passion and unselfish duty towards the state. Odysseus and Diomedes wish to win over Philoctetes and gain victory with his aid, but a Trojan mission offers him the highest reward for his assistance. In the end the Hellenic blood of Philoctetes conquers his desire to avenge the betrayal he suffered. He overcomes his resentment and goes with the Greeks to whom he belongs.

The Sophoclean drama depends, in an entirely different way, on the character of the persons involved; above all on Neoptolemus who is here, in a break with tradition, the companion of Odysseus.

[1] H. L. Crosby, *Dio Chrysostom*, vol. IV (London, 1946), pp. 336–353.
[2] POxy 20/No. 2256 frg. 5.

The young man has inherited the nobility of his father, the greatest of all Greek heroes. When in the prologue Odysseus reveals his plan to obtain the bow, the bringer of victory, by means of cunning and deceit, the boy's whole fine nature rebels against it and he only accepts it with difficulty out of soldierly duty. When he meets Philoctetes in his dreadful misery, abetted by a chorus of sailors, he lies to him on instructions from Odysseus. He tells him that he is so deeply insulted by Odysseus' refusal to hand over his father's arms that he has left the army and is on his way home. He soon gains the confidence of the lonely sufferer, who begs him to take him to his homeland. Here Odysseus actively interferes by sending a spy, disguised as a merchant, who announces that he has seen some Greek ships which are trying to catch Neoptolemus, and also, on the basis of a prophecy of Helenus, Philoctetes. The latter begs even more urgently to be taken away. But even if the ruse has apparently succeeded so far, the first scene has shown us enough of the character of Neoptolemus to allow us to guess how painful it is to be trusted by a man so helplessly deceived. When much later on, at a decisive moment (906), he speaks of the distress he has long felt, his words must refer to his first meeting with Philoctetes.

Soon he will fathom the whole depth of the wretched man's suffering. Before they start Philoctetes has another attack of his illness. He is still capable of giving his bow to Neoptolemus so that he may look after it during the exhausted sleep which always follows the attack. Now Neoptolemus holds in his hands the weapon which will decide the fate of Troy and for which all this deception was set in motion. The ship is near and nothing can prevent the rescue of the precious object. That is how the chorus sees things, but Neoptolemus refuses to comply. He does not state as yet that to deceive a helpless man is a contemptible crime, but points out in solemn hexameters (839) the prophecy's condition which was deliberately omitted from the first scene and will be ignored later (1055): the bow itself will be worthless unless Philoctetes himself is brought to Troy. Sophocles can certainly introduce motifs freely whenever he needs them, to explain Neoptolemus' hesitation. But this lingering in itself also expresses his aversion for the methods of Odysseus. The young man has strayed far from the dictates of his own nature in the service of the clever Odysseus. Here, where he seeks support from the prophecy, he has clearly reached the point from which he will find his way back step by step. When Philoctetes wakes up and thanks him for his loyalty in staying with him, Neoptolemus throws off his disguise and confesses what he came for. He yields once more to the authority of Odysseus and retains the bow, but soon turns back and in spite of the entreaties and threats of his companions he gives Philoctetes his weapon. And with a true Sophoclean hero's refusal to compromise he is now determined to follow his course of action through to the bitter end. He still tries openly to persuade Philoctetes to fight willingly with them against Troy. But when he cannot move the inflexible hatred of the embittered man, he is ready for the last extremity: he will fulfil what previously he had promised deceitfully and take Philoctetes to his homeland, even if this would mean a break with the entire army and the sacrifice of his personal glory.

But someone else is to soften the obstinacy of Philoctetes. His divine helper Heracles shows him the path which will lead, in the struggle with Troy, to healing and fame. This sudden appearance as the bringer of a solution may have a superficial likeness to the *deus ex machina* of Euripides, but here the god's connection with the tragedy goes far deeper.

The persons in this drama are not confronting irrational, intangible forces. Although it was a prophecy that set events in motion, in the actual play their actions and sufferings are entirely prompted from within themselves. And so the *Philoctetes* raises the question which has so far remained unspoken in the background: how is man visualised and represented in Sophoclean tragedies, particularly the later ones? We have already noted that the personality of the hero is of far greater importance than in Aeschylus, for whom divinity was the protagonist, but how is this expressed in dramatic terms?

In trying to answer our question we should examine the relevance of two concepts that immediately come to mind. Figures like Ajax and Antigone have a universal significance and therefore appealed to their own time as they do to ours. May we therefore call them 'types,' in contrast with the richer, more varied individuality of modern stage figures? Such a generalisation becomes unsatisfactory as soon as the literary meaning of the 'type' is defined more clearly. It means a rough delineation of human figures in a few sparse strokes, without the mysterious focal point of human character from which all our actions spring. We know a great many types from the comic stage: the old miser, the braggart soldier, the prostitute of noble character, and many others. Even when such figures are seen in the unusual depth which Menander gave them, there is still a great gulf fixed between them and the great inimitable figures of tragedy. The term 'type,' as it has come to be used in literary history, is therefore inadequate for our purpose.

But these tragic figures also differ profoundly from those in modern character drama. However strong the former's impact as unique personalities, they lack the wealth of individual features – often represented for their own sake – of their modern counterparts. Likewise these latter cannot satisfy us alone. The notion of individual peculiarity was not implied in the term χαρακτήρ up to and including Aristotle. Originally it meant something that made a mark or impression, then that which was impressed; from this it was transferred to the way man expressed himself in action, speech and writing. And when Theophrastus, the pupil of Aristotle, represented 'characters' in his small work of that title, these are really human types, however subtly they are differentiated.

To understand the great figures of the Attic stage, especially those of Sophocles, we must realise that neither the usual concept 'type' nor that of individual character brings us any nearer. Free from the chance, inessential elements of modern individuality, they develop from the very roots of human existence. Therein lies the unqualified validity and conviction for the spectator which mark them as classical creations. They are not determined by typical features that can be repeated at will, but entirely by their own fundamental qualities, and it is this which makes it a great experience to encounter them. We have rejected the terms 'type' and 'character' (in the modern sense); perhaps the best definition is the classical concept of 'personality' as expressed by Herbert Cysarz: 'Personality instead of just interesting individuality, a norm instead of the original and the bizarre.'

It is possible, particularly in the *Philoctetes*, to determine more precisely what this concept of personality means in Greek thought of the period. In a modern character drama an individual and all the different facets of his being are the centre of the action, and the changes that take place in him are frequently shown as well. Euripides – after a revolution in ideas about human nature – was the first to incorporate such changes in his dramatic representations. They do not occur in classical drama, in fact they are alien to its spirit, in a significant way. We saw that the actions of Neoptolemus, in different passages of the drama, were contradictory, but we should misinterpret the play if we ascribed this to a change in him as a person. A different concept altogether is needed to interpret this figure. When Odysseus explains his mission to him, he says understandingly (79): 'I know, young man, it is not your natural bent (φύσις) to say such things nor to contrive such mischief.' With this word *physis* we encounter the notion of an inborn quality in a man, which at that time was considered fundamental to human nature and which will help us to understand this play. Its psychological core is not a change in Neoptolemus but the victorious reassertion of his *physis*, against all temptation and after he had disowned it, however grudgingly. Neoptolemus himself states, at a decisive moment in the drama (902), one of the most profound truths of pre-sophistic Hellas when he speaks of the distress in which man lands himself if he disowns his *physis* and does not act in harmony with it. And his greatest reward for the reassertion of his self are the words of Philoctetes (1310): 'You have shown your nature and true breeding, son of Achilles.'

This concept of *physis* as man's permanent possession, his inalienable, unchanging inheritance, contains a fundamental trait of Sophoclean man. Beyond it lies an idea that was inherent in archaic Greek culture and remained valid up to the end of the great classical period: what man inherited through his descent determined his character once and for all. These theories of an aristocratic society sank deep into democracy, and we can trace their origin from the impression they made on Pindar, the poet of the ideals of nobility. In one of his Odes (Ol.9, 100) he speaks of the power of natural qualities; his phrase about the impossibility of concealing inherited traits (Ol.13, 13) might have served as a motto for the *Philoctetes*. In Ol.9, 28 he says the same thing as the Sophoclean fragment 739 N^2: The essence of man's nature is predestined, inexorably fixed. Goethe therefore uttered a perfectly Greek thought when he wrote in his *Orphische Urworten* (Ancient Orphic Sayings):

> And time will not, nor power, ever dismember
> A form once coined, as living form evolving.

This brings us to the general question of whether the inherited qualities in a man's *physis*, or his environment and education are the decisive factors. The Greeks definitely favoured the former and this determined their attitude to two further problems, one social, one pedagogic. The distinction between people of noble and of low birth (*χρηστοί* and *φαῦλοι*) within ancient Greek society was based less on pride than on the conviction that birth was a decisive factor. We shall see how these concepts become problematical in Euripides under the influence of new ways of thinking. They also imply a certain amount of pedagogic pessimism. A man's worth is inherent in his *physis*; it is not the product of education, although the latter is important, even necessary for the encouragement of what is already there. In this connection it is significant that Pindar (Ol.9, 100) distinguishes natural power from that which can be acquired by learning, *διδακταὶ ἀρεταί*, and considers only the former to be essential. This world of thought is a complete contrast to that of the sophists and of Socrates. Again in Euripides the old tenets dissolve under the impact of a new epoch.

When Sophocles wrote the *Philoctetes* he was nearly ninety years of age. *Oedipus at Colonus* is no less astonishing as a testimony of his inexhaustible creativity. His grandson and namesake had it performed in 401. The play required a fourth actor.

We saw in *Oedipus the King* the type of Sophoclean tragedy in which man is helpless against irrational powers which thrust him into misery and horror. There is not a glimmer of consolation at the end of the play in which those once blessed with happiness have become an abomination to themselves and others. Now Oedipus, an aged beggar, once more appears on the stage accompanied by his loving daughter Antigone. He has experienced more anguish and suffering than any other man, but the gods have pity on him and the words of Apollo bring him to Attica, to the shrine of the Eumenides at Colonus Hippius, where the restless sufferer will be released from his misery and where, as a 'hero,' he will bring blessing to those who befriended him.

In the opening scene he hears from one of the inhabitants that he is actually on the sacred soil which he has been seeking, but it is doubtful if he will be permitted to remain there. When a chorus of citizens from Colonus appears he has to leave the grove and learns that his accursed name produces a sense of horror. Only the arrival of Theseus makes possible the future he has longed for. Theseus here epitomises – as in *The Suppliant Women* of Euripides – all the noble qualities of the ideal Athenian. He feels it his duty to succour those who, though innocent, are involved in crime and sorrow. As king he is conscious of the blessing which according to the prophecy the hero will bring to Attic soil. So it is Theseus who at the end of the play, when thunder and the voice of heaven call the old man to his death, leads him to the place where he will be transfigured.

The passing of Oedipus into the peace of death is hallowed by great poetry. But this motif alone could never give shape to a dramatic play. Before he finds this peace, the powers of this world once more reach out towards the sorely tried man who only wishes to bid farewell to life. After the scene in the first part of the play in which Oedipus and Antigone convince the chorus of citizens from Colonus that they must wait for the arrival of Theseus and his decision on the fate of the helpless man, Ismene enters and introduces violent dramatic movement. While Oedipus is seeking peace in Colonus, life's wild struggle continues outside. Eteocles and Polyneices are contending for the mastery of Thebes. Polyneices, who has been driven out, is raising an army in Argos to fight against Thebes. But a prophecy has declared that the party which Oedipus joins will be victorious. Therefore Creon, who is on the side of Eteocles, now comes to fetch back to the army the man he once banished. He is a very different Creon from the level-headed man in *Oedipus the King*. He is now prepared to resort to any means, and since persuasion does not work, he will use force. He drags away Antigone and Ismene in order to compel their father to return. But here also Theseus is the champion of those in need and does not shrink from using force to bring the girls back to their father. Then Polyneices arrives. He is the elder of the two brothers and has more right to rule than Eteocles, who drove him out. Sophocles, in his characterisation of the two brothers, clearly follows Euripides, who in his *Phoenician Women* turns the 'brawler' of the old saga into a person who had been unjustly driven out by Eteocles. But Oedipus is implacably resentful towards both his sons, who did nothing to prevent his banishment from Thebes. In his uncontrolled severity he utters a curse against them, which will later be fulfilled in their fratricidal combat. He allows Polyneices to go to his doom without consolation or hope. He has done with hateful life and rejects it whenever it reaches out to him with violence or entreaties.

We have already emphasised the importance of action being filled with dramatic incident, but this does not mean that Sophocles grafted some lively action on to the main theme of Oedipus' transfiguration for technical reasons alone. The struggle for Thebes and the end of Oedipus form a compelling whole, though this was not recognised by those who sought to explain the construction of the play by assuming that it had either been re-written or that some parts were added later. The road to peace leads the sufferer once more through life's anguish, and the hallowed end of his journey is all the more moving because it occurs against the background of raging human passions, which he leaves behind to enter into the peace of god.

Even Oedipus' reactions to those around him have an innate consistency. His anger with those who bar his road to peace is in keeping with his inflexible purpose in *Oedipus the King*. Now, having gained wisdom through suffering, he yearns to tread this road.

For many reasons it is significant that this particular play was Sophocles' last work. The words of Odysseus in the prologue to the *Ajax* have been suggested as a motto for the poet's work: lives like our own, fatally caught in suffering and distress and a helpless prey to higher powers, are shown on the stage. These words bore a sinister meaning in the *Ajax* and in *Oedipus the King*. Now, in the aged poet's last work, they gain milder, more peaceful overtones. Apollo's prophecy has cast the king from the height of good fortune into an abyss of misery; now the same god's words show him the way to peace. And the Eumenides are not spirits of damnation, summoning the guilty, they are merciful infernal powers who may hide and resolve man's misery. We have learned to see the difference between the Sophoclean vision of human existence and that of Aeschylus, but even in Sophocles divine grace may grant redemption from terrible anguish. In the peace which suffuses the final scene in the second Oedipus play, the suffering and horror in the first appear in a different light. We become aware of the sublime paradox that the same gods who cast him into abysmal suffering also drew him through it towards themselves. In the messenger's account at the end of the drama, a wonderfully poetic passage which relates the mysterious vanishing of the aged sufferer, the words of the god's summons reveal most movingly how close to him they are:

1623 ... suddenly a Voice called him, a terrifying voice at which all trembled and hair stood on end. A god was calling to him. 'Oedipus! Oedipus!' it cried, again and again. 'It is time: you stay too long.'

Few words have probed more deeply into the mysterious relationship between a great human being and the gods than those which Hölderlin wrote in his first draft of *Der Tod des Empedokles* ('The Death of Empedocles') when he spoke of 'a lovers quarrel'; again at the end of *Hyperion* he writes: 'As lovers' discord are the dissonances in the world.'

But the *Oedipus at Colonus* is also precious to us as a personal confession. The poet stood on the threshold of death when he wrote about Oedipus again. And in his hero's longing for death, his quest, after a stormy life, for peace and silence in the Attic region of Colonus, which was the poet's homeland, we can hear his own voice. Life had given him much, but the longing for it to be dissolved in the utter tranquillity of death was the ultimate wisdom for him also. He speaks to us of this yearning with a rare directness in the third stasimon:

1211 Show me the man who asks an over-abundant share
Of life, in love with more, and ill content
With less, and I will show you one in love
With foolishness.
In the accumulation of many years
Pain is in plenty, and joy not anywhere
When life is over-spent.

And at the last there is the same release
When Death appears.
Unheralded by music, dance, or song,
To give us peace.[1]

Sophocles, whose good fortune was proverbial to the Athenians, had experienced its frailty also, and much that once lit up his life had vanished into darkness. But one thing he retained – with his powerful poetic gift – till the end of his life: his love of Athens. He died before the city's fall, but probably foresaw its coming. So he creates once more, especially in Theseus, the image of Athens' greatness and praises in the play's first song (668) – one of the most beautiful of all Greek poems – the magic of his native soil, watched over by the gods.

A fortunate discovery of papyri in 1911 makes it possible to return to the youthful Sophocles and round off the picture of his creative output with an early work. On the same stem that bore the grave tragedies there grew an enchanting satyr play, of which we possess the greater part: The *Ichneutae* ('The Trackers'). Here the satyrs are 'trackers' who, cowardly and cheeky, roam the woods of the Arcadian mountains under the guidance of Father Silenus, to earn the reward for finding Apollo's stolen cattle. Their keen noses lead them to the cave of Cyllene, where the infant Hermes quickly grew to an incredible size and became capable of equally amazing pranks. The young god – the Homeric *Hymn to Hermes* already knew the story – had stolen his brother Apollo's precious herd and had also, in an idle moment, invented the first lyre in the world, made from a dead tortoise. Now the tones of the instrument, sounding from the depths of the cave, throw the satyrs into confusion. But in the end they have a bright idea: the young inventor who is such a clever thief will soon pacify the brother he has robbed by giving him the lyre, and will make him a close friend.

Here we see the satyr play of the Attic stage as a counterpart of the gay vase paintings of the period. It is quite different from *The Cyclops* of Euripides, who was incapable of gaiety for its own sake. But what makes this play one of the most charming in Greek poetry is the proximity of nature, of which the satyrs are only a part:

[1] Reprinted from E. F. Watling, *Oedipus at Colonus*, by kind permission of Penguin Books Ltd.

Sophocles' vivid pictures of mountains and woods as a setting for the myths of his people. This play rounds off the image of his personality as well as the work which stemmed from it. He saw into the darker depths of life over which we move unawares, and experienced the sheer joy of the radiance with which, in spite of everything, the gods suffuse the world.

CHAPTER SIX

Euripides

THE SURVIVING biographical data for Euripides are scanty, and what little we can rely on is confused by a mass of anecdotes. As one who was the mouthpiece of a new era Euripides became, more than any of his contemporaries, a target for ridicule in comedies. The insolent drollery connected with his name was frequently incorporated in pseudo-history, and the Satyrus-Papyrus[1] gives a good idea of the result.

Not even the date of his birth is certain. The most likely is that given in the Parian chronicle of 484, but another source makes it – perhaps deliberately – coincide with Salamis. His father Mnesarchides, whom comedy turned into a seller of vegetables with his wife Cleito, was a landed proprietor. The poet was born on the family estate at Salamis and many years later people still went to see the cave on the island in which he liked to work, his restless thoughts ranging over the boundless sea. In contrast with Sophocles it is not known if he ever held any state function. But a number of his works will show how he tried to serve his country as a poet in her hour of need.

It may be true that he started life as a painter, but we know that in 455 he obtained a chorus for the first time and performed the *Peliades*. The enormous posthumous influence was dearly bought, for his contemporaries were slow to appreciate his poetry. Since his thoughts were often in sharp contrast to those of the community he aroused their antagonism. This is particularly clear in the comedies of Aristophanes, which are also 'communal art' like the tragedies of his precursors. Euripides obtained a third prize with his *Peliades* and not until 441 did he gain a first; although he wrote some ninety dramas the judges awarded him that honour only three times.

The gossip about the poet's unhappy experiences with both his

[1] POxy 9, No. 1176.

wives, Melito and Choerile (or Choerine), need not be considered. But what we know of the later years of his life is important for our understanding of the man and the poet. In the North, where Macedonian ambition ran also to cultural aspirations, there had developed a sort of centre of the arts. Though less brilliant than its Sicilian counterpart, which Aeschylus honoured with a visit, it housed, in particular, representatives of new artistic trends such as the tragedian Agathon and (probably) the lyric poet Timotheus. In 408 Euripides followed the summons of king Archelaus and there, far from his homeland, he died in the spring of 406 at Arethusa near Amphipolis. He is said to have been torn to pieces by wild dogs, but this is probably another fable.

The love he felt for his Athenian homeland had always been strong, as his work testifies, but his own intellectual estrangement and the political developments at the end of the fifth century must have made this love a source of suffering. His work did not have Sophocles' direct appeal to the hearts of the people, though this was partly because its roots were elsewhere. He may have left his country in great bitterness, but at his death people realised that a great Athenian had gone. At the Great Dionysia when actors and chorus were, as usual, presented to the spectators, Sophocles made them appear ungarlanded and he, on the brink of death himself, wore mourning attire. Athens erected a cenotaph for Euripides and awarded to those plays which were performed posthumously the victories she had stinted in his lifetime.

The political events of his time were not as significant for Euripides as for his predecessors. It is true – and this is one of the many contradictions in the work of Euripides – that there are far more topical passages than in the works of other tragedians, and during the conflict with the Spartans he often spoke out against them. But this kind of political involvement was not the deepest source on which Euripides drew for his tragedies. Such words were often prompted by external events and often sound like propaganda; and usually remain peripheral. The essential character of his work must be understood in the light of the reciprocal relationship between the poet as a person and a movement which was beginning to make a fundamental change in Athens' cultural life.

The word 'sophist' has a bad connotation, due to the parody of the sophist movement in comedy and the criticism of it which is far better known to us from Plato's writing than this criticism's object. It is therefore difficult to grasp the motive forces behind this movement, particularly in a time like ours which realises better than any other the dangers inherent in an enthronement of reason. But a grasp of them is essential for an understanding of Euripides.

Even a brief and tentative characterisation of this movement, which introduced a new epoch in the second half of the fifth century, must start with the famous dictum of Protagoras: 'Man is the measure of all things, of things that exist that they are, of things that do not exist that they are not.' The man who said this came from Abdera, an Ionian colony, as was Leontini, the origin of Gorgias, another spokesman for the sophists. These are not irrelevant biographical details, they indicate that the sophistic movement must be regarded as the penetration into the centre of the Greek world of Ionian habits of thought. It was in these peripheral regions that *ἱστορίη*, that is an unprejudiced questioning of the things of this world, had been developed.

What the words of Protagoras really implied was a complete break with tradition in all spheres of life. They meant a revolutionary demand that anything which concerned human existence, religion as well as the State and justice, should become the subject of rational debate. For these sophists it had become senseless and therefore impossible to allow their thoughts and actions to be directed by the usage sanctified by tradition, by the *nomos*; their norms could only be worked out in their own minds. But this did not give them a unified concept of the world, a religious conviction which either resolved the world's antitheses in a transcendent unity, as in Aeschylus, or at least comprehended them as part of such a unity, as in Sophocles.

Reason can observe things from different, often opposite angles. The sophist finds himself outside the protective security of tradition in a world of antinomies. It reveals a programmatic intention when a work by Protagoras has the title *Ἀντιλογίαι* ('Contradictions'), and what Diogenes Laertius (9.51) says about its author confirms this: 'He was the first to propose the thesis that on every subject there can be two conflicting opinions.' This undoubtedly led to the bad sophistic practice of turning the worse argument into the better one – as a notorious phrase has it – by means of words alone. But what is far more important, the relation between man and the world had changed completely – whatever value we may attach to this change. The individual was not under any obligation to tradition, and conversely tradition no longer gave any support. Man, confronted with antinomies, had to bear the entire burden of decision and responsibility.

Sophistic philosophy remains unsatisfactory even if the traditional distortions are disregarded. That it was practised for gain did much harm, as with any intellectual activity. But its criticism was often aimed particularly at the existing order, for which no new values were substituted. It was this which caused that cultural rift which was unknown to previous generations. Apart from all this, man's aggressive exposure of his self-reliant intellect to the confusion and danger of antinomies is bound to have tragic implications. This, in fact, constitutes the tragedy of Euripides, the poet and the man.

Biographical tradition asserts that he was a pupil of leading sophists such as Protagoras and Prodicus, also of the philosopher Anaxagoras, the friend of Pericles, and of Archelaus. These are stories based on alleged links between the teaching of these men and Euripidean tragedies. In fact, there is no evidence that he embraced any particular doctrine. What was decisive for him was not the acceptance of a system but his surrender to the new ideas of the time, and the particular type of questioning they encouraged. It is therefore hopeless to try to distill a clear, well-defined conception of the world from his plays. Even if many of the utterances in these plays are only regarded as statements by the imaginary figures in question, there still remains a great deal that cannot be fitted into a coherent intellectual development. There is a ceaseless struggle, a passionate search that haunts the poet's work, and precisely because tradition collapses before his questions, and his meditation does not result in clear insight but only reaches the *δισσοὶ λογοί*, the contradictory aspects of things, he must be considered a true pupil of the sophists although he never just propounded their doctrines. For the sophists all knowledge, all decision is centred in man. In their world there exists no power beyond human feeling and thought which might decisively influence the action of an individual. The gods are robbed of this function even if they should exist somewhere, somehow. As

LIBRARY ST. MARY'S COLLEGE

Protagoras said: 'I know nothing about the gods, whether they exist or not and what they may be like, for there are many obstacles to this knowledge; their invisibility, for one, and the short span of human life.'

In this type of argument was also rooted Euripides' criticism of the traditional figures of religious faith, although he does not go so far as to deny – as an atheist would – the existence of higher powers. He agrees that there are such powers and that, unfathomed by man, they fashion destinies. But he is in line with sophistic thinking in regarding man himself as the real centre of events. For him, in a world of insoluble contradictions, human action and divine guidance no longer form an ethical cosmos. This is the complete opposite of Aeschylus' point of view. Whereas for the latter human destiny was only an arena for a higher order to demonstrate its powers, in Euripidean dramas like *The Medea* and the *Hippolytus* this destiny evolves entirely out of man himself and the strength of his passions. Man is no longer guided – as in Aeschylus – by a divine partner on the road to wisdom. But where, as in many of the later plays such as the *Helen*, fate is seen to be dependent on superhuman forces, the power of chance, later called τύχη, begins to take the place of the ancient gods. *Tyche* mixes up people's fortunes and provides the kind of colourful interplay that figures in another genre, namely the comedies of Menander.

The work of Euripides, rooted in the problematical world of sophistic antinomies, is itself distinguished by a number of striking contradictions. The following was of most consequence: the firm belief in the traditional gods had declined and the influence of independent thought and feeling created divinities which were far more akin to the new concept of man than to their mythical prototypes. But however much awareness of the new ideas Euripides shows in his plays, he cannot destroy the structure of traditional literary forms. So the old gods still move on the stage, although their significance has altered for the poet, and the themes are still taken from legends, although their indestructible stories carry a new meaning. Aristotle says (*Poetics* 1451b) that Euripides' contemporary Agathon, whose celebration of a dramatic victory in 416 is the setting for Plato's *Symposium*, took in his tragedy *Antheus* or *Anthos* the step to which Euripides came so close: he freely invented both action and persons. This does not mean that from now on the spacious realm of myth was deserted in favour of bourgeois drama. This experiment remained a mere episode; the link between tragedy as part of the official cult and traditional myth was still too strong, although the core of that tradition was falling into decay. For this reason the content of Euripides' tragedies often reaches beyond the form dictated by their 'genre.' The form of his work shows no compulsion towards organic unity, but reflects the absence of harmony in the several portraits of that austere, thoughtful face which traditionally represents the poet.

We shall deal with the various plays in their probable chronological order, without concerning ourselves about uncertainties of date. It is certainly tempting to group the surviving plays according to their content, but that may easily obscure the diversity of this poet's work.

We have eighteen plays of Euripides, more than we possess of the two other tragedians together. It may be accidental that parts of a very early complete edition in alphabetical order can be added to the plays accepted as canonical. Possibly, however, we owe this edition to the great reputation of the poet in the centuries after his death, as illustrated by the numerous papyri found in Egypt.

As with Sophocles there is no surviving work that can be dated to his early period. The oldest, the *Alcestis* of 438, is separated by a considerable gap from his first effort, *Peliades*, in 455. But although the poet's earliest plays are not known to us, the *Alcestis* has features which link it with classical dramas and separate it from works of the later period, in which the classical style is less strictly maintained.

The play is based on a motif that is well known from the legends and ballads of many lands: the motif of self-immolation for the sake of love. It is gradually becoming clear that several Greek myths incorporated such widely known stories and linked them with their heroic figures. Here it is Admetus, the King of Pherae, who is to be carried away by Death on the day of his marriage with Alcestis. The sinister god is prepared to accept a substitute but the parents refuse to save their son; they love this world too well. Then his beautiful young wife offers herself as a substitute and sacrifices her life for his. Phrynichus had used the motif before Euripides, but little is known about his treatment, and we are probably justified in assuming that the latter altered it decisively and that it was he who brought out the greatness of Alcestis' sacrifice in human terms. In the original story the sacrifice was made immediately after the appearance of the god of Death, but Euripides separated these events by a period of several years. Alcestis had, it is true, immediately declared herself prepared to make the sacrifice in the hour of danger, at the wedding, but she only had to keep her promise much later. We must not ask how she could live with the prospect of this fatal day when Death would fetch her, but must admire the artistry of the poet, who did not allow the bride or newly-wedded girl to make a sudden decision to offer herself. Instead, he shows us the wife and mother, who for years had known the deepest joys of womanhood, going to her death fully recognising the magnitude of what she sacrificed.

In the beginning of the play Apollo leaves the palace of the king whom he had served in payment of a debt and whom he still befriends. He is not allowed to bar the approach of Thanatos, the god of death, who is coming to fetch Alcestis. After the chorus of elders from Pherae have sung of their anxiety and sorrow for the queen, we witness two parting scenes. A maid describes her farewell to home, servants and marriage bed, then she herself enters with Admetus and their children. Modern sensitivity finds it hard to accept that Alcestis does not mention in her last words the love for her husband which leads her to her death. The poet conjures up with appalling vividness her terror of death, revealed in a vision of the journey into the Underworld, and of being seized by the god of death, but she speaks of her sacrifice as something she considers useful and therefore necessary. When she asks Admetus to promise her not to re-marry, she does this for the sake of the children. This Alcestis does not yet make us feel the pathos of subjective feeling; austere and self-contained, she joins those figures of the tragic stage in whom we recognise the features of Greek classicism. But this very austerity throws into relief the significance of her sacrifice and reveals her true stature: she towers above all the Alcestis figures who, speaking or singing, have appeared on the stage in more recent times.

Her small son Eumelus laments her death in a song and the chorus praises her memory. But a visitor arrives at the house of mourning: it is Heracles, on his way to performing yet more labours, who calls on Admetus. The latter does not want to let him go, although Heracles does not wish to be entertained in a house where there is mourning. In order to silence objections Admetus hides the fact that he is burying his wife.

The bier of Alcestis and the procession of the mourners have just arrived in front of the palace when Pheres, the king's father, appears, bringing gifts for the dead. In the hard words with which Admetus rejects the sympathy of the old man, who could by his own death have prevented the loss of a young life, and the equally harsh reply by Pheres, who turns all the reproaches of greediness for life and selfishness back against his son, one of those scenes of conflict flares up which are typical of Euripidean stage craft. It is true that the scene makes sense within the structure of the play because it focuses attention on the greatness of the generous wife against a background of such pettiness; nevertheless this quarrel at the bier of the dead can only be explained by the independent life which the *agon*, the violent dispute, had by now assumed. Here no argument is too poor or too irrelevant: the Athenian passion for legal strife and the sophistic doctrine that there are two sides to every question mutually reinforce each other. Therefore it is quite wrong to make something which is said in one of these scenes for the sake of argument into a key to the understanding of the whole play. The independence of such clearly circumscribed scenes is of great significance for the structure of Euripidean drama. The coherence of a play as a whole is weakened thereby, and that same tendency prevails where prologues, messengers' reports and choric songs acquire a new independence. The danger that they may become stereotyped, a mere routine, is not always avoided by Euripides.

The chorus has followed the body of Alcestis. As in the *Ajax* the stage remains empty for a moment. In the meantime Heracles has been regaled within the palace. We hear this from a servant who does not approve of festivity in a house of mourning. Now Heracles enters in his cups. Critics have often used this scene to characterise Heracles as the mighty carouser of Doric comedy, and to give the play as many burlesque features as possible. Actually this scene is very restrained, and we soon see Heracles in very different light, as a true hero and saviour of people in distress. When he learns from the servant who the dead person is then he does not hesitate, in return for the king's hospitality, to wrest this precious prize from the hands of Death. Here we have yet another motif from popular legend, the contest with Death, which has been combined with self-immolation for love's sake.

Admetus returns with the chorus from the burial. It was as difficult for the poet to create a plausible image of this man, as it is for us to understand anyone who would accept such a sacrifice. The old legend did not concern itself with psychological motives and all Euripides achieves, by his promise to be faithful in the farewell scene, by his attitude towards Heracles as his guest and his bitter lament when he returns from the grave, is that we do not grudge him the happy ending. But at one point his image has been given a new depth: Admetus has realised at the graveside that since he too is doomed to die, he should not have allowed his wife to die for him and that the sacrifice, intended to save his life, has in fact destroyed it. In his words, 'I see it now' (940), there is a change, a disintegration of tragic will and action, which shows that man's position has altered in Euripidean drama.

The difficult problem of the characterisation of Admetus has been dealt with so often, even quite recently, that it is important to make our views quite clear. This means departing somewhat from our earlier definitions. As against the dull, will-less figure of the legend, Euripides shows how the sacrifice of Alcestis affects the man who had accepted it. But it is not the intention of the poet to reduce the myth to absurdity by showing its impossible consequences, nor should we rename the play *Admetus* and make him the subject of the tragedy.

The question of how far we should apply our own psychology to the interpretation of Euripidean characters is at once the most important and difficult in our search for the poet's significance.

When Heracles returns, leading Alcestis, whom he has wrested from Death, veiled and silent by the hand, Admetus must stand a test. Heracles says that he wishes to leave in the king's palace an unknown woman whom he has won in a contest. The horrified refusal of Admetus shows that he desires, in all seriousness, to remain faithful to Alcestis. So he is allowed to recognise his wife and leads her into his house towards a new life. But Heracles does not join in the festivities; his own tragedy, lightly hinted at, forces him to seek new labours.

Antiquity called the poet of the *Alcestis* a misogynist. Aristophanes in his *Thesmophoriazousae* (411) allows the women of Athens to summon him before a most meticulous court of justice, and several anecdotes explained his 'hatred of women' by unfortunate experiences in his own home. Such a biased judgment is understandable since contemporaries were mostly influenced by figures like Phaedra and Stheneboea. We, on the other hand, see Euripides as a poet for whom both the noblest and the vilest of human potentialities were particularly clearly revealed in women. He brought women on the stage who destroyed themselves and others in the flames of their passion. Since in Athens those women were considered most praiseworthy who were least talked about, this appeared as an unheard-of attack on the female sex and gave him the name of a woman-hater. Yet it is to him that we owe those female figures who perform the greatest of human achievements, the complete renunciation of self in an act of sacrifice.

The poet often returned to this theme. Not always were his figures created with the same power and depth as in *Alcestis*, but it is nearly always women who show greatness of heart. In *The Heracleidae* Macaria sacrifices herself for her family; in the lost *Erechtheus* (dated, with *The Suppliant Women*, around 424), there is a daughter who dies such a death and a mother who learns to conquer her grief. There is an outstanding example in one of his last works, where Iphigeneia turns from a wild terror of death to a self-possessed sacrifice of her own life for a greater cause. The poet also proves the depth of his psychological insight where the sacrifice is not made by a woman. In *The Phoenician Women* Menoeceus saves his native city with his life; the courageous act appears as consistent with this boy's youth and innocence as it was with a woman's loving nature. The *Phrixus*, also lost, probably belonged to this group since it dealt with the sacrifice of a young life.

We have evidence that *Alcestis* came fourth in a tetralogy, and thus took the normal place of the satyr play following three tragedies. It was preceded by *The Cretans* which concerned the love affairs of two Cretan princesses; by the *Alcmeon in Psophis*, which according to a Florentine papyrus[1] dealt with the fate of a matricide and the love of a faithful woman; and finally the *Telephus*, in which to the indignation of the Athenians the king of

[1] Pap. Soc. It. No. 1302.

the Mysians appeared on the stage clad in rags. It is pointless to try to find in these plays the unity of a trilogy. Since the poet's main interest was focused on single characters the trilogy's unity made it an unsuitable medium. Nor, because the *Alcestis* came after three lost tragedies in the place of a satyr play, should we look too hard for burlesque features; it was, in spite of the happy ending, a serious play. It is worth noting that among the 75 plays which were considered genuine in the Alexandrian library, there were only seven or eight satyr plays. So it would seem that Euripides frequently rounded off a tetralogy, not with a satyr play but one with a happy ending. This is quite in keeping with his temperament, for he lacked the easy gaiety which we value so much in the Sophocles of the *Ichneutae*. It is very noticeable in Euripides' only surviving satyr play, *The Cyclops*. Although many features, such as the technically skilful use of triangular conversation, point to a fairly late date, this is so uncertain that it may as well be dealt with here.

The theme is the well-known Cyclops episode in the *Odyssey*. It has been turned into a satyr play by the assumption that, for some reason, the satyrs and their father Silenus had been cast away in the land of the Cyclops, whom they are compelled to serve as shepherds – from which chore the wily Odysseus frees them. The way in which these half-bestial creatures are sketched as braggarts, or sometimes as cowards, is not lacking in humour, but we miss the sparkling quality that lights up the Sophoclean poetry. In the satyr play of Euripides there are features reflecting contemporary thought which do not quite fit in. The Cyclops is outspoken about his contempt for *nomos*, and his faith in his own brute strength, in terms which in their garbled form are very like those of Plato's Callicles in the *Gorgias* and Thrasymachus in the *Republic*, who defend the thesis that might is right.

From the very start the poet was fascinated by the daemonic figure of Medea. In the *Peliades* (455) he shows how the sorceress sent the ancient Pelias to his doom by a ruse for which she used the unsuspecting daughters of the king as a tool. Attic legends connected Medea with Aegeus and related an attack on Theseus, who had not yet been recognised by his father. This became the theme of the lost *Aegeus*. We do possess *The Medea* of the year 431 in which the poet's skill is unsurpassed in showing how the daemon in human hearts will shape their actions and their fate. He does not hesitate to introduce such innovations as are needed to give the living forces in his tragedy free play. The daughter of the king of Colchis, whom Jason brought, far from her home, into an alien country where he deserted her, is a woman who counters suffering and insult with immoderate passion. We forget that she is a sorceress skilled in magic, although this motif is used when relevant to the action. This Medea whom Euripides has made the murderess of her own children is daemonic not as a witch but as a human being. He takes great liberties with tradition here, for legend relates that the children were murdered by the Corinthians and honoured with a cult.[1] A variant of this story provides the starting-point for Euripides' innovation: Medea had killed the children accidentally during an attempt to make them immortal by means of magic practices. It is also possible that the legend of Procne who killed her small son to take revenge on her husband Tereus influenced the Euripidean form of the Medea saga.

The level which Euripides' characterisation reached in this play can be gauged by the fact that none of his other dramas was constructed so firmly around the central figure. In the prologue the nurse speaks of Medea's distress over Jason's betrayal, since he wishes to make the daughter of the king of Corinth his new wife: she alternates between wild lament and silence, and the hatred with which she looks at her children makes the nurse shudder with premonition. The attendant who enters with the children brings the news that Creon intends to banish her and her sons, and again (92, 100) the fear takes shape that Medea's desperation may be a danger to her own flesh and blood. Carefully the poet prepares the ground for his own innovations and we are deliberately made to hear, under Medea's cries of distress from the palace, the curses she is directing at her children (113). The nurse warns the children not to come near their mother and the words with which she refers to Medea's passionate nature point beyond their literal meaning to something more significant. These closely related words, *ἦθος, φύσις φρήν* (102 ff.) show a desire to find the most pregnant epithet for these decisive forces in human make-up, and some tentative attempts to arrive at it.

The chorus of Corinthian women enters. They sympathise with

[1] Scholiast on E. Med. 9, 264; Pausanias 2, 3, 6, etc.

Medea's misfortune and wish to comfort and support her. Medea does not refuse to see them, she leaves the palace to talk with them about her sorrow. The composure with which she speaks, now of her own fate and then, in general terms, of highly topical ideas about the social plight of women, provides an impressive contrast with the shrieks of despair which were previously heard from the palace. In the first great speech of Medea Euripides makes her control her emotions, to give maximum effect to the heightened expression of her feelings later on. But Medea's self-control also prepares us for the way in which she will face Creon, the king, who announces her banishment. Here her cool calculating mind masters her passions. She demeans herself to ask a favour, and wrests from her enemy the day's delay which will give her time for revenge. Then follows the first of three great monologues. It is true that Medea first addresses the women of the chorus, but then she seems to be no longer aware of them. She holds a dialogue with herself, plans the revenge on which she is unshakeably resolved, and deliberates where she can find shelter once her revenge on Jason, his bride Creusa and her father Creon has been accomplished. She has forgotten the chorus, even calls upon herself by name (402) to turn her humiliation into a triumph of revenge. It is typical of the heightened emotional tension of this speech that it should end with the general statement that women are particularly gifted for doing evil.

This tragedy also has its *agon* but it is a combat with unequal weapons. Jason, who tries with sophistic arguments to present his faithlessness as an act of wisdom and foresight, cannot stand up to Medea who rejects his despicable offer of assistance and does not spare a single reproach.

The next choric song is followed by a scene in which the Attic king Aegeus calls at Corinth on the way to Delphi and meets Medea. Its episodic character has given rise to all sorts of interpretations and criticism, yet it can be fitted in quite naturally just where it is. A large part of Medea's first soliloquy (386) was taken up by the question of where she might find shelter after her revenge. The Aegeus scenes provide the answer: the king will give her asylum in Athens. As soon as he has gone Medea discloses the plan which she has now fully worked out. The children will bring death to Creusa with poisoned presents and then we hear the dreadful news which was already implied in the first scene: the boys will perish by the hand of their mother, for the man who has deserted her is to experience a loneliness more cruel than the one he had intended for her. In the two lines of the dialogue in which the leader of the chorus and Medea clash (816–17) we sense the daemonic quality of her decision, where every feeling except a desire for revenge is stifled:

> Can you have the heart to kill your flesh and blood?
> Yes, for this is the best way to wound my husband.

The next choric song has a double function. It recapitulates the previous act (we feel justified in using this term because the structure of the drama is clearly marked by the songs) by contrasting Medea's wish to find a home in Athens with the horror of her infanticide. At the same time the mention of Athens in the first two strophes develops into a song in praise of the city whose beauty has never been surpassed. Here we sense the poet's devotion to the soil of his homeland, but we also notice something very personal: when he praises the brilliant clarity of the air above the town he does it in spiritual terms. It is here that the *Erotes* dwell together with Wisdom, and the words express the imperishable fame of Athens:

824 From of old the children of Erechtheus are
Splendid, the sons of blessed gods. They dwell
In Athens' holy and unconquered land,
Where famous wisdom feeds them and they pass gaily
Always through that most brilliant air where once, they say
That golden Harmony gave birth to the nine
Pure Muses of Pieria.

And beside the sweet flow of Cephisus' stream,
Where Cypris sailed, they say, to draw the water,
And mild soft breezes breathed along her path,
And on her hair were flung sweet-smelling garlands
Of flowers of roses by the Lovers, the companions
Of wisdom, her escort, the helpers of men
In every kind of excellence.[1]

[1] Reprinted from Rex Warner, *The Medea*, by kind permission of The Bodley Head and The New American Library.

Jason is now soon caught in the net Medea has prepared for him. He is glad that he can strike such an easy bargain, and will himself support the two children in their request to be allowed to remain in the country. That Medea with them will lose all she has does not disturb him. In the choric song we accompany the children on their way to Creusa and hear how she accepts Medea's gift. There is no turning back now for Medea, but the strength with which she took her decision fails her on the final stretch of the road. The force of natural feeling revolts against a plan so unnatural and gives rise to her last terrible conflict before committing the act of murder. When the attendant comes back from the palace with the boys and announces with joy that their sentence of banishment has been lifted, he finds Medea in a state of profound agitation. After he has left her we witness her inner struggle in a speech which, although it refers to the chorus once (1043), is essentially a monologue. The intensity with which inner experiences are portrayed here is unequalled in Attic tragedy; it also reveals man's tragic potentialities from a new angle. We are not shown, as in the death of Sophocles' Ajax, a rigid predetermination rooted in his *physis*, but a human being as a prey to the contending play of forces which have their source in his soul, and are struggling for mastery over it. It is characteristic of Greek ideas that Medea should experience the most dangerous of these forces as a living entity, which confronts her and to which she can speak. A translation can only tentatively approach the meaning which the word *Θυμός* has for Medea, when she appeals to it (1056), begging it to spare her children. The furious passion in her heart, emotions riding roughshod over reason, all that is implied in the word which Euripides uses. The other, opposing force within her is expressed in the word *βουλεύματα*, which implies the result of thoughtful reflection. This points beyond the urge for furious action to the significance of the act in the world as a whole, and to its consequences. The conflict between these two forces is so violent that Medea alters her decision four times. As a mother she sees the trusting looks, the smiles of the children and is convinced that she cannot do what ultimately she will have to perform. But in the end her daemon triumphs and one consideration is decisive: the children are lost in any case, for if their mother spares them, the revenge of her enemies will strike them down after the death of

Creusa which is taking place at that moment. She now abandons herself to the sorrow of parting, to the last cherished embraces; then she sums up the past struggle in words which have a programmatic significance for Euripidean tragedy of this period (1079): 'Stronger than all my afterthoughts is my fury, fury that brings upon mortals the greatest evils.'

Here more than in any other Euripidean passage it is made clear that the polar tension of a tragic conflict is no longer, as in Aeschylus, one between man and god but exists within man himself. Compared with his predecessors Euripides has perhaps secularised tragedy, but this does not mean that tragedy has become senseless, deprived of the superstructure of an effective order of values. Medea, Hippolytus, Hecuba, with their acts and suffering, are part of a definite world order. Euripides never doubted that this order was essentially divine although the interpretation of it offered by traditional myth had become doubtful.

Medea's great monologue is the climax of the drama; here her inner conflict has found its conclusion. The rest runs its predestined course. A messenger enters and announces the pitiful death scene of Creusa, wearing the poisoned robes and crown. Now the final deed must be done. Once more she turns to the women and justifies her act by calling it inescapable. Again she speaks to herself, to her own hand, which threatens to become paralysed (1244). But then the cries of the dying children are heard through the anxious words of the chorus. Jason arrives too late to rescue them. Completely shattered, he merely watches Medea's escape with the bodies of her children in a dragon-drawn chariot sent by Helios. The sorceress gloating in her triumph over the man she hates provides a powerful dramatic ending. But the woman whom we had seen struggling and suffering, a prey to despair and guilt, has vanished.

The fact that a *Philoctetes* was performed with *The Medea* shows how varied were the themes of Euripidean tragedy, and how loosely connected within the trilogy. We mentioned in connection with the surviving Sophoclean play that the *Philoctetes* of Euripides had some bearing on national problems. We know the period when such questions were bound to come to the fore. At the time when *The Medea* and the *Philoctetes* were performed together with the *Dictys*, in 431, Athens was on the eve of a decisive encounter with her rival Sparta which was to decide her fate and that of Greece. Euripides did not live withdrawn from his epoch or his country, but since his work as a whole was not so immediately rooted in the *polis* as that of Aeschylus, topical material was not always harmoniously integrated into his plays. Historical events, however, do make themselves felt in *The Heracleidae*, which can probably be dated to the beginning of the Archidamian War, around 430. The play has many of the features of Euripidean tragedy discussed above, but does not weld them together. The poet starts with a ready-made situation which recurs in the *Andromache* and the *Heracles* and has parallels in *The Suppliant Women* and the *Helen*: people seeking asylum are crouched near an altar. In our theatre stage curtains can bring such a group suddenly into view. The Greeks must have seen the groups arranging themselves in silence. Here they are the descendants of Heracles, who with his mother Alcmene and his former brother-in-arms Iolaus have fled from his arch-enemy Eurystheus, king of the Argives. This man would like to have them dragged away by his helpers, but here again Athens is the refuge of the persecuted. The son of Theseus, Demophon, values justice higher than force and is prepared to defend it with arms. But before it comes to a fight there is an indication that Persephone requires a human sacrifice and an anonymous daughter of Heracles (another source gives her name as Macaria) offers her young life of her own free will. The Euripidean motif of self-sacrifice which formed the core of the *Alcestis* appears episodic in *The Heracleidae*. Nor do we hear if the sacrifice was actually carried out, and although a scholar with a fine sympathy for Greek tragedy has observed that Euripides was more interested in the courageous offer than in the sacrifice itself, the disappearance of the girl from the scene (601) is all too glib. We cannot help suspecting that *The Heracleidae*, which with its 1055 lines is the shortest of the Euripidean tragedies, was adapted to its present form in the fourth century, although attempts have recently been made to disprove this. Such changes must be taken into account elsewhere, but they are hardly relevant to the episodic character of the sacrifice motif.

In the battle against Eurystheus the Athenians gain a victory and take the king prisoner. The episode of Iolaus, who regains his youth in the decisive combat, gives the play a highlight, but no more than that. In the second part of this loosely constructed drama, Alcmene, the mother of Heracles, who never spoke at all in the first part, becomes a personality in her own right. Here again the furious force *θυμός*, which knows no bounds, dominates the play. Contrary to human and divine justice, and to the protests of the Athenians, Alcmene has the captive king slaughtered. We sense that in the background looms the problem of the right treatment of prisoners of war, which the new war had made urgent again. In the case of Eurystheus Euripides has, as so often, partly rehabilitated the man whom the myth condemned. He goes to his death with manly composure and although his reference to Hera's command which drove him to persecute Heracles is, typically, no more than a mythical insertion into a rational argument, it is intended to exonerate him. Since Athens wished to grant him a prisoner's right to live, he will in return – like another Oedipus – bless the Athenians from the grave if ever Heracles' descendants should start a campaign against the city. To understand this ending we should realise that the Heracleidae are the ancestors of the kings of Sparta who were preparing for war against Athens. But compared with Athena's promise of blessing at the end of the *Oresteia*, and the central significance of the motif in the *Oedipus at Colonus*, it is a mere postscript.

The tragedies of Euripides, which created a new image of man without reference to the old religious concepts, also viewed sexual love from a new angle. We encountered Eros as a cosmic force in *The Danaids* and found the same view expressed in a song in the *Antigone*. But Euripides considers Eros not as an objective force but as a subjectively experienced passion. And since the motive power in tragedies written at the time of *The Medea* is centred in the *θυμός*, it is above all the power of sexual love, intensified to a pathological degree, which appears to fascinate Euripides again and again, and makes him revolutionary compared with the older tragedians.

Both cult and legend in Troezen knew of a hero Hippolytus, a type of Greek youth to which lone hunters belong, denied the pleasures of love. He was a figure who could easily become involved in what we may call the Potiphar motif. In this case it was the young man's own stepmother Phaedra, the Cretan wife of Theseus, whose love brought ruin to him and to herself. This was the tradition as Euripides must have known it, because the maidens of Troezen, who before their marriage sacrificed their hair to Hippolytus, used to tell the story in a cult song. Sophocles wrote a *Phaedra* and we should indeed be glad to know what he made of the theme. For Euripides the emphasis would naturally fall on the anguish of passion. In an earlier version of the surviving play he depicted Phaedra as completely at the mercy of her infatuation. The queen prostrated herself before her stepson and begged for his love. Since the young man hid his face in horror, the play was called *'Ιππόλυτος καλυπτόμενος* (*Hippolytus Veiled*). In this drama Phaedra herself accused her stepson, in front of Theseus, of having tried to seduce her, and she killed herself after his death. It is significant that at the time of the Roman Empire, in the letter in Ovid's *Heroides* 4 and up to a point in Seneca's *Phaedra* – through which Euripides gained such a lasting influence – this crude version was picked out for treatment. The Athenian public rejected it and so the poet produced a further Hippolytus play (*'Ιππόλυτος στεφανηφόρος* – *Hippolytus the Garland-Bearer*) in 428 which won him one of his rare victories.

For the Athenians he certainly made the pathological aspect of the story more acceptable, but it remains curious that both in the prologue and the epilogue he represented the theme as a conflict between two goddesses, Aphrodite and Artemis. Here there is no question, as in the beginning of the *Ajax* or the end of *The Eumenides*, of a devout poet revealing his deepest thoughts on the relation between god and man. Aphrodite and Artemis are for Euripides not the real great powers which give the action its essential significance, they are for him the means, borrowed from popular religion, of crystallising inner experiences. What really matters throughout are those experiences themselves, the motive forces in the actual drama as it develops between the prologue and the epilogue in which Aphrodite and Artemis appear. This shows again the ambiguity of Euripides' work: his dramas are classical in intention and yet they herald the Hellenistic age. The twofold enactment of this tragedy, once between goddesses on a sort of supernatural stage, and again on a human level as an inner psychological drama, makes it an exact parallel to the work of the Alexandrian epic-poet, Apollonius of Rhodes. For in his romance on Medea and Jason the events are first discussed by the Olympians and then shown as conditioned by Medea's psychological make-up. The connection which Aeschylus tried to establish between gods as helpers (συλλήπτορες) and man's free will has here been severed. It had already become much looser in the work of Euripides.

The opening scene with Aphrodite is also important from a formal point of view. The goddess explains the situation and announces that she will take revenge on the youth because he only wishes to serve the chaste hunting goddess. This method of avoiding long expositions by a concise prologue is so typical of Euripides that it has been compared with theatre programme notes. But since Euripides also shows old-fashioned tendencies – another of the contradictions in his work – this might be a revival of the oldest function of the prologue which was discussed in the first chapter. It cannot, however, be denied that this usage continued in comedies from Menander to Plautus. The gradual development of Euripidean prologues again shows how parts of his plays develop independently, but they are not to be considered merely an easy way of explaining an action that is more complex, externally and psychologically, than the traditional myth. In the structure of the play the static quality of the opening speech allows the action to move more swiftly towards the climax of which Euripides was a master.

After the prologue follows a scene in which Hippolytus reveals his single-minded, pure devotion to Artemis, when he sacrifices to his goddess after the chase. His prayer has great poetic beauty. The tranquil, virgin meadows where he gathers flowers for his goddess are a moving symbol of his own purity:

73 My Goddess Mistress, I bring you ready woven
this garland. It was I that plucked and wove it,
plucked it for you in your inviolate Meadow.
No shepherd dares to feed his flock within it:
no reaper plies a busy scythe within it:
only the bees in springtime haunt the inviolate Meadow.
Its gardener is the spirit Reverence who
refreshes it with water from the river.
Not those who by instruction have profited
to learn, but in whose very soul the seed
of Chastity toward all things alike
nature has deeply rooted, they alone
may gather flowers there! the wicked may not.

But when Hippolytus, in the conversation with his servant which now follows, refuses harshly and coldly to do honour to Aphrodite, we realise that such proud chastity, when it implies the denial of a great living power, is at the same time *hybris*.

To balance the Hippolytus scene Phaedra enters, following a chorus of Troezen women. She is a different Phaedra from that of the first Hippolytus drama. She too is in the grip of a passion for her stepson, but still fights for what she, a woman of noble birth, knows to be right. It is one of the most impressive scenes ever created by this great judge of human nature. Phaedra, suffering, racked by pain, is carried on a couch in front of the palace and struggles to keep her secret from the nurse, although she longs to cry it out for all the world to hear. Seneca, who took over this scene from the second version – although his play was largely based on the first – tries to excel the Greek poet by every means in his power; and yet he is far less convincing than Euripides, who subtly allows physical symptoms to reveal inner tension. From a languid state of exhaustion Phaedra suddenly rises up, she – an Attic woman – wants to go hunting in the mountains. She is obsessed by a longing to breathe the same vital air as her beloved; then again she withdraws within herself in shame. But her passion overwhelms her, she feels she must speak. However, once she has induced her nurse to pronounce the name of her loved one, she realises her own weakness in having divulged her secret and sees only one way to save her honour, the way of death. This Phaedra is a fighter who faces within herself the furious conflict between those forces which Medea recognised as *θυμός* and *βουλεύματα*.

Death appears to be a solution, but life asserts itself in the seductive promise by the nurse that love will yet find fulfilment. After a choric song, not about the cosmic ruler of life but about Eros, who with his torch of love reduces human homes to ashes, Phaedra learns how the nurse has carried out her plan. Within the palace she has disclosed the truth to Hippolytus, but all she gets in reply is the horror of the virgin youth, and his self-righteous contempt. The scene is continued on the stage. Phaedra knows herself betrayed, bereft of hope, repelled and despised by the young man she loves. Now only death remains. She had earlier desired to take that road alone, but it is humanly convincing that she now wishes to destroy, with her own death, the self-assured man who has ruined her. She hangs herself and Theseus on his return finds on the body of his wife a letter in which Hippolytus is accused of having driven her to death by his illicit desires. In an outburst of fury the father brings down on his son the anger of his own father Poseidon, and since Hippolytus, in the *agon* with his father, is bound by the oath of secrecy which the nurse made him swear, he must suffer banishment. We hear from a messenger how swiftly the father's curse proved effective for the young man leaving his home. A monstrous bull emerged from the sea and made the horses of Hippolytus shy. They dragged their own master to death. Fatally wounded he is brought on to the stage, but Artemis, his divine helper, reveals his innocence and he dies reconciled with his father. Before she leaves the dying youth Artemis promises him the high honour of a cult in Troezen. The parting of the stern goddess and the dying youth has been rendered with infinite tenderness. What touches us here is far removed from the sphere of profound religious faith; it is nearer to Homeric anthropomorphism, but refined to deepest humanity:

1389 Artemis:
Unhappy boy! You are yoked to a cruel fate.
The nobility of your soul has proved your ruin.
Hippolytus:
O divine fragrance! Even in my pain
I sense it, and the suffering is lightened.
The Goddess Artemis is near this place.
Artemis:
She is, the dearest of the Gods to you.
Hippolytus:
You see my suffering, mistress?
Artemis:
I see it. Heavenly law forbids my tears.
Hippolytus:
Gone is your huntsman, gone your servant now.
Artemis:
Yes, truly: but you die beloved by me.

This solution of the drama by divine intercession, this turning away from human passions as motive forces towards external religious themes – as if to justify the action – often recur in Euripides. They show the heterogeneous character of his tragedies, especially when the link with the drama is less firm than in the *Hippolytus*, one of the most perfect dramas of the Attic stage.

In a series of lost plays Euripides continued to concentrate on erotic passion. Related to *Hippolytus* in character, and close to it in date, is the *Stheneboea*. Here it is the wife of the Tirynthian King Proetus who seduces her husband's guest Bellerophon and pays for her sin with death. Among the tragedies which Alexandrian scholars did not consider to be by Euripides was a *Tennes*. Here the Potiphar motif was connected with the eponymous ruler of Tenedus. The play may have been written by Critias, the radical politician whom we shall meet again as a tragedian.

Three Euripidean tragedies whose main themes are known were wholly preoccupied with pathological love. In *The Cretans* a legend was dramatised which reflected a primeval, pre-Greek myth about the union between the earth mother and the bull of heaven, telling of the unnatural love of Pasiphae for a bull. We possess a song from this drama, which involves a chorus of mystic initiates of the Idaean Zeus and of Zagreus. This song remains unexplained, but this much can be said, that Euripides' interest in such unofficial cults points forward to his experience of Dionysiac religion in Macedonia. The second play, *Aeolus*, dealt with an incestuous love between brother and sister; the third, the *Chrysippus* (produced about 410 with *The Phoenician Women*), with a homosexual relationship. This was not treated as an allowable form of love: Laius, who rapes the son of Pelops, succumbs to a sinful passion and must pay the penalty for his deed.

One of the polarities in Euripides' treatment of human nature is that the same Eros that leads into the darkness of error may also raise the human soul to noble passion. We saw that in the portrayal of Alcestis the erotic element was kept in the background, but in Evadne of *The Suppliant Women* – with whom Laodameia of *Protesilaus* can be compared – we meet a woman whose love survives death. And whereas Sophocles in his *Antigone* refers only briefly and in impersonal terms to the love of Haemon, this love plays a prominent part in Euripides' play of the same name and ultimately brings about the rescue of Antigone. Eros also functions as saviour, in the *Andromeda* (412, with the *Helen*), in which Perseus, a real fairy-tale hero, rescues the princess with whom he had fallen in love from a sea monster.

Euripides' profound exploration of the entire range of erotic motives has had a far-reaching influence on all subsequent dramatic art. Though themes of this kind appear peripherally if at all in old comedy, the new comedy of Menander and his contemporaries is unthinkable without such a central theme. But his influence goes further, it penetrates Hellenistic poetry and from there reaches Rome too. And if in drama, modern drama especially, the absence of erotic subject is a rarity, this too is traceable to Euripides.

Some years after the *Hippolytus* – probably in the 420's – Euripides wrote the *Hecuba*, the tragedy of the Trojan queen. Troy has been destroyed, the Greek fleet is ready to sail home and the captive women are awaiting their fate. Among them is Hecuba, the woman whose suffering has been greatest. She has witnessed the death of her husband and nearly all her children, her town is in ruins, but the ghost of her son Polydorus, who speaks in the prologue, prophesies that her suffering is not yet at an end. He was the son she wanted to save, and had sent him with costly gifts to the Thracian King Polymestor, trusting his hospitality. But Polymestor has killed the boy for the gold he brought and now the boy's ghost announces that the Greeks will demand Hecuba's daughter, Polyxena, as a sacrifice for the dead Achilles. We then hear Hecuba's lament. Her song of sorrow for the fall of Troy is interrupted by the entry of a chorus of captive women, who announce that Polyxena has been chosen as sacrifice for the dead. The mother still resists when Odysseus arrives to fetch the girl: Polyxena is to move him, pleading her youth, but he, though not hard-hearted himself, must obey the army council. Polyxena, however, related in spirit to those other Euripidean heroines of sacrifice, refuses with the noble high-mindedness of youth to beg for her life: it is better to die than to live as a slave in the land of the victors. Her resolve is matched by the manner of her death, as reported by a herald. This willing acceptance of fate, without loss of dignity, is reminiscent of many Sophoclean figures, but there is a significant difference. The core of the drama is not the relationship between man and divinely ordained fate, but a human being only, who courageously accepts this fate.

A servant, sent to fetch water from the sea to wash Polyxena's body, brings from the shore the dead Polydorus, whom Hecuba believed safe in Thrace. The response to this overflowing sorrow is a truly Euripidean upsurge of θυμός, of a passionate desire for revenge. The *Hecuba* is a tragedy of suffering, as so many dramas of Aeschylus and Sophocles. But again we must note the difference. Fate is here not the confirmation of a transcendent power; it does not generate, in its human opponent, the nobility of action of the Sophoclean hero, still fighting in defeat. In this drama the function of fate is to set free the forces of θυμός in the afflicted old woman and to show their uncontrollable fury. Hecuba's revenge is horrifying and she prepares for it in a manner as calculating as Medea. Agamemnon, who has her daughter Cassandra in his tent, gives in to her appeals. She then lures Polymestor and his two small sons into her tent. The innocent children are murdered before the eyes of their father and he crawls blinded from her tent. Before Agamemnon as judge an *agon* takes place between Polymestor and Hecuba, who justifies what she has done. It is decided in favour of the mother, who in her anguish became a daemon of revenge.

Here Euripides, as so often, goes beyond the framework of the actual tragic events into prophecies at the end of the play: Polymestor knows from Dionysus that Hecuba will be changed into a bitch and that Agamemnon will be killed by his wife on his homecoming. The technique of such gratuitous additions, which Euripides often uses in order to link a particular event with a traditional myth or cult, as if he wished to see his own creation either justified or annexed by it, loosens the firm unity of a classical work of art. Such unity has been denied to the *Hecuba* on the grounds that it is divided into a Polyxena and a Hecuba-Polymestor tragedy. But not only does the Polydorus prologue combine the two motifs, only their conjunction makes it plausible that the suffering mother should embark on her uncontrolled revenge. And yet it cannot be denied that in the first part of the play Polyxena is more emphatically a figure in her own right than the role of her fate in the play as a whole would warrant. Here again the autonomy of single parts of the play is not consistent with the unity that is characteristic of a classical creation.

Another structural innovation, which is especially noticeable in this tragedy, is that the part played by the chorus has been considerably reduced compared with that of the actor. A glance at any Aeschylean tragedy will show the change in their relative importance. The shortness of the chorus in the *Hecuba* (629–656), which consists of strophe, antistrophe and epode, and marks the division between the main parts of the action, demonstrates its diminished role. Against this the actor has a greater share, even in the singing, than in earlier tragedy. Euripidean protagonists find in song the proper medium for expressing their more intense emotions. Alcestis, for instance, appears on the stage singing a monody of farewell to the world. Here, as elsewhere, an impassioned, stirring song is followed by reflective utterances in spoken verse, so that the two modes of human self-expression are formally differentiated. The monody by Theseus over Phaedra's body (817) shows that for man overcome by passion or anguish spoken verse, the true medium of the logos, is inadequate. Because of its subject it is not surprising that the *Hecuba* is rich in songs. The prologue of Polydorus is followed immediately by Hecuba's mournful anapaests; these indicate the mood of the play's beginning so that the chorus needs no song of entry, but can start with the announcement that Polyxena's life is threatened. Hecuba expresses her new sorrow in a monody (154) and the lamentation is continued in the commos between herself and Polyxena (177) and concluded in her daughter's song (199). Only with the arrival of Odysseus, who has to make arrangements and give explanations, is the spoken verse resumed. The death of Polydorus again calls forth a lament in song (684) and the anguish and rage of Polymestor is expressed in a monody (1056). Similarly we find a monody in a rarely used elegiac metre at the beginning of the *Andromache*, which was roughly contemporary with the *Hecuba*, though possibly a few years earlier. The *Andromache* contains passages of great beauty, but it is not easy for us to appreciate it, in fact even ancient critics only rated it as 'second-class' Euripides. By taking great liberties with the well-known figures of the saga, the poet has combined them into an extremely confused family history. After his return from Troy Neoptolemus lives in Thessaly, his father's homeland, with two women. He has brought back from the campaign Andromache, Hector's wife, and it is now her bitter lot to live in a foreign land as concubine of the victor, to whom Menelaus has given his daughter Hermione as legitimate wife. But whereas the Spartan princess remains barren, Andromache has borne a son to her new husband. When Neoptolemus undertakes a journey to

Delphi to ask forgiveness from Apollo for the boldness with which he once called the god to account for the death of Achilles, Hermione can no longer control her hatred: Andromache must be got rid of. Menelaus has come over from Sparta to be a worthy helper in his daughter's ignoble task. In the opening scene we see Andromache praying for assistance in the sanctuary of Thetis. In the prologue she explains the situation, but now a servant arrives and tells her that the hiding place of her small son has been discovered and that he is in the hands of Menelaus.

Andromache pours out her woe in the elegiac monody already mentioned, and a chorus of Thessalian women now appearing on the scene responds sympathetically. An *agon* in which Andromache and Hermione confront each other in verbal conflict is followed by lively action brought about by the interference of Menelaus. His threat to the life of her child drives Andromache from her refuge, but then she is told that this was a base trick of Menelaus to abandon her and her child to Hermione's hatred. All seems lost when the aged Peleus enters, the grandfather of Neoptolemus, the ruler of Pharsalus. Menelaus draws back in pitiful cowardice and Hermione must release her prey. She now begins to feel remorseful and anxious, she dreads the return of Neoptolemus. But a new figure appears on the stage and initiates a new phase in the action. Orestes, to whom Hermione had been betrothed before she was given to Neoptolemus, has hastened to Thessaly, his hope rekindled. She is soon prepared to elope with him and there is mention of an attack he has planned against Neoptolemus.

After a short choric song a messenger announces that Neoptolemus has been killed by the inhabitants of Delphi, whom Orestes had incited against him. Careful interpretation must lead to the conclusion that Orestes had organised the attack before he appeared in Phthia, but was not present at the murder. Euripides has done little to clarify the sequence of events. This is all the more surprising because as a rule he takes great care over the *πιθανόν*, the rational probability of the action. But a lack of clarity in several other details suggests that the play was carelessly written.

The last part consists of the lament of Peleus and the chorus for Neoptolemus. Then Thetis makes an appearance – this is more or less justified by her connection with Peleus – and consoles him with a promise of immortality. But Andromache is destined to become, as the wife of her brother-in-law Helenus, the ancestress of a great house of rulers over the Molossians.

We have learned from the *Hecuba* that we must be careful in criticising the lack of unity in Euripidean drama. But in this case not even the most sympathetic approach can blind us to this flaw. Euripides has certainly created a most wonderful woman in the figure of Andromache; the woman who unhesitatingly risks her own life for the sake of her child touches us as closely as the valiant Peleus, but her disappearance in the second half of the play destroys its unity and is not compensated for by the fact that she is mentioned in the prophecy of Thetis. The function of single figures like Orestes is also limited to one part of the action only. The piling up of different themes, the ever-present wish to create new tensions, the accent on single dramatic events that are not properly integrated: these features, though they appear in an extreme form here, also recur in other plays. It is as if, now that the old values of tragedy had been called in question, the poet was tempted towards virtuosity and artifice, but was ever and again held back by his divine gift for higher, more genuine art.

When the representatives of Spartan ideas, Menelaus and Hermione, are made to display all imaginable vileness, Euripides has obviously attempted to combine their dramatic function with an expression of the hatred he felt for the mortal enemy of Athens. But when he allows Peleus to fulminate against Spartan girls (595), who romp half-naked with young men, it is not 'political' poetry in the higher sense, as we find in Aeschylus, but inartistic propaganda.

Topical tragedies which with the *Erechtheus* can probably be dated to around 424 probe deeper than such invectives. In this year the Athenians were defeated by the Boeotians at Delium and the Thebans had, contrary to the general practice, refused to give up the dead. Thus the legend – already used by Aeschylus in *The Eleusinians* – that after the catastrophe depicted in the *Seven Against Thebes* the Athens of Theseus forced the sacred rights of the dead to prevail, acquired a new meaning. And it is an echo of a contemporary event, as well as the sign of a desire for dramatic effect, when in *The Suppliant Women* the force of Athenian arms replaces persuasion.

The opening scene of this play again shows suppliants seeking refuge in a sanctuary. The mothers of the Seven are crouched in front of the temple at Eleusis, and Aethra, the mother of Theseus, describes and explains the group in a singularly undramatic prologue. The mothers of the dead and their servants form the chorus but are not always kept apart in the usual group of fifteen. Neither the mothers nor the dead can, in fact, have been seven in number according to the legend, since Jocasta, for instance, was not among the former nor Polyneices among the latter. We must assume that the poet introduced the 'Mothers of the Seven' formally as a group. Aethra takes it upon herself to support their plea, and this is important, for Theseus has at first refused to come to their aid, and has pointed out to Adrastus, the defeated king of Argos who leads the chorus, the folly of his campaign. Here Euripides inserts a short sketch (201) of the development of human culture from a state of savage barbarism, which echoes contemporary theories on the origin of culture and recalls the problems of the Prometheus trilogy. It also reminds us of the choric song in the *Antigone* about the mystery of man's ceaseless questing, which contrasts with Theseus' obvious complacency in the Euripidean drama when he speaks of the world's design:

199 I believe
That there are more good things than bad for mortals;
If there were not, the light would not be ours.
I praise the god who set our life in order,
Lifting it out of savagery and confusion.
First he put wits in us, and then gave language,
Envoy of words, to understand the voice;
And fruits of earth to eat, and for this food
Watery drops from heaven, to quench our thirst
And nourish the yield of the land; providing also
The fortress winter, against the sun-god's fire,
And commerce over sea, that by exchange
Each country may obtain whatever it lacks.
Things without mark, not clearly visible,
Are brought to light by seers, observing fire
And reckoning from birds and the folds of entrails.
Now, if all this is not enough for us –
So well equipped for living, by God's gift –
Are we not pettish?

Aethra's pleading overcomes the hesitation of Theseus and he prepares for war with Thebes. But first he fights a verbal combat with a Theban herald, in which the latter defends the political programme of tyranny, while Theseus upholds the Attic democracy which still represented an ideal, however much this ideal differed from reality. When he describes a state in which all citizens have equal rights yet only qualified people may give advice, Euripides takes a stand on political principles. But it is revealing to compare this passage with the speech of Athena to her people in *The Eumenides*. We can see how the words about a divine power that was active in the *polis* have changed into the terms of rational debate.

Armed conflict takes place and a messenger announces a victory over Thebes, which the Athenians would gladly have gained in reality. Now the bodies are brought in and the lamentation for the dead begins. The remarkable thing about this ceremony is the speech delivered by Adrastus. It is a proper *λόγος ἐπιτάφιος* such as, in the lifetime of Euripides, was habitually made in honour of the slain. But now – and this is typically Euripidean – the acts and emotions of single people begin to stand out against a background of communal suffering. For Capaneus, who was struck by lightning, a separate pyre is erected on the stage. Above it, on a rock, his wife Evadne can be seen. Her love transcends mortality and, deaf to her father Iphis' entreaties, she hurls herself into the flames. She is the counterpart of Laodameia, in the *Protesilaus*, who in a strange but moving act shares her couch with an image of the dead and remains faithful to him beyond the death of the body. Here the Evadne motif is better integrated with the action than usual. After her death we hear again a lament for the seven slain men, in which boys who carry the ashes of their fathers sing in antiphony with their mothers. Athena herself ends the play and firmly links it with the contemporary situation. What Athens has done for Argos and her dead must form an everlasting bond between the cities, confirmed by solemn sacrifice. To the sons of the dead she promises the victory denied to their fathers.

In the *Alcestis* the figure of Heracles already foreshadowed tragedy. As the principal character in a play which is named after him, this most outstanding of legendary heroes becomes a tragic figure. It must probably be dated around 421, shortly after the peace of Nicias. It is however not the poet's intention to dramatise the Heracles myth; as in *The Medea* he freely invents several important features. He is concerned with human existence and its tragic implications.

The hero, resolute in action, is at his zenith in the first part of the play. He has measured the boundaries of the earth, and gone beyond them in his effort to fetch the hound of hell from the nether world. While he is on this quest the usurper Lycus has made himself master of Thebes and now wants to destroy the family of Heracles. The aged Amphitryon, the hero's wife Megara and her children have fled to an altar, forming another evocative opening scene with fugitives seeking refuge. The chorus of Theban elders cannot assist them and the *agon* between Amphitryon and Lycus only results in a moral victory. When the tyrant threatens the fugitives at the altar with firebrands Megara realises that the final task of those doomed to die is to preserve their dignity. She has already left the sanctuary and has arranged the children for their last journey when Heracles returns from the realm of the dead. He, who has been the saviour of entire countries, now rescues those nearest to him. Mortal anguish melts into joy. Warmly the hero embraces his rescued children with a tender response to their impetuosity. Then he enters the palace where his revenge on Lycus is swift and just. We share the exultation of the choric song and yet, as in Sophocles, it only serves to measure the depth of the imminent fall.

An old legend related that Heracles had murdered his children in a fit of madness and therefore had to serve Eurystheus. But the poet has placed the time of his servitude and his great labours before his madness, for only thus could he create a dramatic figure which epitomised the contrast between triumphant achievement and utter humiliation.

Iris, the messenger of the gods, appears on the roof of the palace accompanied by the goddess of madness, Lyssa, in the form of an Erinys. It is Hera who has sent her to the house of the man she hates, the son of Zeus and Alcmene, although this Fury actually shrinks from reducing to wretchedness the champion of mankind, who brought peace to many lands. But she must obey and a messenger relates how, while Heracles was sacrificing, his mind became shrouded in darkness and he killed the wife and children he had so recently saved. The palace door is opened and we see the hero, who had defied Death in his own realm, amidst the corpses of those he loved. He has been tied to a column when, after his attack of madness, he fell asleep exhausted. Awakening to the terrible reality, he decides upon death. But now a friend intervenes. On his journey to the underworld Heracles has rescued Theseus from mortal danger and brought him back to life. Theseus has hastened to assist his friend against Lycus and now he comes to his aid in a far more wretched situation.

Like Sophoclean heroes Heracles sees himself as cast down by fate: death, he thinks, is the unavoidable way out. But a new attitude is revealed in the speech of Theseus. Man does not preserve his dignity in the face of irrational forces by choosing his own death, but in a courageous acceptance. The terrifying irrationality of fate cannot obliterate human merit, least of all that of Heracles. He must go on living, supported by the affection and loyalty of his friend; such an acceptance is more courageous, more dignified than the hasty settling by death of an account that cannot be balanced.

The hero who triumphed in so many mythical combats now gains a victory in the most difficult struggle of all, the purely human conflict within himself. No *deus ex machina* ends this play, its solution lies entirely within man's own suffering and self-conquest. The dichotomy in the action is externally very marked but, in an almost unique way, both parts are strictly correlated by standing in antithesis, and there are no isolated motifs which obtrude.

Euripides explains the sudden onset of madness in the soul of Heracles by an old legendary motif, namely Hera's hatred, and he brings it before our eyes by introducing Iris and Lyssa. Here we have a concrete example of what was earlier described as a contradiction in the poet's work. Hera and her messenger do not embody the powers of a higher order that were vital to the poet himself. Tradition provides him with the means by which to objectify psychological experiences, but this tradition has become of doubtful value, even worthless to him. Gods who sacrifice Heracles, the saviour hero, to their hatred do not represent a higher world order and can no longer be piously accepted. As Heracles himself says:

1340 Ah, all this has no bearing on my grief;
but I do not believe the gods commit
adultery, or bind each other in chains.
I never did believe it; I never shall;
nor that one god is tyrant of the rest.
If god is truly god, he is perfect,
lacking nothing. These are poets' wretched lies.

These words reflect the famous saying of Xenophanes that Homer and Hesiod imputed to the gods all that is infamous: theft, fornication and mutual deception. And Euripides' beautiful words about the true god who lacks nothing evoke the sublime image of a divine being, serene and with no inner contradiction, which the Ionian philosopher conceived.

Beyond Euripides we can perceive the sophists' enlightened criticism of the gods and, behind this, its very source: the ideas of the Ionian philosophers. Ion, in a play of the same name, also criticises the eroticism of the gods (436), and in the *Iphigeneia in Tauris* the heroine confesses her distaste for the cult of the goddess whom she must serve (380): this goddess turns away those who are polluted by the blood of murder, and yet claims human sacrifice. The messenger in the *Andromache* (1151) speaks in similar terms of the Delphic god, implacably revengeful himself, who insists on a moral code for others. The poet expresses his views in a pregnant aphorism in fragment 292 N^2: 'When gods do evil, they are not gods.'

The enlightened critical attitude towards religion reached its peak in the work of Critias, poet and politician, mentioned earlier as the probable author of the pseudo-Euripidean *Tennes*. In his *Sisyphus* he defined religion as a political invention to inspire a fear of the law. Euripides, however, never became a nihilist in matters of religion, and continued his search for the truth till the end of his life. This will be discussed shortly, in connection with *The Trojan Women*. The poet shows in a beautiful passage of the *Heracles* how pure and unrestricted humanity triumphs over ancient superstition. Heracles has covered his face, as tradition demanded of those who were unclean. When Theseus approaches he warns him to flee from pollution. But Theseus does not allow that there is any danger: a man can no more harm his friend than he can offend the gods by his blemishes. Thus the belief in transgression as a physical uncleanliness has been overcome; a superstition which caused the Athenians to hold a ritual court of justice over every case of accidental killing, even with inanimate objects.

Another protest of the poet against the *nomos* must have appeared even bolder. In one of his later dramas, the *Auge*, the heroine, made pregnant by Heracles, bears her child in the temple of Athena, whose priestess she is. This infuriates the goddess, but Auge protests passionately against the supposition that the spoil from dead soldiers may adorn the temple, while a human birth would desecrate it.

The *Heracles* was written during a short period of peace. In the chorus of the elders the ageing poet, for whom in an ephemeral world art remained the only lasting reality, has sung of his life's task:

673 Never shall I cease from this,
Muses with the Graces joining,
loveliness in yoke together.
I may not live without the Muses.
Let my head be always crowned!
May my old age always sing
of Memory, the Muses' mother,
always shall I sing the crown
of Heracles the victor!
So long as these remain –
Dionysus' gift of wine,
the lyre of seven strings
the shrilling of the flute –
never shall I cease to sing,
Muses who made me dance!

When Euripides produced his *Trojan Women* in 415 peace was over and Athens was preparing for the Sicilian expedition. Those who had doubts and considered this bold westward expansion highly dangerous were voted down, but when the fleet had sailed the doubt remained which would later be so terribly justified. The mood of this period pervades the entire play and is clearly expressed in some passages.

We know that the surviving play came after an *Alexander* and a *Palamedes*, and was performed with the satyr play *Sisyphus*. The three tragedies, performed on the same day, appear to form some kind of trilogy, though from what is known of the content of the lost plays they appear far more self-contained than those of an Aeschylean trilogy. The *Alexander*, as was to be expected, came first. In it Alexander-Paris, who had been exposed in infancy, comes to Troy for athletic games and triumphs over his brothers. These are furious with the interloper and Deiphobus wants to kill him: but he is recognised and there is a happy reunion, in which Cassandra's prophecy of future disaster is ignored. In the brothers' plan to murder Alexander we have one of those motifs which the poet used repeatedly, because he not only believed in the force of human passions but also in the power of destiny in the form of *Tyche*, mistress of chance. She allows unsuspecting persons to raise arms against their own kin and snatches them away at the last moment. This motif recurs in the *Ion*.

The *Palamedes* is known to have dealt with the ruin of this inventive hero through Odysseus' envy and betrayal: a fate so singular that it hardly seems feasible as part of a trilogy.

In *The Trojan Women*, the only surviving play of the three, dramatic action has been dissolved into a series of scenes, but the shadow of the dreadful destruction that ended the great legendary war gives those scenes an emphatic unity. Poseidon described in the prologue the annihilation of the city, whose walls he once built. Athena saw her wish fulfilled, but as she approaches Poseidon we notice that her mood has changed. Ajax has insulted her image and she now wishes to destroy the returning fleet with Poseidon's help. Thus we are told, even before we witness the misery of the defeated in the coming scenes, what fate awaits the victors. In this unholy war friend and foe alike will be the victims of anguish and terror. As background to the drama Athena evokes another image of destruction:

78 When they take ship from Ilium and set sail for home
Zeus will shower down his rainstorms and the weariless beat
of hail, to make black the bright air with roaring winds.
He has promised my hand the gift of the blazing thunderbolt
to dash and overwhelm with fire the Achaean ships.
Yours is your own domain, the Aegean crossing. Make
the sea thunder to the tripled wave and spinning surf,
cram thick the hollow Euboean fold with floating dead.

Then we hear Hecuba's lament in a long monody, which changes into an antiphonal song with the chorus. The herald Talthybius announces new disasters: the fate of Polyxena, the subject of the *Hecuba*, is only an episode here, while Cassandra is to be given to Agamemnon, Andromache to the son of Achilles, who killed her husband, and Hecuba to Odysseus.

Frenziedly, Cassandra sings her own bridal song:

308 Lift up, heave up; carry the flame; I bring fire of worship,
torches to the temple.
Io, Hymen, my lord. Hymenaeus.
Blessed the bridegroom.
Blessed am I indeed to lie at a king's side,
blessed the bride of Argos.
Hymen, my lord, Hymenaeus.
Yours were the tears, my mother,
yours was the lamentation for my father fallen,
for your city so dear beloved,
but mine this marriage, my marriage,
and I shake out the torch-flare,
brightness, dazzle,
light for you, Hymenaeus,
Hecate, light for you,
for the bed of virginity as man's custom ordains.

In a typical Euripidean sequence this stirring and passionate monody is followed by a far more composed, logical speech by Cassandra. Her prophecy is again the poet's means of diverting our attention from the ruins of Troy to the suffering that awaits the victors. Those among them who will reach their homeland, like Agamemnon, will meet their doom there.

Andromache is next to suffer. Before she is led to her new lord, her child Astyanax is torn away from her, to be hurled from the walls of Troy.

Then follows a different scene. The victorious Menelaus appears with the adulteress who was the cause of all this misery. Hecuba hopes that even in all the horror around her she will see justice done. Menelaus plans to punish Helen with death and Hecuba replies to Helen's defence with fierce accusations. She apparently triumphs in the *agon* but Menelaus decides to take Helen with him in his ship and the chorus hints (1107) – where the saga was quite definite – that a weakling like Menelaus will be easy game for a woman of such beauty.

Helen's speech reveals much about the process whereby myth is undermined as soon as it is no longer accepted as a sacred story. When she calls Aphrodite a power of destiny, this is shown up as a spurious argument by Hecuba and Menelaus, and rejected. And when she maintains that her unfaithfulness was the saving of Greece (932) – since otherwise Paris, after Hera's and Athena's promises, would have become the ruler of Hellas – then mythical motifs have been torn from their source and placed in a new context of sophistic rationalism. This procedure had a great following for it is still noticeable in Seneca's tragedies.

Hecuba is allowed to lay out the body of Astyanax on Hector's shield, then the women depart, leaving the soil of Troy and the city enveloped in flames. Again a question of stage management interrupts our analysis of the play. The fire that swallows up Ilium can hardly have existed only in the imagination of the spectators. Hecuba wants to hurl herself into the flames but is kept back by force. Euripides, who makes Evadne in *The Suppliant Women* jump into the flaming pyre, was a producer who loved powerful effects. Here we are ignorant. We cannot go beyond the general statement that compared with the modern stage the means of producing scenic effects were probably very simple. More important to realise that effect is always subordinated to the form of the play as a whole. Staging as an end in itself was almost unknown. It is always a sure sign that theatrical art is bankrupt.

In the first chorus the Trojan Women ponder over their imminent fate. Anywhere, rather than Sparta! Here speaks the Athenian poet, and when the women give Athens first preference, then Sicily and the coast of Southern Italy, he seems to follow his people's dream of a Greek empire in the West. Not frivolously, however; the entire tragedy reveals his ideas on war, just when Athens was embarking on her greatest expedition. War is the ordeal of a whole people and this play differs from the *Hecuba*, whose subject is similar, in that we are not shown even the flaring up of a human passion to relieve the utter gloom. A few years later the poet was commissioned by his city to write an epitaph for the Athenians who perished at Syracuse (Plutarch, *Nicias* 17).

No passage in the known tragedies is more revealing of Euripides as a religious thinker than Hecuba's prayer in her *agon* with Helen:

884 O power, who mount the world, wheel where the world rides,
O mystery of man's knowledge, whosoever you be,
Zeus named, nature's necessity or mortal mind,
I call upon you; for you walk the path none hears
yet bring all human action back to right at last.

Ultimately this prayer goes back to the hymns of invocation, which attempt to reach the highest being by using all his names, as in the hymn to Zeus in Aeschylus' *Agamemnon*. And the phrase ὅστις ποτ' εἶ σύ ('whosoever you be') quoted above has an exact parallel in the ὅστις ποτ' ἐστίν of the earlier hymn. But how different the content, although the form may be similar! Aeschylus, filled with awe, can hardly find words for his god, whereas in Euripides we see a contemplative mind, whose restless search is prompted by feelings no less profound. In his quest he has recourse to philosophical theory. The god of his prayer is the Ether which envelops the earth, and its repeated deification shows the influence of Diogenes of Apollonia. We know the idea of 'mind,' the divine power of *nous*, from the teaching of Anaxagoras, the friend of Pericles who, according to an ancient biography, counted Euripides among his pupils. But more important than these scraps of knowledge is to try to understand the man who never denied the existence of divine power but strove for a deeper insight, beyond a tradition that had become questionable. He is the poet who makes the hero of his *Bellerophon* storm the skies on his winged steed to solve the mystery of the world. But Euripides knew well that the problems which continued to haunt him were insoluble. Bellerophon plunges to earth before he has even reached his goal.

The poet's effort to free himself from tradition is particularly striking when we are able to compare his treatment of a subject with that of the other two tragedians, as in the *Electra*. Since that play mentions the concern of the Dioscuri for the fleet in the Sicilian sea (1347) it can be dated to the year 413. The *Electra* of Sophocles also belongs to his later years. It is a mark of the independence of these contemporary tragedians that it has hitherto been impossible to prove which was the earlier play.

The *Electra* is not acted in front of the palace of the Atreidae.

In the prologue there emerges from a miserable peasant hut the humble man to whom Clytaemnestra has given the king's daughter as his wife. Electra lives in poverty and must decline when women come to fetch her for the festival of Hera. But Orestes is already in the country, finds her and, as yet unrecognised, makes her tell the story of her misery. To entertain him the poverty-stricken household must send for food and wine to the old servant who had once rescued Orestes from the palace of death. The old man arrives and brings about recognition. At the tomb of Agamemnon he has found a lock of hair which Electra must compare with her own. She must also place her foot in the footprint near the tomb to see if it is her brother who has come. These are the signs which in *The Choephoroe* of Aeschylus had led Electra to recognition. When here such proof is repudiated as senseless, we are aware of the rationalistic critical spirit of the poet who took probability (*πιθανόν*) very seriously – a disturbing polemical intrusion. Recent interpreters, however, have raised serious objections to the authenticity of these verses.

Only the scar on the face of Orestes, which the old man recognises, clinches the matter and after the first joy of being reunited careful plans are laid under the guidance of the old man.

Soon a messenger announces the first success: the unsuspecting Aegisthus has been killed at a sacrifice to which he had invited the strangers. When Orestes arrives with the body Electra vents her passionate hatred in a speech in which she covers the dead with ignominy and shame.

Their mother still lives. Electra's fictitious confinement has brought her away from the city and again the poet remains within the bounds of probability when he makes these women, who have not seen each other for a long time, speak of the past. Clytaemnestra's self-defence crumples under her daughter's icy scorn. She can no longer justify what she has done. Inside the hut she receives her death-blow and again the Attic stage reveals her body and that of Aegisthus. But by the side of Orestes now stands Electra, whom Aeschylus never brought on to the stage again after the great commos. Here she has not only urged her brother to do what at the sight of his mother he feels incapable of doing of his own accord: she even shares with him in the death blow. Her *θυμός* is so wholly daemonic that she resembles those women of the older Euripidean dramas, who stepped beyond the limits of humanity.

With Aeschylus matricide is both a fateful necessity and a crime. In this conflict, which finds its solution on a higher level in the poet's religious faith in Zeus, lies the tragic problem of this crime. For Sophocles Apollo's command – a sacred tradition – justifies the act. But in Euripides the matricide lacks any religious implications, it is merely an act committed by human beings who must, but cannot justify it. It is true that the god's command looms behind Orestes, but this legendary theme does not lead to a dreadful antinomy within the structure of the play. Orestes rejects it as he approaches his mother (971), saying that the divine command to murder is senseless, and the Dioscuri confirm this at the end of the play (1245). And so the brother and sister who killed their own mother remain alone to face what they have done and break down under the strain. There is no sense of triumph, of rightful expiation, only horror and fear remain. The Dioscuri, as *dei ex machina*, only produce an external solution: Orestes will be acquitted before the Areopagus and Electra will marry Pylades.

There is an important problem to be faced, especially in this play and the *Heracles*. Both dramas are based on traditional myth and in both the myth is exposed as senseless, unworthy of belief. We have pointed out that such an antinomy came as naturally to a man of Euripides' intellectual character as it was a part of contemporary trends. But it becomes very difficult to pin down the real tragic quality of such plays, since that which the events presuppose has been dismissed by the poet's criticism. Tragedy, as Aeschylus and Sophocles fashioned it, now starts to become a problem. The *Heracles*, for instance, comes very close to the Sophoclean conception of the tragic, yet the ending is far removed from it. For the problem raised at the end of our introduction it is significant that tragedy becomes questionable when the gods of the old faith begin to leave the Attic stage.

The most sympathetic figure in the *Electra*, the poor peasant to whom the princess had been given in marriage, deserves particular notice. He has not touched her, he understands her suffering and alleviates it as best he can. Nobility in a simple guise is to us a well-known theme, but in Euripides it means new ideas. Here the last remnant of the notion that the good and the bad, χρηστοί and

Φαῦλοι, can be distinguished by their birth has vanished and a new image of human values emerges. We meet the simple peasant whose heart is in the right place once more in the *Orestes*, where a similar man, who detests cowardice and meanness, comes to the aid of Orestes when he is hard pressed (917). Although in the *Electra* the *αὐτουργός* (small farmer) is still made to point out that he is of good parentage (35), the poet waives such an explanation in the *Orestes*. Instead we are given a charming sidelight on the man's character. This man of honour in peasant dress is hardly ever seen in the city or market. He sticks to the soil, a simple farmer, one of those who alone keep a country sound and healthy. *The Bacchae* supplements this idea in a negative way. There (717) the shepherd who for his own benefit gives the disastrous advice to catch the Maenads is a real braggart, who has learned his nasty tricks in the town which he frequents at every opportunity. Here we see the dissolution of the *polis* in yet another form: the city as the educator of the right type of man has become questionable; it is contrasted with the country, where goodness still prevails. Euripides often foreshadows the Hellenistic age. Here again he anticipates a mood of that period, though one confined to literature. We know, however, that the poet whose work is permeated by the ideas of the sophists was not blind to the danger of placing the weapons of clever dialectic into the hands of the common man.

There is a new valuation of man, free from former restrictions, in the peasant figures of the *Electra* and the *Orestes*. This innovation is still more striking where human worth is attributed even to a slave. A revolution in traditional notions is contained in the words from the *Ion*:

854 A slave bears only this
Disgrace: the name. In every other way
An honest slave is equal to the free.[1]

There is a connection between the new image of man and the fact that for Euripides the concept *physis*, of central importance in the *Philoctetes* of Sophocles, gradually changes and becomes less definite. Here we can probably trace a development in the poet's ideas from the surviving material. Fragment 810 N² of the *Phoenix*

[1] Similar statements from *Androm.* 638, *Hel.* 730, *Phrixus* frg. 831 N² can also be quoted.

(before 425, because Aristophanes refers to it in his *Acharnians*) states the well-known doctrine that the natural predisposition, the *physis*, is decisive. No fostering or care can make good what is bad. We find the same pedagogic pessimism, the logical consequence of attributing the highest value to the *physis*, in fragment 1068 N², which unfortunately can neither be dated nor identified. A curious wavering appears in the *Hecuba*, written a few years after the *Hippolytus* of 428. Hecuba reacts to the news of Polyxena's courageous death, after an initial outburst of sorrow, with a very strange reflection (592) – in fact she herself points out its strangeness in this context (603). She first states that the good and the bad in man are indestructible. But where do they come from? Are they inherited, or the result of upbringing? The poet definitely favours the latter. The detailed exposition in the speech and the forced nature of its insertion in the play prove that these questions were new and important to him. His notion is stated clearly in *The Suppliant Women* written a few years later, in an important passage at the end of the funeral oration of Adrastus:

913 Manliness
Is teachable. Even a child is taught
To say and hear what he does not understand;
Things understood are kept in mind till age.
So, in like manner, train your children well.

The praise of education in the *Iphigeneia in Aulis* (561 and 926) can also be cited here. These new ideas are the negation of Pindar's τὸ δὲ Φυᾷ κράτιστον ἅπαν (Ol.9, 100), for the distrust which his words express against διδακταὶ ἀρεταὶ is in complete contrast to the first line of the passage just quoted from *The Suppliant Women*, namely ἡ δ' εὐανδρία διδακτός. These changes were obviously due to sophistic influence, even without the testimony of the sophist Antiphon (frg. 60D). For him upbringing is the most important factor in human life. He uses the simile of the soil and the seed, but not in a physical sense, the seed being the educator's contribution which, when sown early, will determine man's character. The threads which lead from here to later philosophers could easily be followed – the name of Socrates comes to mind – but we only wanted to point out that Euripides shares the thoughts of a new era.

The dramatic structure of the *Electra* shows a dichotomy which recurs in two plays written shortly afterwards. The scenes which lead up to and bring about a recognition between two closely related persons after a long separation are followed by a carefully laid plot for their rescue, an 'intrigue' or *μηχάνημα* as it is usually called.

The principle that it is possible to see all things from opposite angles, implied in the *δισσοὶ λόγοι* of the Sophists, is now also applied to mythical figures. Hence the fashion for 'rehabilitations,' already foreshadowed in Eurystheus of *The Heracleidae* and perfected in Polyneices of *The Phoenician Women*. For Helen, the heroine of the eponymous play that was performed in 412, such a rehabilitation was already begun in the sixth century in the palinode of Stesichorus, the Sicilian choral poet. He maintained that the real Helen had been in Egypt during the siege of Troy and that the entire war had been waged for the sake of a phantom, by design of the gods. It is this Egyptian Helen whom Euripides brings on to the stage and purges of the blemishes which he had exposed in his *Trojan Women* and his *Orestes*. This rehabilitation is no accidental parallel with that of Gorgias, whose eulogy of the great adulteress of the legend, argued with a sophist's tricks, had the same purpose.

Helen herself tells in a prologue the story of what had befallen her. She had first found a safe refuge in Egypt (where Hermes had brought her) with Proteus. But after the death of the old man his son Theoclymenus wished her to become his wife. She counters her undeserved reputation by remaining faithful to her husband, and flees to the tomb of Proteus. There she meets a Greek who was stranded in Egypt and learns from him what had happened to her relatives. She explains her wretched situation to a chorus of Greek women, who had been carried off by force to Egypt, and goes with them to the palace, to ask the prophetess Theonoe, sister of Theoclymenus, for more information about her husband, who disappeared seven years before on the voyage back from Troy. Again as in the *Alcestis*, the stage becomes empty; the poet makes room for Menelaus, who has just landed in Egypt, to tell the whole story of his miserable wanderings anew. That is done in the easy form of a new prologue, just as Helen's refuge at the altar in the opening scene merely represented an established formula;

when it suits her for other reasons she does not hesitate to leave the refuge.

The play continues by bringing Helen and Menelaus together. We cannot blame him for beginning to feel at ease only when he is told that on board ship Helen had declared herself a phantom and vanished into thin air. After a joyful reunion they plan his rescue, for as an alien Menelaus is condemned to death according to the barbarous laws of the Egyptians. The couple are in great danger, but Theonoe's magnanimity comes to their aid. She is prepared, for the sake of justice, to conceal Helen's ruse from her brother. And so Helen's *μηχάνημα* succeeds. Menelaus, disguised as a messenger, announces his own death and Helen obtains permission to bring offerings at sea to the husband who is presumed shipwrecked. Theoclymenus, unsuspecting, puts a ship at her disposal and enables the two to escape. The Dioscuri who appeared at the end of the *Electra* and related Helen's transfiguration, thus foreshadowing this play, are again the *dei ex machina* and rescue Theonoe from her brother's anger.

The gods are often mentioned and censured in this play, but in contrast with the *Electra* the question of the justification of their acts has entirely receded into the background. In this play, which is technically well constructed, human beings are exposed to the whims of fate, and in this situation hold their own, but apart from Theonoe they do not present any deeper metaphysical truths. We do hear about the inscrutable decrees of the gods in a choral epilogue to the play – to be further discussed in the *Ion* – but in the manner in which the successful ruse is carried out, the *Helen* reveals the gradual secularisation of the tragic play that was rooted in religious cult. Left unfinished in tragedy, this process became complete in the comedy of the following century.

This process of secularisation also meant the end of the kind of tragedy that had lent grandeur to the Dionysiac festivals of the classical period. We can now answer the question with which we ended our introduction. Greek tragedy in its greatest period does not represent a world view which we may call totally tragic since such a view rejects the idea of the Absolute – of a meaningful universe that is divine in origin. Classical tragedy, on the contrary, presupposes such an order, and its tragic events confirm it. But as the relationship with the transcendent begins to weaken, the conviction and the dignity of tragedy decline. This, at any rate, is true of the Greek world.

The *Iphigeneia in Tauris*, which can probably be dated a year later than the *Helen*, has quite unjustifiably been awarded a special place among Euripidean dramas because the subject was well known in one of Goethe's finest works. But it is even more unwarranted to play off Goethe against Euripides in absurd generalisations about Germans and Greeks. The Greek stage too possesses in Neoptolemus a noble character incapable of deceit, but the antagonist of Iphigeneia is a barbarous Scythian before whom such behaviour would be senseless.

At the end of the *Electra* the Dioscuri had advised Orestes to seek the Areopagus in Athens and had promised that he would be acquitted by equality of votes. That was the Aeschylean version of the story. But Euripides, taking great liberties, elaborates the myth: not all the Erinyes accept the judgment, and some continue to pursue him. Apollo, from whom Orestes forcibly obtains assistance by threatening to commit suicide in front of the Delphic temple, stipulates that he will only rescue him if he brings the statue of Artemis, which had fallen from heaven, back from the Scythian land of the Taurians to Attica. It is quite likely that Aeschylus also took liberties with the myth in his *Eumenides*. The road from Delphi to Athens, which Orestes treads, symbolised a profound religious concept. But such probing into the divinely intended significance of events plays no part in the Euripidean treatment of the subject. Here again we find the contradiction mentioned earlier. The fetching of the Taurian Artemis by Orestes gives the poet a link with the Attic cult of Artemis Tauropolos at Halae – the type of link with an actual cult which he so often seeks to establish. On the other hand these innovations enable him to write a lively play in which recognition and intrigue (*ἀναγνώρισις* and *μηχάνημα*) have a purely human interest and lack all religious connotations. The structure of the play, based on these two elements, has a close parallel in the *Helen*, but the character of the recognition scene makes it the better play. The poet has certainly deserved Aristotle's favourable judgment (*Poetics* 1455a); to us the quality of the psychological transitions which match the changing situations means more than the technical skill. Human nature reveals itself here in a new form: no longer, as in the earlier plays, does the passionate force of the θυμός sweep everything along with it in one direction. The soul now responds to varying pressures as would a stringed instrument, with tones that are full and tender.

Iphigeneia speaks in her prologue of the harsh service of Artemis, which in a barbarous country demands human sacrifice. She has been forced into this service after being carried off from Aulis. Now she is oppressed by a dream which she can only interpret as signifying her brother's death in a far country: she has sprinkled Orestes with holy water as in a ritual for the dead. And yet he is so close to her; he comes on the stage when she leaves it and in a short dialogue with Pylades discloses his difficult task. After the entry of the chorus – here also they are captive Greek women – and its lament with Iphigeneia, the action quickly develops. A shepherd announces, in one of those narratives which are masterpieces of epic in miniature, that two strangers have been discovered, one of whom, in terrible derangement, believes that he is being pursued by the Erinyes. They have now been taken prisoner and will be brought before Iphigeneia to be sacrificed. Her heart goes out to the young men who are doomed to die but Orestes is proud and reticent and only mentions that Argos is his homeland. Now begins a stirring scene of question and answer. Iphigeneia, in painful longing, seeks news of her country and its heroes and about the present fate of her relatives. And Orestes, from the depth of his suffering, relates the events that have taken place in Argos. Again and again the dialogue comes close to the point where the spark of recognition must leap across, only to be sidetracked once more. Brother and sister are unknown to each other, neither suspecting the other's presence, while suffering and the fear of death make Orestes speak tersely. Thus the poet makes entirely convincing their heartrending failure to reach what both so deeply desire. Iphigeneia now wishes to save one of the young men from the Scythians and their barbaric goddess, so that he can make it known in Argos that she is alive. Orestes wins in a noble duel of self-sacrifice. Pylades must go free. Again the manner in which the poet directs the move that leads to recognition is masterly. Iphigeneia gives Pylades a letter and so solemnly enjoins him under oath to deliver it that he, being honest and conscientious, feels he must exclude the possibility that the letter might get lost on the dangerous sea voyage, whereas he might survive. Iphigeneia accepts this and gives him the essentials as an oral message. Iphigeneia is alive. Now brother and sister have found each other in a strange and savage country, in dire peril. Joy and sorrow are mingled, then follows the search for a mode of escape. Here again feminine shrewdness finds the way, and takes the lead until the goal is happily reached. She manages to convince Thoas, the barbarian king, that the strangers, being polluted by murder, have offended the goddess. They and the statue must now be cleansed in the sea. Soon a messenger tells of their escape but adds that the wind is driving their ship back to the shore. This is Athena's cue. In her speech she establishes the link with the cult and festival of Artemis at Halae, and almost as an afterthought commands Thoas to overcome his anger. The play might well have ended without her and again it appears as if Euripides wished to reintroduce at the close the link with the cult whose gods had become irrelevant to the inner structure of his tragedy.

In Euripidean drama the wealth of subjects corresponds to the great variety of their form. The unity and coherence of *The Medea* or the *Heracles* have to be set against tragedies which disintegrate under the weight of extraneous material, or the insertion of well-worn motifs – not to mention contradictions which repeatedly threaten their unity from within. This becomes very clear in *The Phoenician Women*, produced around 410 with the *Oenomaus* and the *Chrysippus* mentioned earlier. The play is centred on the conflict between Polyneices and Eteocles, as in the *Seven* of Aeschylus. But for Euripides the significance of the myth is quite different, and he has gone beyond the central theme to exploit every aspect of the subject. In the prologue Jocasta tells the horrible story of Oedipus; we also hear that Oedipus still lives in the palace, where his sons imprisoned him as soon as they realised their parentage. In his terrible bitterness the blind man has cursed his sons: they will divide their inheritance with the sword. In order to counteract the curse they conclude a pact: each shall rule for a year, while the other leaves the country. But once Eteocles has tasted of power he refuses to relinquish it. He banishes his brother, who finds himself a wife and followers in Argos and now threatens his father's city.

Euripides has boldly reversed the position of the brothers in their conflict. Polyneices, the 'brawler' of the old legend, is the one unjustly driven from his homeland, while the Eteocles, who has true glory in his name, has broken the pact. Jocasta's prologue is followed by Antigone's viewing the battlefield from the walls with her tutor. This episode is clearly borrowed from Homer, but beyond giving an exposition of the scene, turning the stage in front of the palace into a wide battlefield, it provides a link with the final act of the play. The Antigone who sends her sisterly good wishes over the city walls to her brother will also stand up for his rights when he has been killed.

Polyneices obeys the summons of his mother, who hopes to make peace at the eleventh hour. He is now standing on the soil of his native city, which means that as a banished man he is in danger of his life. And Jocasta, between the two hostile brothers, listens to the combat that is as yet being fought with words, and implores and adjures them in vain. Eteocles is doubly free from the bondage laid on him in the *Seven*. He is not – as in the typically Aeschylean form of the tragedy – a conscious tool for the family curse. Although his father's curse is fulfilled in him, this fulfilment is due to his own greed for power, for the sake of which he would reach for the stars or sink beneath the earth (504). Neither is he the representative of the *polis* for which he is responsible. This Eteocles has a lust for power, he is a tyrant, for whom not the community but the throne is all important. We see in this great scene what the loss of the old ties meant for tragedy and what was gained by it: colour and variety in the conflict of individual character, which keeps the play moving. There is the mother, lovingly embracing her two sons as she stands between them, the brutal tyrant and the gentler Polyneices, whom only injustice has driven to violence. Here is a conflict that can only be solved by bloodshed. But first the poet has inserted the Menoeceus episode, mentioned in our analysis of the *Alcestis*. The boy gives his life as the saving sacrifice which Ares demands.

Jocasta is told by a warrior that the attack on Thebes has been repulsed but more is to follow: Eteocles and Polyneices are determined to settle their feud by a duel. With Antigone she hurries outside the city; then another messenger announces that she has found both her sons dying. Near their bodies she commits suicide with a sword. With compelling force the poet has evoked the scene in the messenger's words, but the tragedy has reached the border-line of theatricality. This is also apparent in the final scenes. The three corpses are brought on to the stage and the aged, grey-haired Oedipus leaves his prison to sing the lament with Antigone. But this is not yet the end of the play. Creon banishes Oedipus because Teiresias has prophesied that only thus will the city find peace, and he prohibits the burial of Polyneices. Antigone then defies him on behalf of the dead. She has to give way to force but refuses to remain in the city and to marry Haemon. The end of the play would be rather less cluttered with motifs if all the verses which refer to the burial of Polyneices could correctly be rejected. But it is rather risky to eliminate from a play that was intentionally crowded with subject matter one motif which Sophocles had already firmly linked with Antigone. In the passage where she joins her blind father to embark on a life of misery we experience the full impact of the poet's genius. We see him often enough at the height of his powers in this play; in the Antigone of the opening scenes, in the great meeting of the brothers with Jocasta, and in the farewell speech of Menoeceus, but however much the play was admired in later antiquity, the poet failed to integrate the wealth of images and motifs into final unity.

The chorus of the play consists of Phoenician women, whose appearance on the stage has the rather forced explanation that they were sent from their homeland for service in the temple of the Delphic Apollo. Their songs provide an occasion to survey the different ways in which the later Euripidean choric songs developed. Line 784 marks the beginning of a song in the usual triad system, strophe, antistrophe and epode. But the unusual length of each of these corresponds with a new independence of their content. In fact we can, notwithstanding their uniform dactylic rhythm, distinguish three different songs on the basis of their subjects: Ares, the war lord, Cithaeron as a place of disaster, and the primeval history of the city. This independence of the separate strophes reflects the tendency, throughout the play, for its parts to be self-contained parts – a characteristic of Euripidean tragedy in general. The same applies, in a different way, to the songs about the founding of Thebes (638) and the story of Oedipus (1019), though these have admittedly a function within the play since it deals with the fate of the city and those living in it. The evocation of Theban history acquires a new grandeur by this view of the past. But the form of these verses is that of self-contained songs, not unlike ballads. Kranz rightly calls them, with reference to the dithyrambs of Bacchylides, 'dithyrambic stasima.' Ancient critics have disapproved of this use of the chorus, e.g. Aristotle in the *Poetics* (1456a), and in the case of *The Phoenician Women* particularly, the authors of the *scholia* or ancient marginal comments to this play. But these poems have an undeniable value of their own, although they set the fashion of limiting the function of the chorus to insertions between the acts. According to Aristotle Agathon was the first to use such *ἐμβόλιμα* ('something thrown in'). But for Euripides this was only one form among many. One of the fascinations of his work, and a proof of his genius, is that whenever a form threatens to become a mannerism, it always disappears under a wealth of spontaneous inventions. His last work is the *Bacchae* and here the chorus is so firmly anchored in the structure of the play as to be comparable with *The Suppliant Women* and almost with Aeschylus.

Ancient lyrics can never be fully appreciated because their music has been lost. For Euripides such traces as exist, e.g. the information given by Dionysius of Halicarnassus[1] about the melody of the parodos in the *Orestes*, or a Viennese papyrus with the remnant of a melody belonging to lines 338 ff. of the same play, provide no clues. This is particularly regrettable with this playwright, since we know that in his choric songs he allowed the contemporary music of the citharodic mode and the new dithyramb to be used freely. It is not surprising that the writer of nomes, Timotheus, whose *Persians* has been discovered in Egypt, is said to have been his friend, and an ancient anecdote makes Euripides console his protégé for his initial lack of success. We can only note the innovations in these songs, which are often affected and turgid or again quite simple and casual, and remember that they can only be effective with the aid of music. In the contest of poets in *The Frogs* (1309) Aristophanes, caustic and insolent, made Aeschylus produce a parody of such a song.

The *Ion* belongs to the later tragedies and although it cannot be dated accurately it must be roughly contemporary with *The Phoenician Women.* Its subject is again a remarkably involved

[1] *de comp. verb.* 11.

human destiny and like the *Electra* it ranks high among Euripidean dramas not only for its technical skill, but for its evocation of a human soul as it is affected by changing events. There are few mythical motifs in this play. Ion, who in ancient genealogies was the eponym of the Ionians and the son of Xuthus, is here the son of Apollo and Creusa, the daughter of Erechtheus, and was begotten in a cave of the Athenian acropolis. The god commands his brother Hermes to bring to Delphi the child exposed by Creusa in fear and distress, and there Ion grows up in the service of the temple. Hermes relates all this in the prologue with the detachment which means that the possibility of any form of dramatic climax is left open. When Euripides appears to anticipate essential features of the drama, it is still apparent that precisely when he treats the subject with the greatest freedom he avoids the more obvious theatricalities to concentrate on subtleties.

Ion, the youth who serves his god with a pure heart, is one of Euripides' most beautiful creations. In the still hours of the early morning he sweeps the house of his lord and sings a pious song. We quote the beginning of it because it is a wonderful example of the musical richness of Euripidean lyrics:

82 Look, now the sun's burning chariot comes
Casting his light on the earth.
Banned by his flame, the stars flee
To the awful darkness of space.
The untrodden peaks of Parnassus,
Kindling to flame, receive for mankind
The disk of the day.
    The smoke of unwatered myrrh drifts
To the top of the temple.
The Delphian priestess sits on the
Sacred tripod chanting to the Greeks
Echoes of Apollo's voice.
    You Delphians, attendants of Phoebus,
Go down to Castalia's silvery eddies:
When you have bathed in its holy dews,
Return to the temple.
Let your lips utter no words
Of ill-omen, may your tongues
Be gracious and gentle to those who
Come to the oracle.

As for myself, mine is the task
I have always done since my childhood
With these branches of bay and these sacred
Garlands I will brighten Apollo's
Portals, cleanse the floor with
Sprinklings of water,
Put to flight with my arrows the birds
Who foul the offerings.
Since I have neither mother nor father,
I revere the temple of Phoebus
Where I have lived.

The chorus of Creusa's companions now enters and describes with amazement the sculptures of the temple, a motif used prolifically in epic, mime, epigram and in late Greek romances. Then Creusa appears in front of the temple and mother and son confront each other unsuspecting. The poet shows with great subtlety how these two, so clearly linked by blood, soon gain each other's confidence. Creusa tells why she has come. Her marriage with Xuthus is childless and now the god must help her. When Ion, pitying her, asks if she has ever had a child, she replies (306): 'Apollo knows my childlessness.' These few words, spoken here, reveal the poet's insight into human feeling: a woman hides her error in shame, she laments that it was not given to her to bring up the child she has borne, and finally reproaches the god who took her love and did not leave her a pledge. Ion has touched a wound and now she feels an urge to speak of her sorrow, even if, with mild deception, she pretends it is someone else's fate. She also wishes the god to give her a child, but not a child by Xuthus still to be born, he must give back her own which she had to abandon. Now Xuthus arrives to obtain the god's verdict. Apollo uses the opportunity to foist his own child on to the Athenian king. When the latter leaves the temple he acts as the god had commanded: he greets the first person he meets as his son, and it is Ion whom he, trusting the god, believes to be the result of a fleeting affair at some Bacchic festival at Delphi.

Creusa learns with dreadful bitterness that the god has given to Xuthus what he has apparently robbed her of for ever. As expected in this late period of the poet's work, a monody follows which develops into a passionate indictment of the god for whom human destiny is a plaything to suit his mood:

881–922

O you who give the seven-toned lyre
A voice which rings out of the lifeless,
Rustic horn the lovely sound
Of the Muses' hymns,
On you, Latona's son, here
In daylight I will lay blame.
You came with hair flashing
Gold, as I gathered
Into my cloak flowers ablaze
With their golden light,
Clinging to my pale wrists
As I cried for my mother's help
You led me to bed in a cave
A god and my lover,
With no shame,
Submitting to the Cyprian's will,
In misery I bore you
A son, whom in fear of my mother
I placed in that bed
Where you cruelly forced me.
Ah! He is lost now,
Snatched as food for birds,
My son and yours; O lost!
  But you play the lyre,
  Chanting your paeans.

O hear me, son of Latona,
Who assign your prophecies
From the golden throne
And the temple at earth's center,
I will proclaim my words in your ears:
You are an evil lover;
Though you owe no debt
To my husband, you have
Set a son in his house.
But my son, yes and yours, hard-hearted,
Is lost, carried away by birds,
The clothes his mother put on him abandoned.
  Delos hates you and the young
  Laurel which grows by the palm
  With its delicate leaves where Latona
  Bore you, a holy child, fruit of Zeus.

The pedagogue who accompanies her aggravates her anger and distress: in the palace the bastard will be the king's son whereas she, scorned, will have to stand aside. They hatch a plot to poison Ion at a banquet. A servant relates how the plan was nearly successful. The pedagogue had handed the poisoned draught to Ion when somewhere in the hall a blasphemous word was heard. That was a bad omen and the youth poured the wine away. The plot was discovered through a pigeon dipping its beak into the spilled liquid. The pedagogue confesses and Creusa is condemned to death. She has already fled to the altar when the Pythian priestess hands to the youth the casket in which she once found the child together with swaddling clothes, amulet and wreath. She tells him to take it to Athens, where he may still find his mother. But there is no need for a search. Mother and son, who in a mysterious and fateful confusion sought to kill each other, now embrace and, to make all well, Athena confirms Apollo's paternity and promises him famous descendants. But Xuthus, she commands, must continue to believe that Ion is his own son.

In this picture of bliss Euripides has brought human fate very close. But the gods interfere more decisively than usual in this play, first Apollo, then Hermes, then Athena. The question which can never find a solution in the work of Euripides, least of all in a concise formula, is raised again: What are we to think of these gods on the stage?

Apollo is severely censured: Ion lectures the seducer of young girls (436) and Creusa fiercely reproaches the god who brought misery upon her. And yet the god works everything out for the best. He has brought Creusa to Delphi (67) and guided the Pythian priestess to take the decisive step; she herself is aware of this and Athena confirms it (1565). But that does not mean that the god has been entirely exonerated or that the play extols the rule of divine wisdom above human blindness. It cannot be modern opinion alone which found it strange that the god of prophecy tried to establish his son in the palace of Xuthus by a flagrant lie. In fact the god himself does not feel entirely blameless. Thus Apollo knows that in spite of everything he deserves the bitter words addressed to him; that is why he prefers to send for his sister and to let her speak for him in his own abode (1557). It is impossible to resolve the contradiction between the god who is clearly a ruler and the god who knows that he is to blame and is in any case very different from the great upholder of justice in the tragedies of Aeschylus.

To look for a consistent solution is to misinterpret the work of a poet who was in opposition to his age and who yet belonged to it. He was never an atheist. His first drama, the *Alcestis*, as well as one of his last, *The Bacchae*, end with the same words, which also occur in a slightly different form at the end of *The Medea*, the *Andromache* and the *Helen*:

> Many are the forms of what is unknown.
> Much that the gods achieve is surprise.
> What we look for does not come to pass;
> God finds a way for what none foresaw.
> Such was the end of this story.

The concept God does not mean for Euripides the gods of popular tradition, whom he criticises so harshly, as we mentioned earlier and also in the case of the Apollo of the *Ion* and in the *Electra*. But on the stage divine powers cannot remain the disembodied *numina* which he invokes in Hecuba's words in *The Trojan Women* (884), so they are often represented by the well-known figures of the Olympians, however problematical many of their features may have become in a new era.

We have not finished with this basic contradiction, which cannot be dismissed with the simple rationalistic explanation that Euripides displayed these gods on the surface of his drama in order to undermine faith in their existence at a deeper level. The *Ion* especially opens another perspective. For in spite of all his precautions Apollo, like human beings, is subject to a power which cuts him down to size. What he really intended, says Athena (1566), was that Ion should go to Athens as the son of Xuthus and there all would be revealed to mother and son. But then Creusa's plot intervened and the god had to make a hasty decision. Here his hand was forced not by a *Moira*, the ultimate source of order in the world, whose will transcends the gods. Ion himself names the power that plays with their illusions and plans (1512); it is *Tyche*, who in the lives of thousands exchanges peril for fortune and who had nearly made him his mother's murderer. This notion occurs much earlier, and we see the poet's hesitant probing into the mystery that lies beyond phenomena when Talthybius says to Hecuba in the play named after her (488): 'O Zeus, what can I say? That you look on man and care? Or do we, holding that the gods exist, deceive ourselves with unsubstantial dreams and lies, while random careless chance and change alone control the world?' Again the poet's attitude foreshadows that of the Hellenistic period, when Tyche becomes the great ruler of the world. Her increased influence in some but not all of his later works means a change from tragedies dominated by the elemental force of passion, to a type of drama which shows us human beings scheming and suffering against a background of Tyche's dispensations.

Beyond our analysis of Greek tragedy lies the question: what is the essence of the tragic? We found it in its purest form in Sophoclean tragedies, for instance in the first *Oedipus* where man asserts his own dignity in combat with superior irrational forces. In the Euripidean plays under discussion the situation is entirely different. The individual is not confronted by a world order which, though unfathomable, he accepts in deep faith to be meaningful; all he sees is a capricious game of motley fortunes rising and falling. His attitude is therefore not heroic in the true sense of unbending perseverance, since this would be senseless. He attempts to bend his wits to changing circumstances, a μηχάνημα is what is required in his situation. And whereas in the totally tragic conflicts, for which there is no solution, the hero's physical existence is doomed, here it is triumphantly preserved. The happy ending of the *Helen*, for instance, is not mere superficiality. We saw, especially in the *Ion*, that these plays' significance lay in a most subtle rendering of inner experience related to a superbly constructed sequence of events; but this relegates the problem of tragedy to the background. Are the dangerous situations in which these people find themselves, through the erratic movements of the game of life, still fraught with the seriousness which is inherent in the tragic situations of Aeschylean and Sophoclean plays, even those with a happy ending? It is undesirable to burden fluid expressions with precise terminology, but here we might briefly formulate what we have observed as the transition between tragedy and 'drama' in the modern sense. This would find support in the words of the chorus leader in Anouilh's *Antigone*, mentioned in our introduction. Were there allied factors

LIBRARY ST. MARY'S COLLEGE

contributing to the disappearance of the tragic from Greek tragedy? Perhaps the answer lies in the historical assertion that this disappearance coincided with the loss of religious depth in Greek tragedies.

We should notice, in the surviving plays, how much dramatic tension Euripides has extracted from moments of recognition. This tallies with what we know of lost dramas. In the *Auge* Heracles had got this priestess of Athena with child at a nocturnal festival. She has borne her baby in the temple and is in great distress. But Heracles later recognises her by a ring and rescues her from a painful situation. The recurrence of the motifs of nocturnal festival and ring in Menander's *Arbitration* shows how they were to be developed. In the *Melanippe* the sons, exposed in infancy, grow up unknown to their mother and release her from cruel imprisonment. This Melanippe was called 'the Prisoner' to distinguish her from the 'Clever Melanippe' who, in a speech that became famous, defended her children whom Poseidon had fathered. These had been suckled by a cow after being exposed and were to be burnt as monsters. But Melanippe ensures that nature and good sense prevail. In the *Hypsipyle*, a late play like the other two, mother and sons were again reunited. It contained one curious feature, namely a lullaby accompanied by castanets. In the *Alcmeon in Corinth* father and daughter are brought together.

Tyche's machinations reach their greatest dramatic intensity in the *Ion*, where recognition is preceded by a murderous attack on a near blood relative. This motif had already been used in the *Aegeus*, mentioned in connection with *The Medea*, and in the *Alexander*, which formed a trilogy with *The Women Trojan*. In the *Cresphontes*, which can be dated to the twenties, it is the mother Merope herself, who like Creusa plans to kill her son before she recognises him. The *Antiope*, of which papyrus fragments have been recovered, as in the case of the *Hypsipyle*, is a late work. Here Amphion and Zethus, the Theban Dioscuri, have been commanded by Dirce to tie Antiope, who had fled from her cruel treatment, to the horns of a bull. But a shepherd recognises in her the mother of the two youths whom Antiope had once born to Zeus and abandoned in the mountains.

More important than these motifs common to other plays is the characterisation of the two brothers. They have been contrasted as the representatives of two completely different ways of life. Amphion is the great singer and lyrist, as he proves by performing a citharode on the stage. His life is dedicated to art and the visionary experiences of an artist. He thus represents the *θεωρητικὸς βίος* the *vita contemplativa*, in contrast to his brother, the man of action, who epitomises the *πρακτικὸς βίος* or *vita activa*. The best form in which to demonstrate the tension between the two was the *agon*, since it brought the disparity between their two ways of life into focus. Euripides has touched here on problems which have never ceased to preoccupy mankind. The contrast between Amphion and Zethus reflects an event of the greatest consequence in man's history: the split between thought and action. But in the work of the poet this falling apart of what was once a unity meant that thought often became introspective, no longer the servant of immediate action – independent, but not remote. The pedagogical reflections in the *Hecuba* (592), referred to earlier, are a striking example of this.

The performance of the *Orestes*, the last play to be written in Athens, can definitely be dated to 408. There is a remarkable discrepancy between the influence of this play in Hellenistic and Byzantine times and later opinion which has been persistently unfavourable. The censure of the Alexandrians that its characters were wicked throughout has been echoed in modern times, and Jacob Burckhardt's objections to this view remained for long unnoticed. Only in recent times has more justice been done to the poet.

The play begins with the situation after the matricide. At first we are shown a state of collapse following the act, which is similar to that of Electra. In the dead of night when Orestes collects the bones of the mother he has killed from the funeral pyre, madness overwhelms him and he sees the avenging spirits. Now he has fallen asleep on a couch, exhausted, and Electra is keeping watch. Euripides has made her infinitely gentler here than in the play named after her. Although only an accomplice she did 'all a woman could to help him' (32, 284).[1] And completely feminine she is, in the manner of all the most beautiful characters among Euripidean women, as she nurses her sick brother with complete

[1] In the prayer to Agamemnon she only speaks line 1236, not the preceding half-line.

devotion. She tries to prevent the chorus of Argive women who now enter from disturbing his sleep, and when he awakens enfolds him with her love. After a renewed attack of madness, evoked with a mastery that reminds us of the *Heracles*, she attempts to support him with her own strength.

It was not the poet's intention to represent these young people, who are later joined by their staunch friend Pylades, as criminals who after one dreadful deed plan their next. We should not emphasise their wickedness, as Alexandrian and many modern critics have, but the bitter anguish and the despair with which they must fight for their lives. This is the message of the opening scenes; any other interpretation would make the contrast with what follows unintelligible.

At the same time this play shows an extraordinary progress in dramatic dynamics, which is developed even further in the *Iphigeneia in Aulis*. It is no longer the conflict inherent in *one* situation – and one resulting mode of behaviour – which has been pursued to the end. The position constantly changes and must be met by new plans, new action. This lively interplay between external changes and the characters' internal reactions represents a line of development that begins with the increased dramatic movement of Sophocles and brings us close to modern drama.

Already in Electra's prologue there is a ray of hope for her and her brother. The Argive council is to be held which will decide whether or not those who have been convicted of murder must be stoned to death. But now Menelaus has landed in Nauplia on his return from Troy. He should appreciate what Orestes has done, for was not Agamemnon, whose death Orestes avenged, his own brother? Helen has preceded him and has entered Argos under cover of night. She has every reason to shun the daylight, and after the prologue, before the entry of the chorus, the poet gives in a short scene a brilliant sketch of this selfish coquette with her heartless politeness. Even such oblique touches as that whereby Helen, when she offers her hair to Clytaemnestra, is careful only to cut off the tip of a curl, reveal the growing variety and subtlety of dramatic expression.

The most contemptible figure in the whole play enters in the person of Menelaus, who is supposed to come as a rescuer. When Aristotle (*Poetics* 1454a) calls this Menelaus an outstanding example of a figure who has been needlessly vilified, his judgment is for once mistaken. This portrayal of Menelaus, which is in line with other contemptuous sketches of Spartan character, is indispensable because it alone makes the play's psychology intelligible. The problem of Aeschylean tragedy, namely the meaning and the nature of the family curse, has receded into the background. Orestes has broken down under the strain of what he has done, and as long as he is alone with his conscience his act seems to him unnatural and unbearable. But then the world outside sends its lamentable representative. Menelaus first shows compassion but when Tyndareus, the father of the murdered Clytaemnestra, intervenes with blind hatred, Menelaus draws back faint-heartedly, leaving brother and sister to their fate. In this confrontation Orestes' will to live is rekindled, in spite of his state of collapse in the opening scene. Now, in the face of such antagonists, he defends his act which he could not justify to himself. The twofold significance of this act, as necessity and as crime, resulted in the tragic dilemma of the trilogy's central play; it is characteristic of Euripides that he represents this dilemma as a plausible psychological sequence.

What now follows, the battle which the young people have to fight under strain, can only be understood in the light of the inner dynamics of these scenes. Pylades joins them, he willingly shares their danger and raises new hope. Orestes, he says, must appear in person before the council. But a messenger soon announces that the outcome is unfavourable. Only the simple rustic, mentioned in connection with the *Electra*, takes the part of brother and sister. The way in which Euripides sketches his attitude, and that of the council, proves that judgment on the matricide is no longer the principal motif. Envy and political intrigue lie behind Orestes' and Electra's death sentence, and Orestes can only wring from the assembly the concession that the condemned are free to execute their own sentence.

Now a heroic acceptance of death brings the three together in a final farewell, but again the will to live asserts itself and a reappraisal of the despicable meanness of Menelaus (1056) forms the psychological basis for the development of a new plan. They will kill Helen, and bring a well-deserved revenge on Menelaus. The people of Argos, who hate her, may thus be persuaded to judge more mildly. Should the plan fail then, since they are doomed to die, the palace must become their funeral pyre. But in case it succeeds Hermione, the daughter of Helen and Menelaus, must become their hostage to foil the latter's revenge. The plan seems bound for success, Hermione is caught, and a Phrygian slave sings, in a precipitate rhythm that expresses the panic of the cowardly barbarian, of the murderous attack inside the palace. But again expectations are disappointed: Helen is mysteriously carried away at the last moment. A new course of action is proposed: Hermione is in the power of the three plotters; by threatening her life Menelaus must be forced to offer effective help. For the second time an attack on a defenceless victim must save them and we feel even more repelled than in the case of Helen. It is ethically indefensible but, to do justice to the poet, we should not forget the desperate situation which led to this state of affairs, nor the contemptible character against whom the plan is aimed.

On the roof of the palace Orestes keeps Hermione under the threat of his sword, and torches are in readiness to burn down the palace. Menelaus rages in vain outside the bolted door, he must either sacrifice his child or give in. It is hard to imagine what could have been the outcome of this scene. Menelaus, shown up in the drama as a weakling, might let his child die and the palace burn down rather than submit. But if he should give in, one only needs to visualise a situation with Hermione set free and Menelaus pleading with the Argives to change their mind, to realise its impossibility. So there is only the merest suggestion that Menelaus might give in (1617) and Orestes, as if he had not noticed it, gives orders for the palace to be burnt. Then Apollo appears, just in time, with Helen at his side whom he has rescued from the palace and will lead to Zeus (1684, the second half of 1631 is not original). Orestes must atone for his crime in Athens and then marry Hermione, while Pylades must take Electra to wife. Marriages are hastily arranged to bring about a happy ending.

In the *Orestes* the poet has not hesitated to use spectacular effects, especially in the final scene with its build-up on three levels, Menelaus in front of the palace, the three plotters with Hermione on the roof holding burning torches, and the manifestation of the god higher up in a *theologeion*. But to dismiss the *Orestes* as merely aiming at effect, or to treat it as symptomatic of the decay of

Euripidean art, is going too far. This is a work where his genius is peculiarly alive, although the different elements have not been completely harmonised.

When Euripides went to Macedonia, in the same year that the *Orestes* was performed, the muse to whom he had dedicated his life did not forsake him. The *Archelaus*, a festival play he wrote for his royal host, is probably not a serious loss, but after his death in an alien country three of his posthumous plays won victories in Athens. A son or a nephew of the same name is reputed to have produced them. Two have survived, the *Iphigeneia in Aulis* and the *Bacchae*. They provide, together with the remains of the *Alcmeon in Corinth*, a rich and varied image of the poet's last creative period. Here the whole of Euripides' being is reflected, as he nears the end of his life – also the new phase on which his restless spirit had embarked. In him also creative power was undiminished, even in extreme old age.

In the *Alcmeon in Corinth* Euripides again used the recognition theme, but in a new form. Here Alcmeon, in the vicissitudes of change, recognises his own daughter among the slaves he had bought. This play probably resembled the surviving recognition dramas in style and structure.

The *Iphigeneia in Aulis* stands by itself. Here we find, in a more pronounced form than in the *Orestes*, the new type of dynamic action, the lively movement in which each situation cancels the previous one, and action is still more dependent on character. When this play is compared with the almost contemporary but completely different *Bacchae*, it becomes particularly clear that in that last phase of the poet's work a new dramatic form has emerged, in which psychological subtlety has made the old structure less rigid. Man no longer fights for a particular quality of his *physis*, to preserve it or perish, nor is he a person blindly urged on by the passionate force of his θυμός: man, as a complex and changeable being, has found a perfect expression in the restless dynamics of this new type of drama.

The form of the opening scene in the *Iphigeneia in Aulis* is unusual. Instead of a typical prologue we have a dialogue in anapaests between Agamemnon and his ageing servant. Inserted into this is an iambic speech by the king, of the type that usually occurs at the beginning of a play. This part is so like a Euripidean prologue, and the anapaests are poetically of such a high standard, that both might be ascribed to Euripides. The state in which the ending of the play has been preserved suggests that the poet had not yet made a final revision and a later editor may have combined what were still alternative drafts for the opening scene, iambic prologue and dialogue in anapaests. If either should not be authentic, one would sooner suspect the trimeters.

The opening scene in anapaests is by no means only formally interesting. It is clearly an effort to replace the dry communication of a typical prologue by a scene which immediately conjures up the mood of the play. Aeschylus' *Oresteia* also evokes a mood in the prologue but here nature, as the setting of the drama, has a stronger appeal. Silence reigns in the dead of night, silent are the birds, the waves. In the midst of this tranquillity stands Agamemnon, deeply perturbed. He has summoned Clytaemnestra and Iphigeneia their daughter, ostensibly for her marriage with Achilles, but actually for her sacrifice on the altar of Artemis, who holds the fleet back by adverse winds. Now the father in Agamemnon rebels against the commander-in-chief. The old servant has noticed that he wrote a letter, then broke the seal and destroyed what he had written. We hear of Agamemnon's fearful dilemma whether to send a messenger and prevent the fateful journey. Now he has finally decided to do so. The old man starts out with the letter but after a song by the chorus of Chalcidian women whose curiosity has led them to inspect the army and the fleet, we hear of a turn of events which balks Agamemnon's countermand. Menelaus has caught the old man, taken the letter from him and read it. This leads to a quarrel between the brothers in which neither spares his reproaches. Menelaus tries to touch his brother's sense of honour as commander, since he now hesitates to permit the necessary sacrifice; Agamemnon points out the senselessness of such an offering, made only for the sake of regaining Helen.

Meanwhile events have moved of their own accord: a messenger announces that Clytaemnestra and Iphigeneia are nearing the camp. This produces a new dramatic mobility and completely reverses the psychological situation. Agamemnon breaks into a wild display of grief, now that he finds himself caught in the talons of Necessity. His suffering deeply affects his brother and in a sudden but not unheralded change of heart Menelaus rejects the cruel sacrifice and frankly agrees with Agamemnon's argument in the *agon*. But now that the rescue of his child seems feasible he knows he cannot follow this course. Although the command of the goddess is still a secret shared by few, Odysseus knows of it and he will force Agamemnon, through the army council, to make the sacrifice.

All that has happened so far in the play had little bearing on external events, but the poet has revealed a wealth of inner experience. He has shown that uncertainty can be the subject of dramatic treatment as well as uncompromising determination.

On arrival with her mother and the infant Orestes Iphigeneia greets her father with childlike joy. Agamemnon would have preferred to send back Clytaemnestra immediately, but she wishes to be present at her daughter's wedding and stays on. A choric song which anticipates the coming war is followed by a scene which introduces, for the first time in a classical tragedy, a form of situation comedy whose main exploitation came later, on the comic stage. Clytaemnestra greets Achilles warmly as the future husband of her daughter, but he draws back, baffled and embarrassed. It is the old servant who clarifies the situation, and out of the mother's horror and the hero's indignation that his name has been wantonly used, grows the opposition to the sacrifice. First Clytaemnestra tries entreaties. In an impressive scene she tells Agamemnon that she knows his secret and exposes it as wholly against nature. It is Iphigeneia, however, upon whom she depends to move her father; the girl who clings to life with all the eagerness of youth and who tries to soften his heart with tender memories. But now Agamemnon no longer wavers, the purpose of the war appears vindicated. There is no response to Iphigeneia's lament, her only hope lies in Achilles, who stands by his promise. But his loyalty can only lead to a gratuitous sacrifice of his own life. The army demands the blood of Iphigeneia and threatens to stone him. Already Odysseus approaches with a mob to which even he will have to succumb.

In this tense situation it is entirely from within Iphigeneia's soul that a decisive change is brought about. She has wept and begged for her life when her youth was suddenly confronted with the prospect of sacrificial death. Her young life, and sudden death: she was aware of nothing more. Now her vision has widened. An entire army is watching her, and the fame of a people, her own people, depends on her. In the first part of the play the image of the war oscillated between that of a great panhellenic undertaking and the mere private wishes of Menelaus. Now the former aspect prevails, so the girl who feared for her life becomes the maiden who offers it willingly for the sake of her people's name and honour.

Our observations on the *Philoctetes* show how new the methods of Euripides were. Human character as determined by the *physis* is no longer rigid and unchanging; under an external stimulus it may be decisively changed from within. With this concept of transformation, which is the central motif of the play, Euripides has not only made the classical concept of *physis* more fluid, he has prepared the way for modern drama.

It is true that Aristotle did not appreciate this play. He only saw (*Poetics* 1454a) two different Iphigeneias without perceiving the psychological link between them. Euripides did not in fact succeed in depicting Iphigeneia's transition from one attitude to another in its different phases. Childish terror and heroic acceptance of death represent the extremes in experience of which the human soul is capable.

Iphigeneia meets her death bravely and the chorus sings of the meaning of her death to Hellas. Here the ancient text comes to a sudden stop. The messenger's speech at the play's end is not by Euripides, its second part (from 1578) may even be Byzantine. An isolated fragment[1] enables us to identify a consoling speech for Clytaemnestra by Artemis, and the promise that Iphigeneia will be taken into her company, as the original ending.

The action in this play is entirely dependent on forces within the human soul, on their exertions and their transformation. As such it represents a watershed in the development of the known Euripidean plays. Questions about the religious significance of events, or about gods in general, are insignificant compared with psychological problems. With *The Bacchae*, on the other hand, which we consider the last play Euripides wrote, we find ourselves in the middle of these religious questions. The different subject-matter is matched by a different form. The form of *The Bacchae* is closely knit, often archaic; the chorus plays an important part, usually in connection with the action. Ionic metres predominate in the lyrics and this

[1] Found in Aelian, *VH* 7.39.

results in a hieratic solemnity; the great lyric arias sung by actors have been omitted. In the stichomythia, liberally used, the to and fro of the dialogue has been carefully shaped to fit the verse. In addition to the iambic trimeter, the trochaic tetrameter is used in emotional passages (604). Although some parts, such as the prologue and the messenger's speech, have a distinctly Euripidean character, the play as a whole, in which the conflict between a powerful god and an unbeliever is clearly carried through, has an unusually coherent structure; also an undiluted realisation of a tragic confrontation that is unparalleled in Euripides' later works.

The prologue is spoken by Dionysus who, in human form, leads a band of his Lydian Maenads to Thebes in order to force his cult on the native land of his mother, Semele, against heresy and doubt. The chorus of Lydian women sings a song in honour of the god, which together with the subsequent messenger's story belongs to the greatest monuments of Dionysiac cult. We then see Teiresias, the aged seer who actually belongs to the Oedipus cycle, and Cadmus the grandfather of the reigning king Pentheus, on their way to the ceremony in Bacchic attire. The two old men honour the new cult, but it has also attracted the women of the town to the wooded mountains. Pentheus, who has just returned from abroad to find this Bacchic frenzy in his homeland, scolds them harshly.

The scene with the two old men reveals the power of the god and is intended as a warning to Pentheus; it is the first of its kind in the drama, and is no more heeded than those which follow. Dionysus, disguised as a prophet of the cult, is brought before the king in chains and at his command is locked up in a stable. After a long choric song the miracle of the god's liberation takes place. The earth trembles, the columns of the palace sway, the tomb of his mother Semele glows with fire; with all the signs of a divine epiphany the imprisoned god, now liberated, joins his followers. A new conflict with Pentheus threatens to flare up, when a messenger arrives from the mountains. He makes the first of two announcements, works of art which surpass all other Euripidean speeches of their kind.

The cowherd, driving his flock to the pastures at dawn, saw above him in the woods three bands of maenads led by three daughters of Cadmus, Agave, the mother of Pentheus, Autonoe and Ino. They are lying in the beds which nature has provided, in a deep, chaste sleep. When the lowing of the cattle wakes them, their miracles begin. With blows of the thyrsus they draw water from the rocks, and wine, milk and honey gush up from the earth. Nietzsche, in his *Geburt der Tragödie* ('The Birth of Tragedy'), has understood the poet when he says: 'Not only human bonds are restored by the magic of Dionysus: nature, alienated, hostile and subjected, celebrates her festival of reconciliation with her lost sons, with man. The earth willingly offers her gifts; and beasts of prey from mountain and desert approach in peace.' In this passage the maenads, young mothers, feed fawns and wolf cubs at the breast, and when they invoke the God and dance for him, then mountains and beasts alike, in the mysterious participation of nature, share their exultation.

The cowherds, led astray by one of their number, a braggart from the town, try to catch the women. But these now attack the herds, tear to pieces the strongest of the animals, chase the cowherds and pillage the villages at the foot of the mountain, driving the men before them. The poet reveals, through the messenger's words, his understanding of one of the deepest mysteries of Dionysiac religion: its polarity, in which pure innocence and natural gaiety are one with elemental fury in the service of the god. For Pentheus this story should mean a justification of the maenads against the charge of immorality, and a warning as well. The messenger is aware of both (686, 769) but he is not heeded. Now Pentheus is ripe for destruction. He is easily tempted by Dionysus to watch the maenads himself in the woods. Dressed in the attire of Bacchic women, in a state of strange excitement and confusion and with a pathological sense of power – he believes he can carry Cithaeron on his shoulders – he starts out for the mountains with Dionysus.

In the story of the journey's outcome we are again confronted with the duality of maenadic behaviour, impelled by the ambivalence of the cult. In a few strokes the poet conjures up the image of a high secluded mountain valley with its streams, to which our sense of nature responds as immediately as to the opening scene of the *Iphigeneia in Aulis*, or to the choric song from the *Phaethon* that evokes an early morning. The maenads are at peace again, as is nature; they attend to their costume or sing a song in honour of the god. Dionysus has placed Pentheus at the top of a pine-tree and then disappeared. But his voice is heard from heaven, inciting the maenads against the unfortunate man. He, who thought he could carry Cithaeron, is hurled to the ground with his tree by the supernatural strength of the women, and torn to pieces in their wild fury. In sickening triumph Agave rushes on to the stage carrying the head of her son impaled on her thyrsus, and praising her good luck as a hunter in catching a mountain lion. Slowly Cadmus restores her reason by making her look up to the light of heaven, and she realises what she carries on her thyrsus. The triumph of Dionysus brings the play to an end. This part of the original has been destroyed but we can surmise that he condemned Cadmus and his daughters to the harsh fate of banishment.

This play, the last which Euripides wrote, raises a serious problem. Again and again the poet attacked, in the spirit of the sophists, the gods of the traditional faith. In his later plays such questions receded before his preoccupation with humanity. The process of secularisation continued, when suddenly in one of his last tragedies the play is dominated by Dionysus in whose cult tragedy had originated. It is not difficult to see why Aeschylus dealt in two tetralogies with similar myths about the god's antagonists, myths that belonged to the Dionysiac cycle: the saga of the Thracian king Lycurgus and our own Pentheus story. But what is the attitude of Euripides towards his subject? The answers to this much debated question have usually depended on personal bias, and range between the following extremes: either the poet, faithful to his intellectual background, pilloried the senselessness of tradition so that one might give the play the motto: 'Nonsense, thou art victorious'; or else critics saw in *The Bacchae* the testimony of a conversion, which brought Euripides back to the religious faith of his people, a palinode in which he retracted his animosity against traditional religion.

If the contradictions in Euripides' work have been made at all clear in this survey, no time need be wasted in refuting either of these simplifications. In the first place we are not dealing with a Homeric god who was rehabilitated in this play. This was discussed in the first chapter: the old epic could not or would not know much about Dionysus. It was not the poets who gave him his place in the hearts of men, it was his cult which captured them with its miraculous ecstasy. Euripides encountered this god and his secret rites in Macedonia, in a purer form than was possible in civilised Hellas. It is true that Dionysus is immoderate in his revenge and unjust towards Cadmus, but he is also the bringer of the utmost rapture to mankind. He lifts them from the bonds of despair and leads them, reconciled, back to nature. The poet's intention was not to make a rational protest. What made him write this tragedy was a profound experience of Dionysiac religion with its mysterious polarity of compulsion and liberation, its calm return to nature and vital surging of the secret forces of life, its highest rapture and deepest anguish. And this, if any of his plays, is a genuine tragedy in the strictest sense of the word. Here human will, which in Pentheus is not ignoble although presumptuous, finds its great antagonist and the resulting tension flares up in the tragic conflict of this drama which Goethe called Euripides' finest.

Euripides was no unbeliever but a seeker: this is most clearly shown in Hecuba's prayer in *The Trojan Women*. In these Dionysiac rites his mind was relieved of the burden of a fruitless quest. For how long? We dare not say. We find words in the lyrics which reject *τὸ σοφόν* and thereby the Sophists' programme (395), words which praise the tranquillity of faith. Possibly the poet, in this second ode of the play, which has a programmatic function, allows the chorus to say things to which he does not himself subscribe. But who could fail to recognise in *βραχὺς αἰών* (397) the immediacy of a personal experience? At the end of a long and yet so short life the poet looks back and the result of his contemplation seems small compared with what it had cost him: so small that he begins to doubt the worth of his endless search and is prepared to reject it. Such a mood is understandable in an old man, but it can hardly have been more than a mood. His passionate search, his questioning arose from the very depth of his being, the same depth from which those masterpieces of the tragic stage emerged, which have borne his name across the centuries.

CHAPTER SEVEN

Tragedy in Post-Classical Times

A SURVEY of the richly varied work of Euripides will reveal many signs of a new development. Contemporary ideas are making themselves felt, the relationship between man and the world which surrounds him has altered, producing a change in the inner form of the drama. We are, however, unable to pursue this trend beyond Euripides. It is doubtful whether we could have established any significant development even had the bulk of fourth-century dramas been preserved. One tragedy of this period survives, the *Rhesus*, which was listed among the plays of Euripides because it was known that he had written a tragedy of this name. But even ancient critics refused to attribute it to him. It is the dramatisation of an episode in the tenth book of the *Iliad*, in which Odysseus and Diomede are on a spying expedition. It deals with the killing of the Trojan spy Dolon and of the Thracian king Rhesus, who had just come with his warriors to the aid of Troy.

What is most attractive in this play is its lyrical character, but the influence of tradition is visible everywhere; the morning song of the guard (546), for instance, derives from a song in the *Phaethon* of Euripides. This short drama displays a certain technical assurance. The action is smooth, the gods are skilfully staged; once, when the chorus of Trojan warriors is off stage because it is not allowed to see Odysseus and Diomede, a gap is bridged with a conversation between Athena and Alexander. But the entire play is curiously lifeless. Beyond these figures no problems loom concerning the meaning of their fate, nor are they convincing as human beings. Compared with the great figures of Sophocles or with those who in Euripides' masterpieces are driven by the irrational forces of passion, they are marionettes, enacting a fragment of an epic.

We should not treat the *Rhesus* – whose date is uncertain – as an absolutely typical example of late tragedy, and we must be cautious in our estimate of the plays that have been lost. It can be proved that the fourth century was exceptionally rich in dramatic works. The names of quite a number of poets and plays are known, and many of them dealt with subjects which cannot be found among the many surviving titles of fifth-century tragedies. The dramatisation of myths like that of Adonis and Cinyras was a sign of Hellenistic trends; they had not been used in classical tragedy. Dionysius the tyrant of Syracuse was the first, as far as we know, to use the subject of Adonis. Occasionally, historical subjects were dealt with again. A certain Moschion, who may have belonged to the third century, dealt in the *Pheraeae* with the death of the tyrant of Pherae, Alexander, and dramatised a great historical period in his *Themistocles*. The Carian ruler Mausolus, whose tomb was the original 'mausoleum,' became the hero of a tragedy by Theodectes.

Tragedy was no longer a purely Attic creation, as at its greatest period. We have no reason to doubt that Athens was still leading, both in the production of dramas and in the setting of standards; Aeschylus as well as Euripides had already had tragedies performed at royal courts outside their homeland. But it was in the fourth century that the spread of tragedy throughout the world of Hellenic culture began – a process which was finally completed during the great Hellenistic empires. The theatre became the main focus of culture, even in minor towns; the gymnasium – hardly less important – ranking second. Groups of strolling players became increasingly important in providing the Greek-speaking world with performances of tragedy. But although these circumstances help to explain tragedy's increasing independence of the country where it achieved greatness, there is a more important factor: tragedy grew out of the Attic *polis*, as did the incomparable comedies of Aristophanes. It developed, with the *polis*, from simple beginnings; it reflected the solemn gravity of its great moments in history, as well as the intellectual crises which heralded a new epoch. The end of the old *polis* actually meant the end of classical tragedy, however long its form might survive.

We can only guess how tragedy developed from then onwards. Presumably there was an increase in rhetoric, as well as the growing importance of contemporary music which accompanied the new dithyramb. Above all, the preoccupation with psychological subtlety, as in Euripides, must have affected the core of later tragedy – at the expense of the problems of human existence which were prominent in classical times.

All this remains conjecture and the actual development may have been far richer and more varied than we suspect. But there are a few indications which point to a diminished creativity. The earliest evidence that a classical tragedy was revived dates from 386, and we know from inscriptions that this became a firm tradition from the middle of that century onward. So as early as that fifth-century tragedy must have been considered 'classical' in the sense of an ideal form that could no longer be emulated. Significant also is the increased importance which public opinion attached to stage direction and performance. Attempts at impressive stage setting are already noticeable in Euripides, in the grouping of suppliants round an altar in opening scenes, for instance, or in the final scene on three levels in the *Orestes*, with Menelaus in front of the palace, the group round Orestes on the roof and Apollo and Helen on a *theologeion* that must have been situated higher still. But it is a considerable step to what we read in a scholiast on verse 57 of this drama, that a later stage director made Helen enter the palace in silence, in the opening scene, together with the booty from Troy. Here the intention of the stage direction is not, as it always was and still should be, to express the poet's words; it has become an end in itself. The name and date of this stage director are not known, but his example and similar ones indicate the trend of the new development.

The actors were considered even more important than the direction. H. Bulle was right when he observed: 'The oldest and most dangerous enemy of the dramatic poet was and is his most indispensable helper, the actor.' Under pressure from the actors the functions of poet, actor, stage manager and producer were no longer combined in a single person, as we saw in connection with Sophocles – though the practice may have persisted elsewhere in classical tragedy. As early as the end of the fifth century we find lively discussion about contrasting styles of acting, namely a restrained form in the tradition of Aeschylus, and a more contemporary type which aimed at effect through violent exaggeration. This in turn produced a reaction: in the fourth-century actors sought above all to appear natural. A certain Theodorus was praised because his voice sounded like a real person, not like an actor. His acting made such a deep impression on the notorious tyrant Alexander of Pherae that he had to try to hide his tears from the citizens.[1] At that time the women's parts were still acted by men and it was especially in such parts that Theodorus excelled. Another famous tragic actor of the fourth century, Polus, when acting the part of the Sophoclean Electra, brought on to the stage the urn containing the ashes of his own son, who had recently died, in order that Electra's great scene might be infused with his own suffering.[2] As actors became 'stars' their salaries rose in proportion: rulers who insisted on great performances with first-class actors could not afford to be parsimonious, and towns competed with them. An inscription from the Heraeum at Samos mentions an actor whose salary for one festival performance was so high that he had to give the Samians credit for part of it. These are symptoms of the decay of a great and noble art and it is a bad sign when Aristotle states (*Rhet.* 1403b) that in his lifetime actors were considered more important than poets.

Aristotle is also our source for another phenomenon. In contrast with the general public to whom the actor appeals, we now meet the individual who enjoys the reading of tragedies. *Rhet.* 1413b indicates that apart from dramas intended for performance, there are others which appeal especially to the reader. This was another factor which impaired the coherence of classical tragedies, which were written specifically for performance at the Dionysia, even if they might later appear in book form, to prevent them passing into oblivion.

Hellenistic tragedies of the third century were as numerous as those of the fourth, but equally little is known about them. We have plenty of names for this period, such as the seven Alexandrian poets who formed a Pleiad. Some of these rather ephemeral names will be dealt with shortly.

All the facts and conjectures put forward about fourth-century tragedy apply to the Hellenistic period also. Poets looked for recondite themes, hence the high proportion of fresh subject-matter used in this period. The myth of Adonis, dramatised by Dionysius the tyrant of Syracuse, recurs in Hellenistic tragedy and appeals again to a poet-ruler: Ptolemy Philopator wrote an *Adonis* and so did Philicus, one of the Pleiad mentioned above. There was

[1] Aelian, var. hist. 14, 40.

[2] Gellius, *Noctes Atticae* 6, 5.

an occasional attempt at historical drama. Not only did Philicus write a *Themistocles*, but Lycophron, referred to below, wrote a play dealing with Cassander. It is probable that fourth-century developments were again paralleled in a more rhetorical use of language and an increased subtlety in psychological portrayal. But these are no more than conjectures and the sad loss of evidence precludes us from judging in greater detail. Two works that are complete, or nearly so, survive as probable representatives of Hellenistic tragedy, but there is very little to be learnt from them.

The *Alexandra* by Lycophron, the best-known poet of the Pleiad, is one of the most remarkable works in Greek literature, but not one of the most attractive. Cassandra, the prophetess of Troy's doom, indulges in endless and enigmatic prophecies covering a long stretch of the future. The wording has been deliberately contorted, so that a great deal of scholarship is needed to disentangle its meaning. This monstrous concoction can hardly be called a tragedy. Action, the essence of drama, is completely lacking. It is not our concern to find a proper designation for the *Alexandra* – we can hardly call it an iambus – and it certainly teaches us nothing about Hellenistic tragedy.

The above is more valid – within limits – to the dramatisation, by a Jew called Ezekiel writing in the second century B.C., of those parts of the Old Testament which concern the exodus of the Jews from Egypt. Large sections of this Moses drama called *Exagogus* have been preserved in *Praeparatio Evangelica* by Eusebius. The poetry of this *Exagogus* is mediocre, the language, though it borrows from tragic idiom, rarely takes wings, and the dramatisation of the Biblical story is primitive. Nor does the dexterous introduction of the dream motif – which is historically interesting – and the addition of characters borrowed from the original make up for its deficiencies. The surviving fragments indicate two changes of scene, and a juxtaposition of events occurring at different times, which are technically remarkable. The action has been clearly divided into 'acts.' There were probably five, since Horace, who in his *Ars Poetica* gave a *résumé* of Hellenistic dramatic theories, confirms this division of dramas into five acts (189), which was unknown in classical plays. So little can be learnt about the role of the chorus in the *Exagogus* that it is not even certain that it still existed in Hellenistic tragedy. But the disappearance of the chorus from New Comedy does not seem to have influenced the development of tragedy, since the chorus was not only maintained in Roman tragedy but was referred to by Horace in his theoretical writings. As the division into acts became more rigid, the function of the chorus probably evolved into that of an *entre-acte*, as in the tragedies of Seneca. So there is, on the whole, very little to be learnt from Ezekiel, and the quality of his verse makes it unwise to regard him as a typical representative of Hellenistic tragedy.

Recent papyrus finds have also provided valuable information about later tragedy. One fragment published by E. Lobel[1] contains sixteen verses from a *Gyges* tragedy. They are part of a speech by the Queen on what had happened in her bedchamber, and suffice to show that the content of the play is identical with the account given by Herodotus. The wording here and there seems to point to an earlier tragedy, and it was first thought that Phrynichus might be the author. However, the notion that Herodotus simply copied his story from an existing tragedy is in itself most unlikely, and recently the later dating of the play – to the fourth or third century – has been proved beyond doubt. We may assume that this derivative dramatisation of a historical legend could no more dispense with changes of scene than Ezekiel's work.

The satyr plays of this period, which apparently flourished independently, had some peculiar features. Contemporary Alexandrian theories about the origins of tragedy showed, as we saw, a strong tendency to think in terms of rustic simplicity. Hence a return to the old form of satyr play. The poet Sositheus is praised in a second-century epigram[2] by Dioscorides for having revived the satyr play in its ancient ribaldry. We know of a *Daphnis* by Sositheus in which Heracles killed the ogre Lityerses and liberated Daphnis. His rediscovery of his beloved was at the time a well-worn motif.

Our information about satyr plays that made a butt of contemporary figures points to another tendency. The play *Agen*, which has been attributed to Python, by others even to Alexander the Great, still belongs to the fourth century; it poked fun at Harpalus, who fell from the king's grace, and at some ladies of easy virtue. For the Hellenistic period proper there is a record of a

[1] Proc. Brit. Ac. 35, 1950. [2] Anth. Pal. 7, 707.

Menedemus by Lycophron, in which the philosopher is taken to task in a whimsical, bantering manner. In a satyr play by Sositheus another philosopher, Cleanthes, became the target. These works represent a completely different trend from that shown by the revival of the old plays: the admixture of personal ridicule brings them closer to Old Comedy. They are, in fact, hybrid literary forms, symptoms of a period of decay.

We have now exhausted what little evidence is available for the later development of tragic plays. Equally important, for its influence on European literature, is another form of drama which succeeded fifth-century tragedy: New Comedy, known from the Menander discoveries in 1905 and from the comedies of Plautus and Terence. Satyrus, in his biography of Euripides,[1] made the inescapable observation that many motifs and figures from Euripidean tragedy persisted in this New Comedy. We should also realise the extent to which New Comedy continued the tradition of Aristophanes' comic plays. But motifs like the exposure of children, recognition, and many others which depend on *Tyche's* dispensations, have exact parallels in Euripidean tragedy and Menander himself likes to hint at the connection. Perhaps it is even more significant that this poet, who dominated the Athenian stage in the second half of the fourth century, perfected in his subtle character sketches what Euripides foreshadowed. Tragedy, linked as it was with religious cult, could never strip off its mythical garb, even when it had become a constraint. It is this tension between form and content which explains many features of Euripidean plays. Much of what was new in Menander's work found its appropriate form only in secular drama, which is precisely what we should consider Menander's plays to be. Here contemporary figures are no longer dressed up in a manner prescribed by myth; they move in complete freedom, smaller, less significant than those great figures who were rooted in the living myth and the living *polis*. And yet we are drawn to these human portraits, in their depth and richness, because at a time of vanished greatness they retain some of the precious light of Attic grace (*χάρις*).

This brief sketch of later developments has also attempted to explain ancient drama's far-reaching influence on Western culture. Classical and Hellenistic tragedy bore fruit in Roman authors,

[1] POxy 9/No. 1176.

especially in the type of tragic play which, in the work of Seneca, had such a profound influence in time to come. For a long time Seneca was practically the only representative of the classical tragedians for European authors, until the discovery of the Greek originals gave a new perspective to ancient culture and Greek tragedy began to exert a direct and powerful influence. It must remain a source of pride to the German people that they responded wholeheartedly to this influence in producing great and original work. Plato has expressed most beautifully how the strength of a nation can best prove itself in such creativity.

Greek tragedy's indirect influence on German, English and French literature, through the medium of the comedies, should not be underrated. We can only indicate this influence here, but they suffice to justify the words of Ulrich von Wilamowitz-Moellendorff: 'Without Attic drama, all we are familiar with in Europe would not exist, regardless of whether Greek influence was direct or indirect.'

We turn again to the thoughts with which we started this survey. The significance of Greek tragedy for the cultural life of those peoples who were the heirs of Hellas has been tremendous. But this does not explain why we return to it so often, nor what makes it great. More important than these connections with later cultures, we have tried to show that fifth-century Greek tragedy, so closely linked with the *polis*, is a unique historical phenomenon. As an expression of man's profound reflection on the problems of his existence, it has a timeless validity.

Notes on the Transmission of Texts

AN ACCOUNT is given by U. von Wilamowitz-Moellendorf in the third chapter of the introduction to his edition of the *Heracles*.[1] This is also an impressive contribution to cultural history. It should be compared with the relevant section of K. Ziegler's article 'Tragoedia' in Pauly-Wissowa-Kroll, *Real-Encyclopädie der classischen Altertumswissenschaft*.[2]

The subject, with its specialised literature, is studied further in the writer's *Die tragische Dichtung der Hellenen*,[3] and in his series of articles on tragedy and tragic poets which began in 1948 in *Anzeiger für die Altertumswissenschaft* and which it is planned to continue during 1968.

Attic tragedy was intended for performance at the festival of the Dionysia. During its greatest period in the fifth century, it was never intended only to be read. This did not, however, prevent tragedies – once they had been performed – from being circulated in manuscript form. This is proved by the comedies of Aristophanes, which presuppose a widespread and exact knowledge of tragic poetry which could only result from the practice of reading. These manuscripts no doubt took the form of rolls of papyrus, the writing probably being similar to that of contemporary inscriptions cut in stone. This would have meant that words were not separated and that there was hardly any punctuation. Choric songs would be treated as prose and not divided into sentences or verses. The two centuries which followed Attic tragedy's climax (before Alexandrian scholarship began to assert itself) were the most precarious for the survival of tragic texts. We do not know how far the texts were altered by copyists, but there is no reason to be too pessimistic on this account. More information is available about another danger: the previous chapter described the increasing importance of actors, who could thus take greater liberties with the text. There is direct evidence for this, e.g. from Quintilian who speaks of alterations to an Aeschylean tragedy for a revival in Athens, and of

[1] Berlin, 1889. The first four chapters were reprinted as *Einleitung in die griechische Tragödie* (Berlin, 1910).

[2] II Reihe, 12 Halbb., 2067 ff.

[3] Göttingen, 1956; 2e. 1964.

the public's approval of such practices.[1] It is extremely difficult to locate such changes in the surviving texts. Denys L. Page has dealt with this matter very thoroughly.[2] We should not jump to the conclusion that we are faced with an actor's interpolation whenever our sense of logic or aesthetic sensibility is jarred, but the seriousness of these threats to the authenticity of the texts in the period between the classical age and Alexandrian scholarship is made clear by the report of a counter-measure. According to Pseudo-Plutarch[3] the orator and politician Lycurgus ordered, as part of his reform of the theatre (about 330), that an official copy of the plays of the three great tragedians be made and held in safe keeping. These texts would be binding for all future performances, and would preclude arbitrary changes. Here the main concern was not with questions of scholarship bearing on single words but with violations of the text which affected the entire structure of the play.

The men who founded the great library at Alexandria, in the first half of the third century, under Ptolemy Philadelphus, were probably well aware of the importance of the official Athenian texts. Therefore a late report (second century A.D.) in the physician Galenus' explanation of Hippocrates' *Epidemics* (607 Kühn) may be accepted as basically reliable. According to this Euergetes, the third of the Ptolemies (history would point rather to the second, Philadelphus), brought to Alexandria, at great expense and by some rather doubtful manoeuvres, an Athenian edition of the three great tragedians. This can hardly have been anything but the official text of Lycurgus.

We have no evidence of work on the tragedians by earlier Alexandrian scholars, though this does not preclude its possibility. Aristophanes of Byzantium (about 257–180), an outstanding director of the library at Alexandria, made a decisive contribution to the preservation of Greek tragedy. His work in the service of the great Greek authors – including Homer, the lyric poets, and his namesake – is clearly attested in the case of Euripides. But he must have dealt with the other two tragedians and the texts which now, in their various copies, form the basis of our editions presumably bear his mark. His work included a corpus of reliable texts, the scansion of choric songs – which he also established for the Greek lyrists – and elucidations, the traces of which can still be found in the commentaries to the manuscripts, the so-called 'scholia'.

This type of scholarship continued after Aristophanes, but little is known about it. When the great period of Alexandrian learning and scholarly creativity had passed, and its rich results were being dissipated,

[1] *Institutio Oratoria* (10, 1, 66).
[2] *Actors' Interpolations in Greek Tragedy* (Oxford, 1934).
[3] *Vitae Decem Oratorum*, 7.

one scholar, known to have been a contemporary of Cicero, took up the task. Didymus of Alexandria was less gifted than his great predecessors, but this man, who was such a hard worker that his contemporaries called him χαλκέντερος ('with brass bowels') collected the work of his predecessors in commentaries and in a special lexicon and so preserved them for posterity. His name has become a focal point from which to trace the influence of Alexandrian scholarship in later times.

When we read that the library at Alexandria considered 123 of the Sophoclean plays to be genuine whereas only seven now survive, not counting the *Ichneutae* fragment, we realise the extent of our loss. But this difference is not only the result of accidental losses. Other causes can be established, including one which was decisive. The tragedians gradually became too hard to understand, the knowledge of language and poetry which they demanded being too irksome; their reading finally became an academic pursuit, at the expense of lively current interest. The students could not read all the plays, so a selection was made and editions with explanatory notes were introduced. These did not require the standard of serious scholarship formerly taken for granted. Some such lowering of standards must have occurred during the development of classical culture, particularly in the second century A.D.

At about this time a school edition must have been produced whose contents were decisive for the preservation of ancient tragedies. The survival of single plays which were presumably intended to be used for comparison – such as the *Seven against Thebes*, *Oedipus the King*, *The Phoenician Women*, and the three tragedies which deal with Electra – indicates that the choice of works by the three great tragedians was probably made by one man, who thus prescribed for his age and ours.

The important points about the Euripidean tradition are discussed below, but generally speaking it was the selection just mentioned on which all knowledge of Attic tragedy has depended. This knowledge survived the barren period between the closing of the University of Athens (529 A.D.) and the emergence of diligent scholarship in Byzantium in the ninth century. Then, when such men as Photius and Arethas applied their care and zeal to the texts, their permanence was assured. Next the Byzantine copyists set to work. These have long been the scapegoats of modern scholars, who have made them responsible for some too hastily assumed corruptions as well as actual ones. Thanks to more recent research and to the occasional check provided by papyrus fragments containing remnants of ancient editions, their conscientiousness is now receiving due praise and gratitude. However, the work of Byzantine scholars from the thirteenth century onwards is a different matter. Philologists, Demetrius Triclinius for example, dealt high-handedly with the texts and made arbitrary alterations. It is obvious that whenever the history of individual manuscripts is much older, as with Aeschylus and Sophocles, we have a better chance of coming close to the Alexandrian text.

Sources of error have been numerous on the long road of transmission, both before and after Alexandria. We cannot discuss in detail the research which remains to be done, but generally speaking additional knowledge has increased our confidence in the texts as they have come down to us.

From Byzantium the texts reached the West by routes which can sometimes be followed in detail. Instances of this important traffic will be mentioned in connection with Aeschylus and Euripides. Thus the great Greek tragedians became the common property of European culture, and their influence could spread far and strike deep. This could only be indicated in our sketch of post-classical tragedy.

For each of the tragedians a brief account of the actual transmission of their manuscripts is given below in the relevant part of the bibliography.

Bibliography

To the bibliography given in the appendices of the German edition has been added a representative selection of English titles.

WHAT IS TRAGEDY?

THE EXTREMELY full bibliography for this chapter shows how animatedly the subject has been discussed. We have mainly quoted works which have a bearing on the problems dealt with in the introductory section.

M. Scheler, 'Über das Tragische'. *Die Weißen Blätter*, 1914, 758. (Abhandlungen und Aufsätze 1, Leipzig, 1915, 275).

J. Volkelt, *Ästhetik des Tragischen* (4e., Munich, 1923).

P. Friedländer, 'Die griechische Tragödie und das Tragische' (Die Antike 1, 1925, 8).

J. Geffcken, 'Der Begriff des Tragischen in der Antike' (*Vortr. Bibl. Warburg*, 1927–28, Berlin, 1930, 89).

O. Walzel, 'Vom Wesen des Tragischen' (*Euphorion* 34, 1933, 1).

Th. Haecker, *Schöpfer und Schöpfung* (Leipzig, 1934).

J. Bernhardt, *De profundis* (2e., Leipzig, 1939) 141: 'Der Mensch in der tragischen Welt'.

M. Kommerell, *Lessing und Aristoteles* (Frankfurt a.M., 1940).

J. Sellmair, *Der Mensch in der Tragik* (2e. Krailing, Munich, 1941).

F. Sengle, 'Vom Absoluten in der Tragödie' (*German Quarterly Review* 20, 1942, 265).

E. Staiger, 'Kleists Bettelweib von Locarno' (*German Quarterly Review* 21, 1943, 287).

A. Weber, *Das Tragische und die Geschichte* (Hamburg, 1943).

W. Hamilton Fyfe, *Aristotle, The Poetics* (Oxford, rev. ed. 1964).

H. Bogner, *Der tragische Gegensatz* (Heidelberg, 1947; cf. *Gnomon* 21, 1949, 211).

K. Jaspers, *Von der Wahrheit* (Munich, 1947). The section on Tragedy is also published separately (Munich, 1952).

H. J. Baden, *Das Tragische* (2e. Berlin, 1948).

B. von Wiese, *Die deutsche Tragödie von Lessing bis Hebbel* (Hamburg, 1948).
G. Nebel, *Weltangst und Götterzorn* (Stuttgart, 1951; cf. *Gnomon* 25, 1953, 161).
M. Dietrich, *Europäische Dramaturgie* (Vienna, 1952).
C. del Grande, ΤΡΑΓΩΙΔΙΑ (2e. Naples, 1962).
H. Weinstock, *Die Tragödie des Humanismus* (Heidelberg, 1953; cf. O. Regenbogen, *Gnomon* 26, 1954, 289).
M. Pohlenz, *Die griechische Tragödie* (2e. Göttingen, 1954).
K. von Fritz, 'Tragische Schuld und poetische Gerechtigkeit in der griechischen Tragödie' (*Studium Generale* 8, 1955, 194 and 219). This important study has now been included in the volume of essays: *Antike und moderne Tragödie. Neun Abhandlungen* (Berlin, 1962) whose other sections are also of importance for the problem of the tragic in individual plays.
M. Untersteiner, *Le Origini della tragedia e del tragico* (Turin, 1955).
G. Else, *Aristotle's Poetics: The Argument* (Cambridge, Mass., 1957).
W. Schadewaldt, 'Furcht und Mitleid?' (*Hermes* 83, 1955; cf. also the introduction of his edition of Hölderlin's translation of Sophocles in the Fischer Library, 1957).
J. Jones, *On Aristotle and Greek Tragedy* (London, 1963).
A. C. Schlesinger, *Boundaries of Dionysus* (Harvard U.P., 1963).

COLLECTIONS, FRAGMENTS, WORKS ON THE ORIGINS OF TRAGEDY

J. L. Klein, *Geschichte des Dramas* I (Leipzig, 1874), is still a valuable contribution. U. von Wilamowitz-Moellendorff's history of the transmission of the texts has already been mentioned on p. 209. M. Pohlenz, *Die griechische Tragödie*, in two volumes (2e. Göttingen, 1954), deals with the entire subject in detail and emphasises the connection between the works and their political and historical background. The second volume with the notes contains valuable information on special subjects. The writer's *Die Tragische Dichtung der Hellenen*, which appeared in 1956, was referred to on p. 209. H. D. F. Kitto, *Greek Tragedy: A Literary Study* (3e. London, 1961), provides an excellent, lively survey; as does the same author's *Form and Meaning in Drama: A Study of Six Greek Plays and of Hamlet* (London, 1956). D. W. Lucas provides a good introduction in *The Greek Tragic Poets* (2e. London, 1959). The vital points are brought out by J. de Romilly in her study *L'évolution du pathetique d'Eschyle à Euripide* (Paris, 1961). Ph. W. Harsh, *A Handbook of Classical Drama* (Stanford, 1948), is well organised and provides a crisp, comprehensive study of the whole field of Greek and Roman drama.

W. Schmid contributed important monographs on each of the three tragedians in the relevant sections of his *Geschichte der griechischen Literatur:* for Aeschylus and Sophocles I/2 (Munich, 1934), for Euripides I/3 (Munich, 1940). To these can now be added the corresponding chapters in the writer's *Geschichte der griechischen Literatur* (2e. Bern, 1963; *A History of Greek Literature*, London, 1966).

The excellent work on Athenian inscriptions by A. Wilhelm, *Urkunden dramatischer Aufführungen in Athen* (Vienna, 1906), has made a great contribution to the history of Greek drama. And we can still recommend, as a brief introduction to the complex problem of this evidence, the review of Wilhelm's book by W. Reisch in *Zeitschr. f. österr. Gymn.* (1907, 289 ff.). The inscriptions are now also easily accessible in a book we shall refer to again: *Dramatic Festivals* by A. Pickard-Cambridge, whose treatment is excellent.

Some monographs on individual parts of the Attic tragedies should be mentioned because of the interpretations they contain. Walter Nestle, 'Die Struktur des Eingangs in der attischen Tragödie' (*Tübinger Beiträge* 10, Stuttgart 1930); W. Schadewaldt, 'Monolog und Selbstgespräch' (*N. Phil. Unters.* 2, Berlin, 1926); W. Kranz, *Stasimon, Untersuchungen zu Form und Gehalt der griechischen Tragödie* (Berlin, 1933); J. Duchemin, *L'ΑΓΩΝ dans la tragédie grecque* (Paris, 1945); W. Jens, 'Die Stychomythie in der frühen griechischen Tragödie' (*Zetemata* 11, Munich, 1955); Leif Bergson, *L'epithète ornamentale dans Esch. Soph. et Eur.* (Uppsala, 1956); W. Kraus, 'Strophengestaltung in der griech. Tragödie', I: Aisch. u. Soph. (*Sitzb. Öst. Akad. Phil.-hist. Kl.* 231/4, 1957); H. F. Johansen, *General Reflection in Tragic Rhesis* (Copenhagen, 1959); H. H. Bacon, *Barbarians in Greek Tragedy* (Yale U.P., 1961); R. Lattimore, *Story Patterns in Greek Tragedy* (London, 1964).

K. Heinemann examines the survival of tragedy in *Die tragischen Gestalten der Griechen in der Weltliteratur* (Leipzig, 1920). A great deal of material can also be found in H. Hunger, *Lexikon der griechischen und Römischen Mythologie* (3e. Vienna, 1956), and in Käte Hamburger, *Von Sophokles zu Sartre* (Stuttgart, 1962). There is also a relevant chapter in Margret Dietrich, *Das moderne Drama* (2e. Stuttgart, 1963).

Since archaeology has uncovered the structures of many ancient theatres new problems have arisen which have been widely studied. M. Bieber gives a good general introduction in her *Die Denkmäler zum Theaterwesen im Altertum* (Berlin, 1920) and in *The History of Greek and Roman Theater* (2e. Princeton, 1961); so does A. Pickard-Cambridge in *The Theatre of Dionysus in Athens* (Oxford, 1946). L. Sechan,

Études sur la tragédie grecque dans ses rapports avec la ceramique (Paris, 1926), is concerned with the attractive, though difficult to establish, connections between theatre and vase painting, while R. Löhrer, *Mienenspiel und Maske in der griechischen Tragödie* (Paderborn, 1927), deals with questions often raised by those who are used to the lively facial expressions of modern actors. G. Capone, *L'arte scenica degli attori tragici greci* (Padua, 1935), and A. Spitzbarth, *Untersuchungen zur Spieltechnik der griechischen Tragödie* (Diss. Zürich, 1946), deal with the same subject. On the subject of masks, the relevant article by M. Bieber in the 14th vol. of the *Real-Encyclopädie der class. Altertumswissenschaft* is very useful. Two excellent works on the ancient theatre are A. Pickard-Cambridge, *The Dramatic Festivals of Athens* (Oxford, 1953), and T. B. L. Webster, *Greek Theatre Production* (London, 1956). This latter has an exhaustive list of the monuments; the same author has now provided a bibliography in *Lustrum* 1956/1 (1957), and two exceptionally useful surveys: 'Monuments Illustrating Tragedy and Satyr Play' (*Bulletin of the Institute of Classical Studies*, University of London, Supplement 14, 1962) and *Griechische Bühnenaltertümer* (Göttingen, 1963). R. C. Flickinger, *The Greek Theater and its Drama* (4e. Chicago, 1960), gives information about stage techniques. P. Arnott puts forward the view that the Greek stage thoroughly renounced the use of illusion in two books: *An Introduction to the Greek Theatre* (London, 1959) and *Greek Scenic Conventions in the Fifth Century B.C.* (Oxford, 1962).

We add here the collections of fragments of Greek tragedies which have not been attributed to known poets. A. Nauck, *Tragicorum Graecorum Fragmenta* (2e. Leipzig, 1889), is still of basic importance. Since its appearance a number of papyrus finds have added considerably to our knowledge. Roger A. Pack, *The Greek and Latin Literary Texts from Greco-Roman Egypt* (Univ. of Michigan Press, 1952; new ed. 1965) is a useful guide here. The writer's *Geschichte der griechischen Literatur* (mentioned above) and the learned journals should also be consulted regarding recent discoveries. A number of important papyrus fragments of tragedies have been published in a volume of the Loeb Classical Library with translation and commentaries by D. L. Page: *Greek Literary Papyri* (London, 1941, new revised edition, 1950).

T. B. L. Webster provides a sound, comprehensive assessment of fourth-century tragedy in his essay: 'Fourth Century Tragedy and the Poetics' (*Hermes* 82, 1954, 294), and in his book *Art and Literature in Fourth Century Athens* (London, 1956); see also his *Hellenistic Poetry and Art* (London, 1964). F. Schramm deals with the pitiful remnants of Hellenistic tragedy in *Tragicorum Graecorum hellenisticae quae dicitur aetatis fragmenta eorumque de vita atque poesi testimonia collecta et illustrata* (Diss. Münster, 1929). D. L. Page, in a new chapter in *The History of Greek Tragedy* (Cambridge, 1951), takes a different view on the Gyges fragment to that taken in the present work. The same material is dealt with by Ziegler in an article in the *Real-Encyclopädie* which we shall mention presently. The *Exagoge* by Ezekiel, which Schramm did not include, has been published by J. Wieneke in *Ezechielis Judaei poetae Alexandrini fabulae quae inscribitur ΕΞΑΓΩΓΗ fragmenta* (Münster, 1931). The text has now also appeared in an edition of the *Praeparatio Evangelica* by K. Mras. G. F. Else, in his commentary on Aristotle's Poetics, already mentioned in the section 'What is Tragedy?', has useful remarks on fourth century tragedy.

Most important for the problems of the origin of tragedy is A. Pickard-Cambridge: *Dithyramb, Tragedy and Comedy* (Oxford, 1927), of which T. B. L. Webster has produced a second edition with a wealth of additional material (Oxford, 1962). The latter has also written an interesting article on the subject in *Fifty Years of Classical Scholarship* (ed. M. Platnauer; Oxford, 1954). Surveys of these extraordinarily complex problems and the way they have been dealt with more recently are given by K. Ziegler in his article 'Tragoedia' in the *Real-Encyclopädie* 6A, 1937, 1899, by C. del Grande in *ΤΡΑΓΩΙΔΙΑ Essenza e genesi della tragedia* (Naples, 1952; second revised and enlarged edition, Naples, 1962), and in the writer's *Die tragische Dichtung der Hellenen*. M. Untersteiner, *Le origini della tragedia e del tragico* (Turin, 1955), puts forward some very bold hypotheses. The link with the Dithyramb being thus asserted, H. Patzer rejects the connection with satyr plays in *Die Anfänge der griechischen Tragödie* (Wiesbaden, 1962). Br. Zucchelli provides a good survey of an ancillary problem in 'Hypokrites' (*Studi grammaticali e linguistici* 3. Paideia, 1963). A notable short survey is given by R. Browning, 'A Byzantine Treatise on Tragedy' (*Acta Universitatis Carolinae of Prague*, 1963; *Graeco-Latina Argensia*, pp. 67–81).

AESCHYLUS

In our history of the transmission of texts we spoke of a selection of tragedies made for schools. For Aeschylus only one copy of this edition, containing seven tragedies, safely reached Byzantium. This manuscript, which in its writing and with its added variants probably resembled the famous Menander papyrus, was the basis of the Byzantine copies. Of these only one containing all the seven plays has survived: the Mediceus Laurentianus 32, 9, which is also the oldest and most reliable copy. It was transcribed in Constantinople about 1000 and brought to Italy by the humanist G. Aurispa – who collected manuscripts systematically – in 1423. This copy reached the library of the Medici at Florence, the Laurentian, in the second half of the fifteenth century. From the plays which came down to them the Byzantines made an even smaller selection: the *Prometheus*, the *Seven*, and *The Persians*. The oldest witness for this group is the Ambrosianus (C inf. 222) of the thirteenth century, in Milan. The *Agamemnon* and *The Eumenides* were later added to this Byzantine triad. Apart from the Laurentianus 31, 8, which dates from the end of the fourteenth century, we should mention here a manuscript of between 1316 and 1320 written by Demetrius Triclinius himself, the copyist we mentioned earlier. This manuscript, now in Naples, is a good example of his irresponsible methods. All the data concerning the transmission of the texts is given in the best editions (see below) and in A. Turyn, *The Manuscript Tradition of the Tragedies of Aeschylus* (New York, 1943). Note also R. Dawe, *Collation of the Manuscripts of Aeschylus* (Cambridge, 1964). The Mediceus Laurentianus 32, 9 is by no means the source of all the other manuscripts. The copies of the Byzantine triad especially point to a common model which in turn goes back to that ancient selection which we must assume to have been the basis of our entire Aeschylean tradition.

Among the older editions we must mention that of G. Hermann, which appeared posthumously and is available in the second edition (Leipzig, 1859). We cannot overestimate the merit of this great philologist: it becomes evident in view of the kind of text W. von Humboldt had to use for his translation of the *Agamemnon* (1816), which led Goethe to admire Aeschylus. U. von Wilamowitz-Moellendorff has dedicated to the memory of Hermann his fundamental edition (Berlin, 1914; a minor edition, 1915). Together with this he brought out a volume of *Aischylos Interpretationen* (Berlin, 1914). Among the latest editions are: P. Mazon, 2 vols. with French translation (Paris, 1920–25, now available in the fifth edition, 1949); H. W. Smyth, 2 vols. with English translation and the fragments (London, 1922–26; vol. 2 revised by H. Lloyd-Jones, 1957); G. Murray (Oxford, 1937, 2e. 1955); M. Untersteiner (Milan, 1946–47). The recent papyrus discoveries in Egypt, which produced unexpected material on Aeschylus, have been dealt with by H. J. Mette in *Supplementum Aeschyleum* (Berlin, 1959); he followed this with a volume of commentary, *Der verlorene Aischylos* (Berlin, 1963).

Among English translations those by G. Murray (London, 1920–30) are renowned. E. Hamilton has rendered the *Prometheus Bound* and the *Agamemnon* (N.Y., 1937). All the seven plays are included in *The*

Complete Greek Tragedies, the outstanding series of translations edited by David Grene and Richmond Lattimore (Chicago University Press). Penguin Books have brought out the *Oresteia* (Harmondsworth, 1959) and *Prometheus Bound, The Suppliant Maidens, Seven Against Thebes,* and *The Persians* (Harmondsworth, 1961), all translated by P. Vellacott. All the plays are translated by G. M. Cookson in a volume in the Everyman Library (London and N.Y., 1956).

We note the following monographs: J. T. Sheppard, *Aeschylus and Sophocles – Their Work and Influence* (London, 1927); Br. Snell, 'Aischylos und das Handeln im Drama' (*Phil. Suppl.* 20/1; Leipzig, 1928); Walter Nestle, 'Menschliche Existenz und politische Erziehung in der Tragödie des Aischylos' (*Tüb. Beitr.* 23, Stuttgart, 1934); G. Murray, *Aeschylus the Creator of Tragedy* (Oxford, 1940, Paperback edition 1962); W. B. Stanford, *Aeschylus in his Style* (Dublin, 1942); F. R. Earp, *The Style of Aeschylus* (Cambridge, 1948); K. Reinhardt, *Aischylos als Regisseur und Theologe* (Bern, 1949); F. Solmsen, 'Hesiod and Aeschylus' (*Cornell Studies in Classical Philology* 30; Ithaca, 1949); A. Maddalena, *Interpretazioni Eschilee* (Turin, 1951); E. T. Owen, *The Harmony of Aeschylus* (Toronto, 1952); G. Thomson, *Aischylos und Athen* (Berlin, 1955); J. de Romilly, *La crainte et l'angoisse dans le théâtre d'Eschyle* (Paris, 1958); E. R. Dodds, article on 'Religious Ideas in Aeschylus' (*Trans. Proc. Camb. Phil. Assoc.*, 1960); and A. Rivier, 'Eschyle et le tragique Études de lettres'; (*Bull. de la Fac. de Lettres de l'Univ. de Lausanne et de la Soc. des Et. de Lettres*, Serie II tome 6, Lausanne, 1963, No. 73), with its radical denial of the existence of free will in Aeschylus' characters.

Among editions with commentaries E. Fraenkel's takes pride of place, his monumental *Agamemnon* in three volumes being important for the entire study of tragedy. The edition of the same play by D. L. Page and J. D. Denniston (Oxford, 1957) should not be overlooked. Excellent also are a number of Dutch commentaries: *The Suppliants* by J. Vürtheim, the other plays by P. Groeneboom. H. D. Broadhead's edition of this play (Cambridge, 1960) offers a thorough commentary; he has also produced *The Persae of Aeschylus* (Cambridge, 1960). W. Kraus has dealt with the *Prometheus* in the *Real-Encyclopädie*, 23, 1956, 666.

SOPHOCLES

The Mediceus Laurentianus 32, 9, is here also the most valuable basis for our knowledge. The Sophoclean text, transcribed in the eleventh century, was later bound together with those of Aeschylus and

Apollonius of Rhodes. There exist moreover 95 manuscripts from the eleventh to the sixteenth centuries, the vast majority of which (70) in fact contain only that triad (*Ajax*, *Electra*, *Oedipus the King*) which the Byzantine editors also had again selected. The long-standing assumption that only one copy, the basis of all further transcriptions, survived into the Middle Ages is very much open to question today. Apart from the Laurentianus, the Parisinus gr. 2712, which dates from the thirteenth century, has been considered of special significance. However the important works of A. Turyn, the latest being 'Studies in the Manuscript Tradition of the Tragedies of Sophocles' (*Illinois Studies* 36, Urbana 1952), reopened the question of the Sophoclean tradition and made the value of this manuscript doubtful.

Among the editions that of R. C. Jebb (Cambridge, 1883–96; reprinted with few changes in 1902 and 1908), with critical apparatus and commentaries, is outstanding. Jebb also brought out a students' edition with a shortened critical apparatus (Cambridge, 1897). The reliable Schneidewin-Nauck edition with commentary has appeared revised in small single volumes, which are a valuable introduction to Sophoclean tragedy: E. Bruhn, *Oid. Tyr.* 1910, *Electra* 1912, *Antigone* 1913; L. Radermacher, *Oid Kol.* 1909, *Philoktetes* 1911, *Ajax* 1913, *Trachiniae* 1914 (all Berlin). Valuable also is the 8th volume of this collection (Berlin, 1899; reprinted 1963), in which E. Bruhn deals with Sophocles' use of language. Among the translations of the Dutch classicist J. C. Kamerbeek, that of *The Women of Trachis* should be noted (Leyden, 1950). P. Masqueray provides a French translation in his edition (2 vols., second revised edition, Paris, 1929–34). Three volumes of a new edition in the *Collection des Universités de France*, by A. Dain with P. Mazon's translation (Paris, 1950–60), have appeared which include the surviving tragedies; a further volume containing the *Ichneutae* and the more important fragments was to follow. A. C. Pearson's edition (Oxford, 1924) makes full use (after the Laurentianus) of the Parisinus gr. 1712 manuscript. W. B. Stanford's edition of the *Ajax* (London, 1963) has an excellent commentary.

The papyrus finds which gave us Sophocles' *Ichneutae* have been conveniently assembled in their original form by E. Diehl in *Supplementum Sophocleum* (Bonn, 1913). They have also been incorporated in the great 3-volume edition of the Sophoclean fragments, with commentary, by A. C. Pearson (Cambridge, 1917). This was intended as a supplement to Jebb. The references in the general bibliography should be noted.

Translations into English by G. Murray include *Antigone*, *Trachiniae*, and *Oedipus at Colonus* (London, 1941, 1947, 1948). E. F. Watling has done *Oedipus Rex*, *Oedipus at Colonus*, and *Antigone* (Harmondsworth, 1947 and 1949; N.Y. 1947) and *Ajax*, *Electra*, *Women of Troy* and *Philoctetes* (London, 1953), all for Penguin Books. All the surviving plays are included in *The Complete Greek Tragedies*, mentioned under Aeschylus. Also Th. Howard Banks, *Antigone*, *Oedipus Rex*, *Oedipus at Colonus* (Oxford and N.Y., 1956). H. D. F. Kitto has translated three plays (Oxford, 1963–64).

For a long time the impressive forcefulness of Aeschylus and the rich variety of the work of Euripides caused Sophocles to be somewhat neglected, but more recently scholars have largely concentrated on the latter, with the result that we now have quite a number of good books on Sophocles. Tycho von Wilamowitz, *Die dramatische Technik des Sophokles* (Berlin, 1917) rather antedates this renewed interest, but at that time the emphasis on the technical aspect of the plays, as against interpretations *in vacuo*, was extremely important. A reaction against overrating the technique of the writing was bound to follow. It is implicit in a number of recent Sophoclean books of which we select the following: T. B. L. Webster, *An Introduction to Sophocles* (Oxford, 1936); F. R. Earp, *The Style of Sophocles* (Cambridge, 1944); C. M. Bowra, *Sophoclean Tragedy* (Oxford, 1944, repr. 1947); K. Reinhardt, *Sophocles* (3e. Frankfurt a.M., 1948), probably the most penetrating of all Sophocles studies, and a pioneering work for its elucidation of the poet's later style; H. Weinstock, *Sophocles* (3e. Wuppertal, 1948); A. J. A. Waldock, *Sophocles the Dramatist* (Cambridge, 1951); C. H. Whitman, *Sophocles: A Study of Heroic Humanism* (Cambridge, Mass., 1951); R. F. Goheen, *The Imagery of Sophocles' Antigone* (Oxford, 1951); J. C. Opstelten, *Sophocles and Greek Pessimism* (Amsterdam, 1952); V. Ehrenberg, *Sophocles and Pericles* (Oxford, 1954; German edition Munich, 1956), a most illuminating work since it emphasises the intellectual tension which determines the inner structure of the classical plays; B. M. W. Knox, *Oedipus at Thebes* (Yale U.P. and O.U.P., 1957); G. M. Kirkwood, *A Study of Sophoclean Drama* (Ithaca, 1958); H. D. F. Kitto, *Sophocles: Dramatist and Philosopher* (Oxford, 1958); A. Maddalena, *Sophocle* (2e. Turin, 1963); J. H. Kells, 'Problems of Interpretation in "Antigone" ' (*Bull. Inst. Class. Stud. London*, 1963). The Wissenschaftliche Buchgesellschaft has brought together three essays on Sophocles (by Diller, Schadewaldt and Lesky), in *Gottheit und Mensch in der Tragödie des Sophokles* (Darmstadt, 1963). The research report by H. F. Johansen, 'Sophokles 1939–59' (*Lustrum* 1962/7), is an outstanding aid to study. According to Franz Egermann's essay 'Arete und tragische Bewusstheit bei Sophokles und Herodot' in *Vom Menschen in der Antike* (Munich, 1957, 1–128) the major part of the literature on Sophocles, including the present book, is utterly mistaken. Implicitly, everything Aristotle, Goethe and Hölderlin have said about tragedy and the tragic goes overboard. It would be inappropriate and distasteful to embark on old-fashioned polemics here. Instead the writer prefers to quote Egermann himself (p. 94): 'It is not surprising that Lesky cannot agree.'

EURIPIDES

For the tradition of Euripides our material is more copious. A. Turyn's 'The Byzantine Manuscript Tradition of Tragedies of Euripides' (*Illinois Studies in Language and Literature*, Volume 43, Urbana, 1957) is a basic work. Here also our first encounter is with traces of an ancient edition with commentary, from which one line of transmission has handed on nine plays: *Hecuba*, *Orestes*, *The Suppliant Women*, *Andromache*, *Hippolytus*, *The Medea*, *Alcestis*, *The Trojan Women* and *Rhesus*. Since it is possible that *The Bacchae*, which has been preserved through another line of transmission, originally belonged to this group, we might have here a selection of ten plays with commentary. For this the best witness is the Marcianus 471 which dates from the twelfth century. This contains the first five plays of the series. For Euripides there is no text of the same age and significance as the Laurentianus 32, 9, but the greater number of important manuscripts have proved very helpful. The Parisinus 2712, of the thirteenth century, comes next in importance to the Marcianus, to which it adds *The Medea;* then there is the Vaticanus 909, also thirteenth century, which contains the nine plays mentioned, and the Parisinus 2713 (twelfth–thirteenth century) which lacks the last two plays of this series.

B. Snell (*Hermes* 1935, 119) has given a plausible explanation of how it happened that the total of ten plays from the original selection (including *The Bacchae*) was increased by nine. A papyrus edition of Euripides, in which each play was written on a single roll, was stored in vessels containing five rolls each, arranged in alphabetical order. Of these jars two reached the Byzantines. One contained *Hecuba* (which already existed in the edition with commentary), *Helen*, *Electra*, *Heracles* and *The Heracleidae;* the other *The Cyclops*, *Ion*, *The Suppliant Women* and the two Iphigeneia tragedies. These remnants of the complete alphabetical edition form the second line of transmission and can be added to the plays of the selection. Proof of this group can be found in the Laurentianus 32, 2, which was transcribed at the beginning of the thirteenth century, appeared at Avignon in 1348, and reached the private library of the Medici in the fifteenth century. Of the nineteen dramas, only *The Trojan Women* is lacking here. A second manuscript which combined Palatinus 287 and Laurentianus conv. suppr. 172, is now considered to be a copy of Laurentianus 32, 3. This contradicts the earlier opinion of P. Maas (*Gnomon* 1926, 156). A new book by G. Zuntz tells us that the plays with no commentaries are copied direct from the Laurentianus, after Triclinius' preliminary corrections, while the plays available in the selection were taken from a copy of their common archetype, also amended by Triclinius. For the Euripidean tradition the work of E. Fraenkel, 'Zu den Phoen. des Eur.' (*Sitzb. Bayer. Akad. Phil.-hist. Kl.*, 1963/1), is important, for here the question of how far our text has been defaced by interpolations is energetically taken up again.

A. Kirchhoff's edition (Berlin, 1855) was the first to create a sound basis for modern textual criticism. The edition of the great philologist A. Nauck in three volumes (3e. Leipzig, 1892–95) is still very useful. Outstanding today are G. Murray's three volumes (Oxford, 1902–10), and the bilingual edition in the *Collection des Universités de France* (Budé) by L. Méridier, L. Parmentier, and H. Gregoire, of which six volumes have appeared (Paris, 1923–61), with *Iph. Aul.*, *Rhes.* still lacking. A bilingual edition has started to appear in Spain: A. Tovar, *Eur. Tragedias*, Vol. 1: *Alc.*, *Andr.* (Barcelona, 1955), and by the same author with R. P. Binda, Vol. 2: *Bacch.*, *Hec.* (Barcelona, 1960). Among the editions with commentary the *Heracles* of U. von Wilamowitz-Moellendorff (2e. Berlin, 1909) is still outstanding. He brought out the *Hippolytus* in 1891 and the *Ion* in 1926. H. Weil in *Sept Tragédies d'Euripide* (Paris, 1896–1907) has given a subtle analysis of *Hipp.*, *Med.*, *Hec.*, *Iph. Aul.*, *Iph. Taur.*, *Alc.*, *Or.* The Oxford editions with commentary are eminently useful: D. L. Page, *Med.* 1938; M. Platnauer, *Iph. Taur.* 1938; J. D. Denniston, *El.* 1939; A. S. Owen, *Ion*, 1939; E. R. Dodds, *Bacch.* 2e. 1960; A. M. Dale, *Alc.* 1954; W. Barrett, *Hipp.* 1964.

Translations into English: G. Murray, *Hippolytus* and *Bacchae* (London, 1902) and *Eight Plays* (2 vols., Newtown, 1931); P. Vellacott, *Hipp.*, *Iph. Taur.*, *Alc.* (Penguin Books, London, 1953), *Bacch.*, *Ion*, *Trojan Women*, *Helen* (Harmondsworth, 1953), and *Med.*, *Hec.*, *Electra*, *Heracles* (Harmondsworth, 1963). All the works are available in the *Complete Greek Tragedies*, mentioned under Aeschylus.

The papyrus finds have been far more productive for Euripides than for any other tragedian. So it is important to use the works mentioned in the general section in addition to what is contained in H. von Arnim's *Supplementum Euripideum* (Bonn, 1913). E. G. Turner presents new fragments in the 27th volume of the *Oxyrhynchus Papyri* (London,

1962). The *Telephus* is treated by E. W. Handley and J. Rea in an Institute of Classical Studies bulletin (Supp. No. 5, London, 1957). Fragments which Nauck has identified from authors' quotations have been brought together by Br. Snell (*Wien Stud.* 69, 1956, 86). E. Schwartz has produced an exemplary edition of the 'scholia,' 2 vols. (Berlin, 1887–91), which for Euripides are particularly copious. Other works: G. W. Bond, *The Hypsipyle of Euripides* (Oxford, 1963); W Ritchie, *The Authenticity of the Rhesus of Euripides* (Cambridge, 1964).

The introductory book by G. Murray, *Euripides and his Age* (London, 1922; 2e. Oxford, 1946) is still worth reading. We should mention D. F. W. van Lennep, *Euripides ποιητὴς σοφός* as an instance of those who go too far in applying modern psychology. A. Rivier's *Essai sur le tragique d'Euripide* (Lausanne, 1944) tries to do justice to the poet rather than to the thinker. Further monographs are F. Martinazzoli, *Euripide* (Rome, 1946); W. H. Friedrich, 'Euripides and Diphilos' (*Zetemata* 5, Munich, 1953), with a good analysis of the structure of single plays: W. Ludwig, *Sapheneia, Ein Beitrag zur Formkunst im Spätwerk des Euripides* (Diss., Tübingen, 1954), and H. Strohm, 'Euripides' (Zetemata 15, Munich, 1957), which also give valuable structural analyses. W. Zürcher in 'Die Darstellung des Menschen im Drama des Euripides' (*Schw. Beitr. z. Altertumswissenschaft* 2, Basle, 1947), deals with the important question of how far psychology is significant for Euripidean drama, showing extreme caution where psychological interpretations are concerned. G. Zuntz, *The Political Plays of Euripides* (Manchester, 1955), makes an excellent contribution for *The Heracleidae* and *The Suppliant Women.* O. Reverdin has edited seven lectures on the poet by various scholars, in the sixth volume of the Hardt Foundation's *Entretiens sur l'antiquité classique* (Vandoeuvres, Geneva, 1958). G. M. A. Grube, *The Drama of Euripides* (London, 1961) is the only book of criticism on the whole of Euripides readily available in English. Two works worth noting are: R. P. Winnington-Ingram, *Euripides* and *Dionysus* (Cambridge, 1948); L. H. Greenwood, *Aspects of Euripidean Tragedy* (Cambridge, 1953). Among the best pronouncements on Euripides are the essay by K. Reinhardt, 'Sinneskrise bei Euripides', in *Tradition und Geist* (Göttingen, 1960, 227; formerly *Neue Rundschau* 68, 1957, 615); A. Garzya, *Pensiero e tecnica drammatica in Euripide* (Naples, 1962); R. Goossens, *Euripide et Athènes* (Acad. Royale de Belgique; Classe de lettres et de sciences mor. et pol. Mem. Coll., in 8° 55/4, 1962). Also recommended: T. B. L. Webster, *The Tragedies of Euripides* (London, 1967).

INDEX

Printed in Great Britain
by Fletcher & Son Ltd,
Norwich